Redeeming Beauty explores the richness of orthodox Christian tradition, both Western and Eastern, in matters of 'sacral aesthetics' – a term used to denote the foundations, production and experience of religiously relevant beauty.

Aidan Nichols investigates five principal themes: the foundation of beauty in the natural order through divine creative action; explicitly 'evangelical' beauty as a quality of biblical revelation and notably at its climax in Christ; the legitimacy of making and venerating artworks; qualities of the self in relation to objective presentation of the religiously beautiful; and the difficulties of practising a sacral aesthetic, whether as producer or consumer, in an epoch when the visual arts themselves have left behind not only Church but for the greater part the public as well. The thought of theologians such as Augustine, Aquinas, Balthasar, Ratzinger, Bulgakov, Maritain and others is explored.

Ashgate Studies in Theology, Imagination and the Arts

Series Editors:

Trevor Hart, St Mary's College, University of St Andrews, Scotland
Jeremy Begbie, Ridley Hall, UK
Roger Lundin, Wheaton College, USA

What have imagination and the arts to do with theology? For much of the modern era, the answer has been, 'not much.' It is precisely this deficit that the proposed series will seek to redress. For, whatever role they have or have not been granted in the theological disciplines, imagination and the arts are undeniably bound up with how we as human beings think, learn and communicate, engage with and respond to our physical and social environments and, in particular, our awareness and experience of that which transcends our own creatureliness. The arts are playing an increasingly significant role in the way people come to terms with the world; at the same time, artists of many disciplines are showing a willingness to engage with religious or theological themes. A spate of publications and courses in many educational institutions has already established this field as one of fast growing concern.

This series taps into a burgeoning intellectual concern on both sides of the Atlantic and beyond. The peculiar inter-disciplinarity of theology, and the growing interest in imagination and the arts in many different fields of human concern, afford the opportunity for a series which has its roots sunk in varied and diverse intellectual soils, while focused around a coherent theological question: How are imagination and the arts involved in the shaping and reshaping of our humanity as part of the creative and redemptive purposes of God, and what roles do they perform in the theological enterprise?

Many projects within the series have particular links to the work of the Institute for Theology Imagination and the Arts in the University of St Andrews, and to the Theology Through the Arts programme in Cambridge.

Other titles in the series:

The Passion in Art
Richard Harries

Faith and Beauty
A Theological Aesthetic
Edward Farley

Baptized Imagination
The Theology of George MacDonald
Kerry Dearborn

Redeeming Beauty

Soundings in Sacral Aesthetics

AIDAN NICHOLS, O.P.

John Paul II Lecturer in Roman Catholic Theology,
University of Oxford, UK

ASHGATE

Published by
Ashgate Publishing Limited
Gower House
Croft Road
Aldershot
Hampshire GU11 3HR
England

Ashgate Publishing Company
Suite 420
101 Cherry Street
Burlington, VT 05401-4405
USA

Ashgate website: http://www.ashgate.com

British Library Cataloguing in Publication Data
Nichols, Aidan
   Redeeming Beauty: Soundings in Sacral Aesthetics. –
   (Ashgate Studies in Theology, Imagination and the Arts)
   1. Christian art and symbolism. 2. Aesthetics. I.Title
   246

Library of Congress Cataloging-in-Publication Data
Nichols, Aidan.
   Redeeming Beauty: Soundings in Sacral Aesthetics / Aidan Nichols.
      p.   cm. – (Ashgate Studies in Theology, Imagination and the Arts)
   Includes index.
   1. Aesthetics – Religious aspects – Christianity. I. Title.
   BR115.A8N53 2007
   230–dc22
                                              2006018459

ISBN 978-0-7546-5895-5 (hbk)
ISBN 978-0-7546-6001-9 (pbk)

This volume has been printed on acid-free paper.

Printed and bound in Great Britain by TJ International Ltd, Padstow, Cornwall.

Contents

Preface

For many people in modern British society beauty is perhaps the only available way into metaphysics and religion, as an atheist Provost of King's College, Cambridge acknowledged when he proposed to close the Chapel outside hours of service with a view to protecting visitors from 'irrationality'. Beauty, whether in nature or art, provides an intimation of the transcendental order. That is a fact, whatever difficulty philosophers may have in furnishing a satisfactory account of it. Some of the material presented in this book throws light, I hope, on this obscure subject.

The present writer is a historical theologian, not a constructive metaphysician. But here weakness in one respect might be strength in another. The Christian tradition, Western and Eastern, has vast conceptual and imaginative resources for coming to terms with this subject. The 'sacral aesthetics' of my subtitle means both an approach to beauty in the natural ontological order, and exploration of the iconologies generated when that order has been lifted above its own communicative capacities by divine grace. It is appropriate that a world surmised to be already gift should contain further surprises. Biblical revelation is in its own modalities 'beautiful' too: '*redeeming* beauty'. Its prolongation in Christian iconography is not especially easy to achieve in our time. There are resources here for an ampler 'art of the Church' as well. This is chiefly a study of the beauty which when seen pleases. In my Conclusion, however, encouraged by – especially – Maritain, I cast the net wider to take in by analogy other arts besides.

Blackfriars, Cambridge

Memorial Day of Saints
Basil and Gregory, 2006

Acknowledgements

The author and publisher are grateful to: Peeters of Leuven for permission to re-use in chapters 3 and 4 some material already published in W. van den Bercken and J. Sutton (eds.), *Aesthetics as a Religious Factor in Eastern and Western Christianity* (Leuven, Paris, Dudley, MA, 2005); the editors of *Nova et Vetera* for permission to use an earlier version of chapter 5 published in Vol. 5, No. 2 (2007); the editor of *New Blackfriars* for permission to use an earlier version of chapter 6 published in Vol. 88, No. 1013 (2007).

They are especially grateful to the Director of the Fitzwilliam Museum, Cambridge, for permission to reproduce as the cover image of this book Marlay cutting It. 13A: Don Silvestro dei Gherarducci (1339–1399), 'The Presentation in the Temple', historiated initial from a Gradual dated 1371–1375.

PART 1
Foundations, in Creation and Grace

Chapter 1

Aesthetics in Augustine and Aquinas

Introduction

Our first task is to investigate the foundations of beauty in the natural order through divine creation, and, furthermore, the specificity of explicitly 'evangelical' beauty, considered as a quality of biblical revelation – notably at the latter's climax in Jesus Christ. Thus this opening chapter lays out the account of these first two themes in the two principal theologians of Latin antiquity and the Middle Ages: Augustine and Thomas Aquinas.

Except in the question of the metaphysics of beauty, which Neo-Scholasticism, to its credit, found worthy of investigation and expansion, it might be thought that Thomas's works are not especially susceptible to the treatment called, in the wake of Hans Urs von Balthasar's raids on the tradition, 'theological aesthetics'. Balthasar, theological aesthetician par excellence, did not think fit to include Thomas among the representatives of the theology of God's glory, beauty's revelatory analogate, in the series of monographs which constitute volume two of his *Herrlichkeit*. It is Bonaventure, not Thomas, who saves the honour there of the Western high mediaevals, filling the gap between Anselm and John of the Cross. That absence is the more striking given the pivotal role Thomas plays elsewhere in *Herrlichkeit* – specifically at the very midpoint of the third double volume, which considers metaphysics. There Thomas's ontology is seen as the paradigm of a study of being that does justice simultaneously to being's abundance and indigence, and more especially to the kenotic aspect of being, *Sein*, whereby it so gives itself as only concretely to be in existents, *die Seienden*.[1]

Of course, the metaphysics of beauty picked out of Thomas's writings by authors as different as Jacques Maritain and Umberto Eco is itself no bagatelle.[2] It is a valuable area of enquiry with an important background in Augustine's

---

1   This, for Balthasar, shows how deeply evangelical Thomas's metaphysics are – such that, when his 'moment' in the history of thought passed, later generations could fill its place only by the practice of holy folly among the Baroque saints, who in their own lives made kenotic gestures of self-squandering that replicated in their own fashion what Thomas took to be the dynamic structure of being itself. If, as Balthasar in the last analysis thinks, 'love alone is beautiful', that too is pertinent to theological aesthetics. See A. Nichols, OP, 'Von Balthasar's Aims in his Theological Aesthetics', *Heythrop Journal* 40 (1999), pp. 409–23.

2   J. Maritain, *Art et scolastique* (Paris 1927, 2nd edition); U. Eco, *Il problema estetico in Tommaso d'Aquino* (Milan 1982, 2nd edition).

creation metaphysics and theological cosmology. When to Augustine's influence there is added that of Denys we might even speak (as we shall see) of Thomas's vision of reality as 'pankalic' in character. In some sense – just what, remains to be established – all things are beautiful. But the question can also be raised: is there not implicit in Thomas's presentation of creation and salvation an evocation of beauty *more specifically revelatory and evangelical in character*, just as there is, surely, in Augustine's, for in his mature writings Augustine proved ready to bring together the *content* of the Gospel revelation with the *concept* of the beautiful?

Augustine

That is the discovery of the Durham patrologist Carol Harrison in her study *Beauty and Revelation in the Thought of Saint Augustine*[3]. In that book she describes how, after Augustine's early sorties in the realm of thinking about the beautiful, a shift was prepared to a more 'incarnational' aesthetic. Her underlining of the term 'temporal medicine' as a key to the mature Augustine's theological aesthetics is helpful, for the 'shift' in Augustine's attitude, which not for nothing coincides with his increasing ecclesial responsibilities as in turn *servus Dei*, presbyter and bishop, can be explained by his enhanced concern for pastoral care. Pastoral utility guides Augustine to discern the temporal medicine to be found in creation, in the language of Scripture[4], in man as the image of God and, supremely, in Jesus Christ. Harrison dislodges a sometimes lamentably exclusive focus of attention on Augustine's *ex professo* discussions of what we might term the 'nominally' beautiful in his early, more philosophical, writings, and points up instead the significance of what we might call by contrast his 'adjectival' use of the language of the beautiful to qualify the theological realities with which the mature homiletic and dogmatic texts that have come down to us largely deal.

Augustine's first literary effort was directed to aesthetics, the *De pulchro et apto*. No copy was extant by the time he was writing the *Confessions* less than 20 years later, in 397. Judging by the account given there[5], it appears to have been a mishmash of pagan sources with a definitely Manichaean cast to it. In all probability it was based on anthologies by doxographers, those 'chroniclers of intellectual gossip in antiquity'.[6] The distinction of terms found in the title seems to resolve into two kinds of aesthetic fittingness: one, the *pulchrum*, is the pleasingness of the widest possible whole; the other, the *aptum*, the fittingness to some whole of a part. What Serge Lancel has called 'the varied readings and temptations of the still very eclectic

---

3   C. Harrison, *Beauty and Revelation in the Thought of Saint Augustine* (Oxford 1992).

4   For Augustine, it becomes important that the Scriptures contain not only the rule of faith but sufficient linguistic art and beauty to persuade to that rule: thus *De doctrina christiana* IV. 13. 29.

5   *Confessiones* IV. 13. 20–15. 24.

6   M. J. Edwards, *Origen against Plato* (Aldershot 2002), p. 8.

Augustine'[7] stood in utter contrast, however, to a work he read some few years after this youthful effusion which later, when a bishop, he found somewhat embarrassing. Plotinus's *Peri tou kalou*, with its superlatively anti-Manichaean account of the sheer transcendence of the eternal intelligible realm of the Supreme Beauty, was surely one of the *libri Platonicorum* which helped Augustine towards the acceptance of the Gospel as understood in Milanese Catholicism, in the circle of Ambrose.[8]

In 386, at Cassiciacum, the live-in seminar on that Lombard estate looking toward the Alpine foothills, Augustine is following the twofold path of philosophy and Christianity. From the texts of that time, his ontology of beauty is indeed indebted to Plotinus, whose discussion of the Supreme Beauty by reflection of which all beautiful things are lovely had come as such a revelation to the Manichee hearer. It is with the help of the Neo-Platonists that in the *Soliloquies* he recognises beauty as a Name of the true God,[9] as will Thomas, by way of commenting the treatise of the Syrian monk Denys on the Names of God, eight centuries later. However, we remember that at Cassiciacum while Augustine re-read the Platonists he also read the Psalms. Augustine will retain a 'facility for marrying the symbolism of the Scriptures with the Plotinian dialectic of degrees'.[10]

The lion's share of Augustine's theoretical discussion of the beautiful comes from the early period of his writing – which has enabled the impression to be formed that his aesthetic is ultra-spiritual, and even rationalistic.[11] For the *Contra Academicos*, where *Philokalia* and *Philosophia* are compared,[12] beauty is in principle synonymous with Wisdom – or what in the famous ecstasy scene at Ostia Augustine calls 'the Principle of all that is, has been and will be, without having been made'.[13] The Beauty (capitalisation appropriate here) we should seek dwells in the realm of reason and the soul. Conversely, the beauty found in things of sense captivates negatively through ensnaring the mind on ground level. But not, be it emphasised, because the very ontology of material things embodies what is evil. Rather, as the *De quantitate animae* will explain[14]: since the soul is in the divine image,[15] it is itself the closest to divine truth of all creatures in the hierarchy of existence – a doctrine

---

7   S. Lancel, *Saint Augustine* (ET London 2002), p. 53.

8   *Confessiones* VII. 9. 13. For Olivier du Roy, the writings of Plotinus form the core of what Augustine meant by the *libri Platonicorum*: thus his *L'intelligence de la foi en la Trinité selon saint Augustin* (Paris 1966), pp. 69–70.

9   *Soliloquia* I. 2.

10   S. Lancel, *Saint Augustine*, p. 118.

11   K. Svoboda, *L'Esthétique de saint Augustin et ses sources* (Brno 1933); R. J. O'Connell, *Art and the Christian Intelligence in Saint Augustine* (Oxford 1978).

12   *Contra Academicos* II. 7.

13   *Confessiones* IX. 24.

14   *De quantitate animae* I. 70–79.

15   Augustine's account of the *imago Dei* probably came from Ambrose's preaching on the *Hexaemeron*, the Genesis account of creation in six 'days'. The strong stress on the soul and its spirituality reflects controversy with the Manichees, who had mocked the Christian Creator God for (seemingly) possessing, like his creatures, a human body. The conviction will

anticipated in the *Soliloquies* and confirmed in the *De immortalitate animae*. The soul, accordingly, should turn to itself, and then from there to its Source with a view to finding Beauty directly.

Those imperatives reflect the mystical experience of Augustine's first or intellectual conversion described retrospectively in the *Confessions*,[16] where, as Lancel writes, that experience is:

> put into words which evoke specifically Plotinian themes, but are freely adapted in a spiritual context that may already be said to be Christian.[17]

In the words of the *Confessions* themselves,

> I felt myself drawn to you by your Beauty, but soon was dragged from you by my own weight and fell groaning to the ground. That weight was my carnal custom.[18]

Here the context of Plotinian ascent is, evidently, biblical, and especially Pauline, post-lapsarian struggle. But if the early Augustine recommends a flight from the senses, this is in no paranoid religious temper. Looking back, he explains in the *Retractationes* how in the *De immortalitate animae*:

> Through the intermediary of corporeal things I myself wanted to attain or lead others to attain, incorporeal things.[19]

In particular, Augustine recognises the nobility of sight and hearing, as Aquinas will do likewise. For Augustine, the superiority of these senses lies in the way their objects yield to judgement by rational categories.[20] The delight hearing and sight afford is itself rational – something Augustine characteristically understands as *well-measured*. Thus, in the *De musica*, music's optimal expression is not so much its actual performance as the knowledge it affords of number and metrics. Whether writing at Cassiciacum, in the *De ordine*, with its study plan for the liberal arts, or, on his return to Africa, at Thagaste, in the *De vera religione*, that treatise on the essence of Christianity, he applies to the world of sense ideas of beauty expressed in largely rational and especially mathematical terms. He uses for illustration such things as the proportion and symmetry of windows and doors in architecture, the rhythmical movement of a dance, or the measured syllables of a verse in poetry. [21]

In the perspective of theological aesthetics, this is the most modest of beginnings. But owing especially to the deeper ecclesial rooting Augustine acquired through

---

endure: in the *De Trinitate* XII. 12, the image of God dwells only in that part of the soul which cleaves to eternal things to contemplate them or draw inspiration from them.

16 *Confessiones* VII. 16–23.
17 S. Lancel, *Saint Augustine*, p. 85.
18 *Confessiones* VII. 23.
19 *Retractationes* I. 6.
20 *De ordine* II. 32.
21 *De vera religione* 54; *De ordine* II. 34.

commitment as ascetic, presbyter, bishop, his thinking became increasingly shaped by the Church-carried revelation, to inevitably transforming effect.[22] In Carol Harrison's words:

> The Christian doctrines of Creation *ex nihilo*, of the Incarnation, of a historical revelation, and of the resurrection of the body, to mention but a few examples, have the effect of making Augustine's thought much more positive concerning the beauty of the temporal realm.[23]

The shift concerned is to a point of view more appropriate to a religion where the divine placed itself, by Incarnation, in the order of signs, thus enabling the apostolic witnesses to affirm, in the words of the Johannine Prologue, 'we saw his glory, ... full of grace and truth' (John 1:14).[24]

The shift did not come unprepared. Balthasar makes the interesting suggestion that the Latin language itself affected the *Wirkungsgeschichte* – *the historical influence* – of the Platonic tradition, with consequences for Augustine. Plato's *idea* transmutes when it re-appears in Latin dress through the binomial pair *forma* and *species* with their directly aesthetic connotations. Balthasar writes:

> Being inevitably includes being of a certain kind (*species*) or, what comes to the same thing, a form (*forma*), two words which both imply 'essence' and 'beauty' and are immediately understood by Augustine in this duality (*speciosus* and *formosus*, 'beautiful', 'well-formed').[25]

As Harrison comments,

> Here *forma*, the Latin translation and equivalent of the Platonic Idea, is understood not only as an outward appearance (though it does mean this) but as that which constitutes the existence of a particular thing in the fullest sense of the word: it is *forma* which gives it its life and being. Furthermore, and most importantly, it is *forma* which constitutes its beauty.[26]

---

22 Peter Brown noted how, on his return to Africa, 'the centre of gravity of Augustine's thought had begun to shift', *Augustine of Hippo* (London 1967), p. 134. The questions of a correspondent (Nebridius of Carthage, his old student and friend) who was fascinated by questions raised by Neo-Platonism and the occult, are led back to 'the central mysteries of the Christian faith; his little group must repudiate everything in philosophy that was not consistent with the Catholic creed, while believing that there was nothing in this creed that could not be contemplated by a philosopher', ibid., p. 135, with reference to Augustine, Letter 11, 2 and the *De vera religione* 7, 12.

23 C. Harrison, *Beauty and Revelation in the Thought of St Augustine*, p. 32.

24 For a wide-ranging survey of 'sign' in Augustine, see C. P. Mayer, *Die Zeichen in der geistigen Entwicklung und in der Theologie Augustins* (Würzburg 1974).

25 H. U. von Balthasar, 'Augustine', in *The Glory of the Lord: A Theological Aesthetic, II. Clerical Styles* (ET Edinburgh and San Francisco 1984), p. 115.

26 C. Harrison, *Beauty and Revelation in the Thought of Saint Augustine*, p. 38.

These words in effect paraphrase a passage in the *De immortalitate animae* where Augustine asserts that 'its form, *specie*, gives the body its being', and draws the conclusion that:

> the body is the more perfect, the better formed, s*peciosus*, it is, and the more beautiful, *pulchrius*.[27]

Insofar as 'form' is deficient, or man loses it by sin – an important corollary which shows the importance of a moral and spiritual dimension in this aesthetic, to that extent a being not only becomes deformed but ceases to be. Harrison scarcely exaggerates when she writes:

> The implications of these ideas ... [for] Augustine's aesthetics cannot be overestimated: since beauty ... is thus inseparable from existence given by and orientated towards God, the whole of the Christian revelation – in God's formation of his Creation, His image or form in man, His forming and ordering of history and His incarnation of Divine Form in the Son – all assumes an aspect of beauty which is at once immanent within the temporal, mutable realm, but which yet belongs to and originates in transcendent Divine Beauty.[28]

In the 'new' perspective, calling corporeal beauty the 'lowest' beauty still serves in one way as a warning. When we contemplate the beauty of nature we are not to become curiously absorbed in creation's number, form and measure but to treat its glory as a sign of its Creator (thus the *De libero arbitrio*).[29] There is an obvious parallel with Augustine's discussion of goodness. God is the supreme Good but what is mutable and corruptible, while low down on the ontological scale, is also good, since created by God.[30] But precisely when it is recalled how creatures' existence, form, beauty are – like their goodness – *received from God* does it become apparent that creatures can also in another way be for us *medicina temporalis*, a 'temporal medicine'.[31] *By means of* creatures we should strive to know those realities of which carnal things bring in and of themselves no knowledge. As the *De vera religione* insists, true religion actualises a programme of salvation to achieve ends impossible for Neo-Platonism. It has to invoke the authority that requires from us the intervention of faith, but this in itself prepares man for an enhanced intervention of reason, working on finite, mutable things to bring us understanding.[32]

---

27 *De immortalitate animae* 13.

28 C. Harrison, *Beauty and Revelation in the Thought of Saint Augustine*, p. 39.

29 *De libero arbitrio* II. 43 and 45.

30 And indeed not only *bonum* but *ens*: thus *Confessiones* VII. 17, which text is found almost exactly reproduced in *Enarrationes in psalmos* 134, 4.

31 *De vera religione* 45.

32 Augustine famously loved to cite in this connection Isaiah 7:9: 'Unless you believe, you will not understand'. So reads the prophetic text in the Latin Septuagint. It first appears in his corpus as early as the *De libero arbitrio* and the *De magistro*: see A. M. La Bonnardière, *Saint Augustin et la Bible* (Paris 1986), p. 44.

For Harrison, the notion of temporal medicine, when combined – through Augustine's growing awareness of the flaws in human nature – with a heavier placing of emphasis on the Fall, leads, paradoxically, to a more positive account of mortal beauty than is found in the early works. In the new context, it is beauty's pastoral utility that becomes uppermost. As Augustine remarks in the *De vera religione* (and really this citation is the controlling text of Harrison's monograph):

One must lean on the place where one has fallen in order to pick oneself up.[33]

When man can no longer see and understand beauty in its rational, spiritual concept – the *subtilissima ratio* of the Platonists, God can nevertheless use earthly beauty – not only in *creation* which, writes Augustine, 'proclaims that its maker could have been none other than God, the ineffably and invisibly beautiful',[34] but also in *history*, through the 'beauty' of its ordered succession of changes,[35] in *man* through the beauty of soul which animates the body[36], and above all, in *the Incarnate One* and the economy Jesus Christ introduces, in order to draw fallen humanity to himself in faith, hope and love. On this last: in its temporal dispensation, Providence heals man from undue attachment to the senses through *another* beauty which is shown to us with *auctoritas*, 'authority',[37] in Christ's miracles, his works of love, the Scriptures and ceremonies of the Church, and also – by a motif increasingly sounded in Augustine's preaching – the *humility* with which the Word assumed the form of man. Augustine had been on the way to becoming *peritus*, 'learned'. But, he tells us in the *Confessions*,[38] had he continued thus he would have finished up *periturus*, 'about to perish'. As he asks rhetorically, 'Where indeed was that charity which builds on the foundation of humility, which is Jesus Christ?' Since the beauty of God disclosed in the *forma* which constitutes the being and loveliness of creation in man, history and, supremely, the incarnate Word, cannot be grasped in its fullness in temporal, mutable reality, man must have *faith* in that divine beauty as mediated by its kenosis, so that his sight – the eyes of his heart – may be healed. In that way he can *hope* for the vision of it. And, more than these, by *love* he should move towards it.

The gracious presence of beauty in God's revelation in the temporal realm inspires not only love, but – as Augustine will increasingly emphasise – delight: a word with powerfully aesthetic resonance and to whose referent Augustine gave an ever enhanced role in the motion of will that, so he writes in the *De diversis quaestionibus*

---

33   *De vera religione* 45.

34   *De civitate Dei* 11. 4. Among many other texts that could be cited Harrison selects *Sermones* 241, 2; *Confessiones* X. 6, and *Enarrationes in psalmos* 61, 17.

35   *De diversis quaestionibus LXXXIII*, 44. It should be noted, however, that Augustine has particularly in mind the framing by these sequential stages of the birth of the Redeemer.

36   *De Genesi ad litteram Liber imperfectum* 59.

37   The contrast yet complementarity of 'authority' and 'subtlest reason' comes from *Contra Academicos* III. 20. 43.

38   *Confessiones* VII. 26.

of his episcopal period, 'can have no motive unless something presents itself to delight and stir the mind'.[39]

How divine Providence could use sense and not just time to reform man in and by beauty is shown above all in the Incarnation, and not least – so Augustine daringly claims – in the crucified Christ who was deformed so as to make beautiful ugly man. As the *Enarrationes in psalmos* have it in a positive cornucopia of 'adjectival' beauty:

> He then is beautiful in heaven, beautiful on earth; beautiful in the womb; beautiful in his parents' hands; beautiful in his miracles; beautiful under the scourge; beautiful when inviting to life; beautiful also when not regarding death; beautiful in 'laying down his life'; beautiful in 'taking it again'; beautiful on the Cross; beautiful in the sepulchre; beautiful in heaven.[40]

As this passage suggests, Christ is the climax of the administering of temporal medicine, its maximum saving efficacy. This is an evangelical presentation of revelation with a strongly soteriological rationale. The divine aim is to have done with the deformity of sin. In his homilies on the *Epistles of St John*, Augustine tells his hearers that we shall become beautiful 'by loving him who is always beautiful'[41]. Inasmuch as love grows in us, so beauty grows, since love *is* the soul's beauty'. At one level that is – shades of the early works – a Christianisation of Plotinus, who remarks in the *Enneads* that 'the Supreme Beauty, the absolute and primal, fashions its lovers to Beauty and makes them also worthy of love'.[42] But it can also be expressed in terms drawn from the New Testament, especially the Pauline corpus, the early Fathers and Liturgies. In the words of the *Enarrationes in psalmos* again,[43] the divine One who formed us will reform us – a reflection of the great 'idea of reform' in ancient Christianity to which Gerhart Ladner's classic study was dedicated.[44] Ladner emphasises that Augustine's reform idea is increasingly that of *renovatio in melius* – a reforming to a more wonderful form than Adam's had been

---

39   *De diversis quaestionibus* 2, 21. There is a near-synonymity of the terms 'love' and 'delight' in Augustine's writing – sometimes playing on the similarity of *dilectio* and *delectatio* – for example in *Enarrationes in psalmos*, 118, 10, 6. (In effect, *dilectio* for Augustine is a synonym of *caritas*. Together they serve the function of the Greek *agape*. *Amor* has a broader connotation and can be used with both positive and negative meanings, as the Greek *eros*.) Inevitably this linkage to delight introduces an aesthetic element into everything Augustine says about love, since the marvel and joy implicit in delight are of course essential traits of aesthetic responsiveness. Nor is this surprising since what love is to bring man to is the vision of the God one of whose Names is Beauty (see above, note 9).

40   *Enarrationes in psalmos* 44, 3.

41   *Homilia super Ioanni epistolas* 9, 9.

42   Plotinus, *Enneads* I. 6. 7.

43   *Enarrationes in psalmos* 103, 1, 4.

44   G. B. Ladner, *The Idea of Reform: Its Impact on Christian Thought and Action in the Age of the Fathers* (Cambridge, Mass. 1959), pp. 153–283.

in the primal innocence.[45] This is a gradual reformation through the faith, hope and love which the revealed, yet veiled, nature of God's beauty inspires, and comes to term only in the final condition of the City of God.

Thomas Aquinas

Until recently, discussion of Thomas's aesthetics has had much the same character as earlier twentieth century accounts of the aesthetics of Augustine. Largely philosophical in temper, it has tended to restrict itself to Thomas's *ex professo* discussion of *pulchrum*, the 'fourth transcendental' (after *verum*, *bonum*, *unum*) as recognised by some, if not all, later Scholasticism. Certainly, Thomas's explicit discussion of the beautiful is important – not least because some of its characteristic vocabulary seeps into his theological language in a variety of doctrinal areas. But just as, through the undergirding idea of 'temporal medicine', Harrison was able to show how the Augustinian appeal to beauty far exceeded the bounds of a fundamentally philosophical ontology, so in the case of Thomas a subjacent appeal to beauty permeates, it has been argued, his entire corpus wherever reference is made to the idea of the *convenientia*, the well-suitedness, of the means divine Wisdom has chosen for the salvation of the world. [46]

In Thomas's case, unlike Augustine's, there is really no question of seismic shifts in inner development. At whatever time in his writing, Thomas can touch altogether positively, when speaking of beauty, on a range – not vast, but varied – of concrete examples which overarch the abyss between the uncreated and the created, and the distinction between the moral–spiritual and the corporeal orders. Impressionistically surveyed, these examples take us from the heights of the sublime – the beauty of the pre-existent Son, a doctrinal motif Thomas inherited from Hilary and Augustine – to the depths of delight in playing games. The Son is beauty as the Father's perfect Image, proportioned to him, resplendent with expressivity as his Word.[47] Elsewhere, Thomas's most frequent example of beauty is the human body, for in man spiritual and material elements interweave in 'an ample play of proportions'.[48] Human beauty, for Thomas, has especially to do with the wonderful calibration of body and soul (Thomas mentions specifically human hands, 'the organ of organs', which fit the human being to be craftsman, for any kind of production by artifice.) We should not, however, pass over in silence Thomas's praise of the beauty of music – notably in the question of the *Summa theologiae*'s *Secunda Pars* which asks whether it is appropriate to laud the Deity by means of sacred chant.[49]

---

45 Ibid., pp. 158–62.

46 G. Narcisse [OP], *Les raisons de Dieu: argument de convenance et esthétique théologique selon saint Thomas d'Aquin et Hans Urs von Balthasar* (Fribourg 1997).

47 *Summa theologiae* Ia., q. 39, a. 8.

48 U. Eco, *Il problema estetico in Tommaso d'Aquino*, p. 160. A good example is found in Thomas, *Summa theologiae*, Ia., q. 91.

49 Ibid., IIa. IIae., q. 91.

Actually, insofar as beauty includes proportion Thomas will say that there is a sort of musicality in all cosmic order.[50] As to the game, *ludus*, and word-play, *iocus*, there is a delight in their proportioning to human activity and connaturality with it. Fittingly, men seek recreation after labour, and that brings the playful within the bounds of beauty likewise.[51]

A preliminary wider question such a survey should prompt in us is, are these examples really instances of a far more pervasive 'pankalic' reality? Here Thomas is above all 'Aquinas the Dionysian'.[52] Thomas's commentary on *The Divine Names* was written late in his life, probably in the years 1265–66; but once his master, Albert of Cologne, had opened his eyes to this text the question remained with him of how to do justice to Denys's 'pankalic' vision of the real. He was challenged to think of beauty both as attribute of the triune God and in its causality and creative diffusion in finite things.

Though, as we shall see, Dionysian 'pankalicism' profoundly affects Thomas, it need not rule out some sort of Augustinian contribution in the matter. As early as the second *lectio* of the opening chapter of Thomas's *Commentary on the Divine Names*, Aquinas lists 'beauty' and 'wisdom' among the Names of God. At this juncture, Thomas seeks to unify these two Names by reference to the divine activity *ad extra*. He does so very much in the spirit of Augustine, or what Eco terms 'a sapiential aesthetic of Augustinian origin',[53] pointing out how *harmony* – that Thomas evidently considers here synonymous with beauty – naturally belongs to wisdom, whose office it is to 'order things and render them commensurate'. The divine ordering, work of wisdom as it is, is necessarily a source of beauty.

More directly focussed on God in himself, however, is the *Commentary*'s fourth chapter. Thomas follows the example he had already established in the paradigm case of the good – *bonum*, which he treats as a predicable 'Name' eminently proper to God, but subsequently manifested in the angels and shared in by corruptible creatures. Reproducing this pattern, he first deals with the beautiful, *pulchrum*, as a divine attribute before treating it in its causality and creative diffusion. God is the 'supersubstantial *pulchrum*', who bestows beauty on all creatures according to the properties of each. He is not beautiful under one or more aspects. Rather is he beautiful *simpliciter*, and as the One who is 'in himself beautiful', *pulcher in seipso*, he is the pre-existing generator of beauty in whatever exists, *fons totius pulchritudinis*,

---

50   Ibid., Ia., q. 25, a. 6.

51   Ibid., Ia. IIae., q. 32, a. 1, ad iii.

52   Along with other mediaeval doctors, Thomas drew an account of the beautiful from the combined wells of Scripture's Sapiential books, the Pythagoreanism of Boethius – whose musical–mathematical concept of the universe was inevitably aesthetic, from Platonist sources – not this time Plotinus but Plato himself in the Latin translation of the *Timaeos* by Chalcidius, and, supremely, from the treatise *De divinis Nominibus* by the Pseudo-Denys. These three main streams of inspiration, biblical, Pythagorean, Platonist, had been those of Augustine himself, though for obvious chronological reasons the Pythagoreanism and Platonism reached him by different routes.

53   U. Eco, *Il problema estetico in Tommaso d'Aquino*, p. 46.

the 'fount of all beauty'. The lections of this chapter stress that the divine Beauty is not only the efficacious cause of being but its final and exemplary cause as well. All things are turned toward the Beautiful and Good, desiring God as their end, and, on account of the Beautiful and Good, seeking after him 'as the exemplary cause they have as the rule for their *operatio*', their activity.[54] Everything aspires towards the beautiful, then, just as everything is constructed by reference to it.

However, because Thomas never explicitly writes *pulchrum et ens convertuntur*, 'beauty and being are convertible', whereas he *does* write, *pulchra ... dicuntur quae visa placent*, 'Those things are called beautiful which please on sight', the way was open, in some Thomistic quarters, to a subjectivising interpretation of his ontological account of what beauty is. This was, one suspects, notably the case where Thomas's commentary on Denys was treated as a historical curiosity and left unread. In *Art et scolastique* Jacques Maritain was a creditable exception in the weight he gave to Thomas on Denys. That he came down on the side of beauty as really a transcendental is, in consequence, unsurprising.[55] And yet to speak for the other side, there is a problem here. Surely, not everything is delectable to everybody, so how can the beautiful compete in universality with being, goodness and truth?[56] For Thomas we see things as beautiful only when we see them in their formal structure – and some things we never see in that fashion precisely because we do not intend to view them *sub ratione pulchri*, 'in the perspective of the beautiful'. This answers a worry of Augustine's in the *De vera religione*: if all lovely things are so objectively, why do not all subjectively delight us? The Thomasian reply would, in effect, run: yes, the beautiful *is* constituted by an intentional relation between the knowing subject and the reality in question. *But* the reality in question possesses a structure of such a kind that integral elements therein offer themselves for the contemplation that delights. Yes, there must be *subjective* visualisation. But *objective* conditions must also be met if the beautiful is to be. Hence the importance of Thomas's account of these conditions – *claritas*, *integritas*, *proportio* – if we are to get hold of just what subjective aesthetic vision, or apprehension, entails. The conditions are, to say the least, very generously instantiated in Thomas's view of the world.

The sheer range of analogous examples of *proportio* Thomas can put forward witnesses to the truly transcendental range of the *pulchrum* whose primary formal criterion is proportion.[57] Yet reflection on proportioned form suggests other characteristics that further display the perfection of form: *integritas*, on which

---

54 Thomas, *In Dionysium, De divinis Nominibus*, IV, lect. viii.

55 J. Maritain, *Art et scolastique*, p. 183.

56 Thus M. de Munnynck, 'L'esthétique de Saint Thomas d'Aquin' in Auctores varii, *S. Tommaso d'Aquino* (Milan 1923).

57 Not only does Aquinas maintain that matter is proportioned to form and form to matter, but he also holds that essence is always proportioned to act of existence, for on the former's nature turns the latter's intensity (*Summa contra Gentiles* II. 53). As Eco remarks, this throws light on the transcendentality of the beautiful; for it follows that a thing is proportioned by virtue of the fact that it is: the 'act of composition between essence and existence ... is a *proportio*, a concording, a harmonising', *Il problema estetico in Tommaso d'Aquino*, p. 114.

Thomas has little to say[58], and *claritas* on which he has a great deal more. Rather as with proportion, the ubiquitous variety of *claritas* language astonishes and, for some, perplexes.[59] It was Thomas's master Albert who had integrated the language of *claritas* into Aristotelian hylomorphism where it took its place in the metaphysics of form.[60] Here *pulchrum* emerged at last as *splendor formae, resplendentia formae*. For Albert, such *resplendentia* is the clarity of achieved order in being's manifestation of itself. And something of the same absolute objectivity obtains when Thomas writes his commentary on Denys's treatise, *The Divine Names*. Denys. Denys had spoken of 'divine rays' which bestow on all creatures a certain refulgence. Thomas understands this as a metaphor in the metaphysics of participation. But, as he goes on to explain, it has its referent in *form*.

> All form, through which something has being, is a certain participation in the divine *claritas* ... Things are beautiful ... according to their own form.[61]

Thomas never took this further, because the beautiful was not among his primary explicit preoccupations (on this Balthasar is correct if not perhaps for the right reason[62]). But, clearly, 'pankalicism' here is a fair – in the sense of a 'just' if not, considered as English, in the sense of 'beautiful' – term. But can we go beyond this, and say that Thomas has, at least tacitly, a sense of the wider theological beauty which covers all of revelation, salvation, sanctification, as with Augustine?

Starting from Thomas's favoured word *convenientia*, it has proved possible to claim so. The statistics of the word's use are impressive. Gilbert Narcisse informs us that in Thomas's corpus there are in all nearly nine thousand instances of *convenientia* vocabulary. The adjectival form *conveniens* alone crops up 1,500 times. And this still leaves out of account such near-synonyms as *competit, pertinet, congruit, expedit, decet*. It is suggestive that it occurs with greater frequency in the prologues to Thomas's works or their major sub-sections, for the crucial role of these

---

58   The only discussion is at *Summa theologiae*, Ia., q. 39, where Thomas seems to consider it a kind of proportion, the adequation of an object to what it ought to be, and so its complete realisation of itself.

59   Eco writes, 'The concept of light is contradictory in Thomas because it is so in the whole mediaeval tradition', *Il problema estetico in Tommaso d'Aquino*, p. 135. One need not accept the word 'contradictory' here: 'plural', or, better, 'analogical' would serve. To take the two extremes in Thomas's range of usage: with their 'heraldic' feeling for colour, the Middle Ages loved elementary tones caught in the strongest light – and yet they also inherited a patristic repertoire of light metaphors for the supreme theological realities.

60   There is a continuity here with the *Summa* of Alexander of Hales and his confrères.

61   *In Dionysium, De divinis Nominibus* c. IV, lect. 5.

62   For Eco, Thomas's vision is so pervasively aesthetic that he had no need to emphasise the theme as such: see *Il problema estetico*, p. 146. Or again, in a universe where '*la manifestatività dell'essere*' is the language God speaks to man, given objective proportion and vision, *claritas* follows ineluctably: ibid., pp. 150–51.

has often been marked.[63] Statistical analysis shows that recourse to the language of *convenientia* increases as Thomas's writing career unfolds. *Convenientia* words cluster most thickly when the topic of the Incarnation comes into view. These computations already establish that Narcisse is surely correct to say that appeal to *convenientia* constitutes for Thomas an intrinsic aspect of the 'habit' of theology.

But just *what* about the habit of theology does this linguistic phenomenon disclose? For Narcisse the answer is: an entire theological aesthetic, albeit one that is tacit in Thomas's doctrinal work. He takes as his guide a proposal by Thomas in question 93 of the *Prima Pars*, when dealing with that key tenet of Christian anthropology, the doctrine of the *imago Dei* in man.[64] Thomas suggests that what the image of God doctrine points to – namely, the analogical unity which holds good between God and man – is a kind of *convenientia*, because there is a *proportio* involved, and, as we know, *proportio* is a formal element of the *pulchrum*. This close connection of *convenientia* with *proportio*, and accordingly, with *pulchrum*, must not be forgotten when in a different context, but still in regard to the works of creation, we find Thomas stating as a general principle that God cannot do something which is not *conveniens* with his wisdom and goodness: that is, does not fit beautifully with them.[65] Hence Thomas's confidence in invoking *convenientia* language in a wide range of doctrinal areas affecting the works of re-creation, the economy of redemption; for example, in his account of the missions of the Son and the Spirit, or his description of the indwelling of the divine Trinity in the human soul by sanctifying grace. Whether Thomas has in mind creation or recreation, the work of God is, Narcisse writes:

> only *convenientia* founded in the free love of God, from whom a cascade of particular 'conveniences' flows down.[66]

Significantly, perhaps, the same metaphor – 'cascade' – occurred to Eco when attempting to capture the essence of Denys's cosmology of the beautiful. Denys's treatise, wrote Eco, portrays the universe as 'a cascade of beauties pouring forth from the primordial fount'.[67]

Pointing out the great suppleness of thought made possible by the *convenientia* idea, Narcisse argues that *convenientia* is everywhere present in Thomas's theology not necessarily as an argument but in the mode of an implicitly conceptualised 'ontological convenience' between God and man. By contrast to Balthasar, Thomas carried out his theological project above all as a theological logic, working through the making of distinctions. But a Thomasian theological aesthetic is subjacent, and can be drawn out by showing the essential coherence of revelation's 'grand lines' as Thomas's theological thought presents them. Narcisse largely presumes on the

---

63   G. Narcisse, *Les raisons de Dieu*, p. 35.
64   Thomas, *Summa theologiae* Ia., q. 93, a. 1, ad iii.
65   Ibid., q. 21, a. 4, corpus.
66   G. Narcisse, *Les raisons de Dieu*, p. 54.
67   U. Eco, *Il problema estetico in Tommaso d'Aquino*, p. 43.

quasi-synonymity of *convenientia* with the beautiful, trusting to the long-standing connections of *conveniens* talk with notions of harmony and proportion. The two themes, *pulchrum* and fittingness, can be said to converge 'fairly spontaneously'.[68] Theirs is a relation to which Thomas alerts us in telltale remarks as when he ties together the lovely and the 'suitable' in the words of the *Secunda Secundae*: 'what appears beautiful, *decorum*, to perception is held for *conveniens*' as well as 'for good'.[69]

The climax of Narcisse's efforts to present Thomas as a theologian of evangelical beauty just as Harrison did (unbeknownst to Narcisse) for Augustine, is Christology (just as it was for her). As is well known, Thomas portrays the return of man, the *imago Dei*, to God, his exemplar Source, as coming about by way of Christ's earthly life, predominating as this does in the *Summa theologiae*'s *Tertia Pars*. And here it is hardly possible, thinks Narcisse, *not* to notice the continual recourse to *convenientia* language – taking place, then, at revelation's divine-human heart's core. [70] Thomas invokes it for the hypostatic union itself and for all the principal mysteries of the life of Christ – since, as Aquinas stresses, the kind of life the Redeemer lived, in its sequential order, had to be in a condition of *convenientia* with the goal of the Incarnation.[71] Narcisse leaves this – clearly vital – topic until the last in his survey because he wants to draw attention to three things. First, Christology – and more especially the union of natures in the person of the Word – is where Thomas will speak of the *convenientissimum*, the 'super-*conveniens*', the most fitting thing in the world. The superlative form is uniquely required when we consider, marvelling, how the ontology of the union stands in relation to its purposes – negatively, the abolition of the consequences of the Fall, and, positively, our inheriting of eternal life. Secondly, it is in the discussion of Christ's mysteries that Narcisse can best show how *convenientia* concerns the *proportion* (key formal property of beauty as this is) of means to end, something explicitly stated by Thomas in regard to Christ's miracles.[72] Thirdly, Thomas's reflections on various features of the Gospel narrative can persuade us that *convenientia*-thinking can lead to theological *profondissements*, taking us deeper in such matters as, for example, why it was fitting that the Lord did not personally write. As Narcisse sums up:

> The fittingness (*convenance*) of a means reaches its maximum in a rich plurality of realities that concur in the same end. Now in the Incarnation, the work of God reaches its wonderful maximum of density.[73]

Narcisse believes, surely rightly, that so metaphysical a theologian as Thomas could not have deployed *convenientia* on such a scale unless he considered it ontologically

---

68   Ibid., p. 203.
69   *Summa theologiae* IIa. IIae., q. 145, a. 2, ad i.
70   G. Narcisse, *Les raisons de Dieu*, p. 63.
71   *Summa theologiae*, IIIa., q. 40.
72   G. Narcisse, *Les raisons de Dieu*, p. 74.
73   Ibid., p. 100.

well founded. What is only implied in his corpus may be spelled out – and possibly in so doing, Narcisse throws light on the presuppositions of Augustine's mature aesthetic. *Convenientia*, so Narcisse suggests, depends, first, on some version of the analogy of being, on some version of the analogy of faith, and on some account of the relation between 'theology' and 'economy', God and his saving design. First, then, in some way the *analogia entis* is involved. As Narcisse explains:

> Analogy presupposes a *rapport*, an accord, a proportion, a likeness – themes very close to the concept of *convenientia*.[74]

Convenientia depends, secondly, on the *analogia fidei*, the interrelated unity of all themes in sacred doctrine. Here Narcisse comments:

> The *analogia fidei* presupposes the *analogia entis*. It develops within the faith, seeking to consider no longer the unity of created being [that is the task of *analogia entis*] but the unity of the plan of God.[75]

And *convenientia* depends, thirdly, on a relation between (in the language of the Fathers) 'theology' and 'economy' – between the triune God and his saving work. Or as Narcisse puts it, referring to a well-known reading of the shape of the *Summa theologiae* as one of the going out of creatures from God and their return to him:

> The ceaseless dialectic between the economy and the theology espouses all the *convenientiae* harmonised by the *exitus-reditus* movement, which itself is super-determined by the Christological movement of the coming and return of Christ.[76]

With this threefold foundation, Narcisse's claim is credible that the 'logic' of *convenientia*, itself midway between the logic of arguments *ex ratione* and the logic of arguments *ex auctoritate*, gives metaphysics, theology and the ecclesial sense a more 'perfect reciprocity'.[77] Its appearance as a fresh aesthetic style of thinking about divine things is just what we should expect when the light of faith creates a novel 'proportion' in adequating human intelligence to the new reality of the revelation of the supernatural order in Jesus Christ, inviting human reason to the 'contemplative, silent prolongation of the mystery' which will be seen with unveiled eyes in the Age to Come.[78] One does not have to be a Balthasarian to see how the beautiful can legitimately furnish a basic kind of theological judgement in Christian dogmatics.

---

74 Ibid., p. 89.
75 Ibid., pp. 89–90.
76 Ibid., p. 91.
77 Ibid., p. 145.
78 Ibid., p. 146.

Conclusion

One need not be a Balthasarian, but it might be helpful to be a Balthasar-sympathetic Thomist. This indeed is Narcisse's position. We need to remember that Balthasar's own ontology is drawn from Thomas; the real distinction of essence and existence, and all its corollaries, are common ground. What is distinctively Thomistic – and hence distinctively non-Balthasarian (though not counter-Balthasarian) in Narcisse's approach is the emphasis he would place, in a future Thomasian theological aesthetics, on exemplarity – in particular the exemplary causality of the mysteries of the life of Christ, the perfect Image of God, as conforming to him the lives of Christians by sanctifying grace. In the hands of Thomas, such exemplarity is manifested by multiple *convenientiae*, for what could be more beautifully appropriate than for Christ's humanity to save us by transmitting conformation to itself? This is the imitation that 'opens out to an infinite and eternal originality'.[79] An 'authentic Thomasian theological aesthetic'[80] will be, above all, an aesthetic of configuration. As the image of the triune God in man, defaced by sin, is restored that way by Christ, the entire moral and spiritual content of Thomism can thus be covered.[81] In a future theological project, to:

> deepen the sense of the *convenientiae* of exemplary causality is at the same time to favour the attraction exercised by the mysteries of Christ …[82]

Here, in such configuration, is where the theological aesthetic dimension appears, and what is it if not to bring out the beauty of revelation centred on Jesus Christ such as Augustine celebrated it in the *Enarration* on Psalm 44, and took as the starting point of the *renovatio in melius* of the image of God in ourselves? For Augustine and for Thomas, and not only for Balthasar, it is *convenientissimum* that by visible things are shown forth the invisible attributes – and the saving design – of God.[83]

---

79   Ibid., p. 447.
80   Ibid., p. 439.
81   Ibid., p. 450.
82   Ibid.
83   Thomas, *Summa theologiae*, IIIa., q. 1, a. 1.

Chapter 2

The Origin and Crisis of Christian Art

Introduction

In this chapter, we move on from questions of beauty at large, natural or Christian, to consider the visual art for which the claim is made that it embodies the upshot of reflection on the first two themes. The earlier sections of the chapter will look at the genesis of Christian art, the later sections will explore the greatest of the counter-reactions, Byzantine Iconoclasm, and review the reasons for the restoration of icons as seen from the two extremes of the Christian world of the time: Arab East and Frankish and Celtic West.

So far, much has been said about beauty – including the beauty of God and his saving design, but little or nothing about the artworks, and especially the *visual* art, in which such beauty might be signalled. (No particular theory of the beautiful is presupposed here, save the theologically minimal – yet adequate – position that in the striking form produced by iconographers the wonderful quality of the goodness and truth comprised by divine revelation becomes manifest.) We must address this now. Only the earlier period of such 'signalling' will be treated here. But that is no drawback. Quite apart from the fact that origins are always crucial, one can hardly consider the origin and development of Christian art without becoming aware of the constancy of its basic formulae. That constancy derives from the presence, as its inspiring source, of the historic revelation attested in Scripture (as read in Church tradition). And this revelation, at least in the way classically minded Catholic theologians would see it, is one and identical, albeit capable of fresh exploration and suggestive ramification, throughout the course of time.

As an unexpected consequence, Christian art lends itself rather well, then, to the school of art history that is associated with the names of two highly influential scholars, Aby Warburg and Erwin Panofsky. Originating in German scholarship of the 1920s and 1930s, the 'formalist' iconology they recommended deals basically with standardised images or *typoi* – 'types', just as its counterpart in literature deals with stock themes – *topoi* – which if the English language were itself predictable we should call 'topes'! Art historians who see themselves chiefly as 'iconologists' tend to note how not only motifs and themes but also formulae for representing those motifs and themes constantly recur. Considered as a scholarly movement for the investigation of the history of Christian art, iconology has been described as possessing a threefold focus: firstly, 'continuity of images (iconography per se)';

secondly, a close relation to the 'systematically examined literary text'; thirdly, the 'interaction of artistic image with cultural context'.[1] The iconographic image is:

> stored, coded passion that is perpetuated in a kind of determining collective memory and very strongly conditions (or completely governs) the artist's depiction of a particular motif.[2]

But the *genesis* of Christian art is, even – or, rather, especially – on this view of things, unique. For the basic repertoire which this process will presume is here first being constituted. 'The artistic achievement of the fourth and fifth centuries lay in the creation of an art which was Christian in content and purpose.'[3] The iconographic themes on which a thousand variations will be played, through Giotto, or Poussin to David Jones and Georges Rouault, are now first being sounded. Their composition – that is, the transposition of the verbal forms of 'Scripture read in Tradition' into art – is getting underway. And this is happening, to continue the musical analogy, through the pressing into service of the notes of that 'scale' that is Hellenistic art in its vast geographical deployment, from Rome to Egypt to Mesopotamia, in the world where the Gospel itself was born. In the words of John Lowden, historian of early Christian and Byzantine art:

> Early Christian and Byzantine artists invented and defined the Christian tradition in visual representation that dominated European art until recent times. The images and structures they created to embody the visible and invisible worlds of religious experience and belief were visually and intellectually so satisfying that their tradition was maintained, even through periods that sought self-consciously to throw off the burden of the past.[4]

---

1   N. Cantor, *Inventing the Middle Ages: The Lives, Works and Ideas of the Great Medievalists of the Twentieth Century* (New York 1991), p.173. The same writer further notes in this passage that appeal to texts here is 'absolutely essential and thereby differentiates German iconography from freewheeling French impressionist art history'. He ascribes the key role of interactions with cultural context to 'the influence of Jacob Burckhardt, the revered nineteenth-century historian of Renaissance Italian civilisation, and friend of the classicist and philosopher Friedrich Nietzsche'. For a very clear explanation of the approach, with examples not only from Christian art (Giotto) but a Greek urn, an Indian *Birth of Buddha*, and Paul Gauguin, see L. S. Adams, *The Methodologies of Art: An Introduction* (Boulder, Colorado, 1996), pp. 36–57.

2   N. Cantor, *Inventing the Middle Ages*, p. 73. See for the thought of Warburg, Panofsky and others, M. Prodo, *The Critical Historians of Art* (New Haven, Conn., 1982), and M. A. Holly, *Panofsky and the Foundations of Art History* (Ithaca, N.Y., 1984). For an example of how the text and image approach works, see W. Stammler, *Wort und Bild. Studien zu den Wechselbeziehungen zwischen Schrifttum und Bildkunst im Mittelalter* (Berlin 1962).

3   C. Mango, *Byzantium. The Empire of the New Rome* (London 1980), p. 260.

4   J. Lowden, *Early Christian and Byzantine Art* (London 1997), p. 4.

Iconography and the Bible

Despite the background of Israelite aniconicism (the absence of a cult of visual images for the divine in Old Testament religion),[5] and the danger, identified by ancient Jewish writers, both within the Biblical Canon and outside it, of how pagan idolatry could affect Judaism,[6] a case can be made for saying that the fundamental theological thrust of the Judaeo-Christian revelation necessarily bursts through these constraints.[7] A faith based on divine Incarnation will eventually find expression in the realm of the *visible*. The First Letter of St John opens:

> That which was from the beginning, which we have heard, which we have seen with our eyes, which we have looked upon and touched with our hands, concerning the word of life – the life was made manifest, and we saw it, and testify to it, and proclaim to you the eternal life which was with the Father and was made manifest to us – that which we have also seen and heard we proclaim also to you, so that you may have fellowship with us; and our fellowship is with the Father and with his Son Jesus Christ. And we are writing this that our joy may be complete. (John 1:1–4)

We can hardly fail to notice the importance of 'seeing' words in this short passage. Again, in his letter 28, the fourth-century Greek father St Basil the Great comments:

> All things that are in the Father are beheld in the Son, and all things that are the Son's are the Father's; because the whole Son is in the Father and has all that the Father has in himself. Thus the person of the Son becomes as it were the form and face of the knowledge of the Father, and the person of the Father is known in the form of the Son.[8]

In these two texts, one biblical, the other patristic, we have an anticipation of the theological shape of Christian iconography. What is revealed in the humanity of Jesus is the divine Logos, but the Logos in his relations with the other Trinitarian Persons (or at least, for Basil has nothing to say here explicitly about the Spirit, with the Father). And he *is* so revealed – this John makes clear – within the interplay of the apostolic fellowship, and therefore within what the major twentieth-century

---

5   For this topic in Old Testament times, see W. Zimmerli, 'Das Bildverbot in der Geschichte des alten Israel', in idem, *Studien zur alttestamentlichen Theologie und Prophetie. Gesammelte Aufsätze* (Munich 1974), pp. 247–60. For the later Jewish attitude, see J. Leeven, *The Hebrew Bible in Art: The Schweich Lectures of the British Academy, 1939* (London, 1944), and J. Gutmann, 'The "Second Commandment" and the Image in Judaism', in idem, *No Graven Images: Studies in Art and the Hebrew Bible* (New York 1971), pp. 3–16.

6   Notice, however, that the question of whether all nations are called to Yahwistic faith, and hence required to leave off the practice of pagan cults, is not completely resolved in the biblical literature. See J. Carleton-Paget, 'Jewish Prosyletism at the time of Christian Origins: Chimaera or Reality?', *Journal for the Study of the New Testament* 62. 2 (1996), pp. 65–103.

7   This is the thesis of A. Nichols, OP, *The Art of God Incarnate: Theology and Image in Christian Tradition* (London 1980).

8   Basil, *Letter* 38, 8, at *Patrologia Graeca* 32, 330C.

practitioner of theology in an aesthetic mode, Hans Urs von Balthasar, called 'a co-human constellation' of other figures too. This is something that will eventually license the entry into iconography of Mariology and hagiology – the depicting of Mary and the saints – as well.

The Old Testament background

In one sense, as the continuing antipathy of Orthodox Judaism to sacred art of a figural kind shows us, this is a great surprise – a rupture indeed – in the predominantly aniconic or even anti-iconic tradition of the Scriptures of Israel. But how did that tradition itself arise?

The commandment not to make 'graven images', as found in the Book of Exodus, is closely associated with the primal command to have 'no other gods' but Yahweh – God as named by and to Moses. There is no compelling reason not to accept here a kernel of meaning going back to Moses himself. After all, the command makes sense as a ban on the use by Israelites of motifs drawn from the art of the cult-image with its partly anthropomorphic (man-shaped) and partly theriomorphic (beast- and bird-shaped) – gods which would have been well known to Jewish émigrés from Egypt. Yahweh is not to be imaged in symbols drawn from 'the heavens above, the earth beneath and the waters below the earth' (Exodus 20:4). These phrases indicate, of course, the three basic habitats of creatures.

Probably there was, unofficially, *some* iconic cultus of the God whom the Mosaic tradition worshipped. In the Book of Judges, Micah's house-Levite, a kind of private chaplain, has an 'ephod' or 'ependytes', a star-studded cloak for an image representing the heavenly glory of Yahweh (Judges 18:14). In the Book of Genesis (notably at chapter 31), the patriarchal sagas refer to 'teraphim': images of the 'God of the fathers', the typical pre-Mosaic designation for the God of Abraham, Isaac and Jacob. (These, on the standard source-critical analysis of the Pentateuch current for most of the twentieth century, are stories passed over without comment by the 'Yahwist' writer.)

And indeed the *official* cult has images – but not directly of God in his own nature. In Exodus 25 and 26 we hear of figures of the cherubim cast in gold and placed over the ark and others woven on linen with blue, purple and scarlet thread to adorn the veil of the holy of holies in the Tent of Meeting. These may be called images to identify and adorn the invisible throne of God the Lord.

The Deuteronomic movement was more radical in its interpretation of the Mosaic commands. There was a fear of the contamination of the purity of Mosaic Yahwism by the syncretistic addition of elements from Canaanite religion. In the so-called Shechemite Dodecalogue, a ceremonial expansion of the Ten Words, we read:

> Cursed be the man who makes a graven or molten image, an abomination to the Lord, a thing made by the hands of a craftsman and sets it up in secret. (Deuteronomy 27:15)

A wider aniconicism – that, de facto, can be paralleled here and there in a variety of west Semitic cultures – has here become 'programmatic' with a vengeance. What lies behind such passion?[9] Deuteronomic theology is controlled by the idea of the sovereign freedom of God's action. It construes the making of religious images as a usurpation of divine initiative. Its stance is reflected in the extreme apophaticism of certain strands of the prophetic tradition, as in an oracle ascribed in the dominant modern scholarship to the 'Second' Isaiah:

> To whom then will you compare me, that I should be like him, says the Holy One. (Isaiah 46:5)

This is in part a response to idolatrous cultus in the nations around Israel, but it leads to a problem for Israelites themselves. In what sense is such a hidden God disclosed in his creation at all?

Another of the Hebrew Bible's many sources attempts to answer this question. The 'Priestly Writing', conventionally dated to the period after the Exile to Babylon if also relying on older traditions, includes the first of two creation accounts in Genesis' opening chapter. And there an answer is offered to the – actually, rhetorical – question in the scrolls of Isaiah. God may not be like man, but man is like God – to the extent, at any rate, that the human being has been so created as to be a possible vehicle for divine communication. He or she is made 'in the image of God' (Genesis 1:26–7). Although this text is rarely cited in the rest of the Old Testament it illuminates the collected Scriptures of Israel in a remarkable way.

In its light we can see how the prophets, for instance, embodied the divine feeling or attitude towards Israel (the divine 'pathos' is the phrase often used), whether this be positive or negative, delight or anger. The text on the human imagehood of God also makes sense of much of the seemingly anthropomorphic, 'man-shaped', language of the Old Testament when it comes to divine existence: what this language is doing is, not least, to forward a theomorphic, 'God-shaped', picture of man. Or to put this in another way, humanity's being in the divine image enables language to be bipolar, reflecting in different ways God as well as man. All in all, the text on man as the image of God enables us to read the Old Testament theologically as the account of a God who in some sense wills to enter history in a human manner.

---

9   The Swedish scholar of Israelite aniconicism Tryggve Mettinger has argued that such a text is unlikely even to mention the significance of the *empty* divine throne, upheld by figures of cherubim, in the Jerusalem temple. To say God's *Name* dwelt in the temple seemed less alarmingly anthropomorphic than to place his throne there. Thus T. N. D. Mettinger, *The Dethronement of Sabaoth: Studies in the Shem and Kavod Theologies* (Lund 1982), pp. 50–52; idem, *No Graven Image?: Israelite Aniconism in its Ancient Near Eastern Context* (Stockholm 1995), p. 17.

The New Testament and Jewish art

In *what* sense God wills this becomes clear, for the New Testament successor to the Old, only with the career of Jesus, whom the Letter to the Colossians proclaims as 'the image of the invisible God' (1:15–20). '*The* image': the unique, definitive image. His life, death and resurrection are the revelatory form for God's relation to the world, and are thus bathed in the 'glory' which is the biblical term for the overwhelmingness of that difference from the world by which God is God.

And just as the key to Jesus's ministry, with its culmination in his Passion, is its sacrificial charity, which was the form of his life, so what this images or reflects is the divine love which in this way becomes in Christianity the central divine attribute, around which the others must revolve. And if in this fashion his particular way of embodying divine imagehood has implications for the doctrine of God, for theology proper, it also has implications for a Christian doctrine of man, for theological anthropology as well. As the Second Letter to the Corinthians makes clear, the form of Christ's humanity is the medium by which human beings generally can realise the image and likeness of God in their own lives. As Paul writes to Corinth:

> We all, with unveiled face, beholding the glory of the Lord, are being changed into his likeness, from one degree of glory to another; for this comes from the Lord who is the Spirit [i.e. who now lives in the Spirit of God]. (II Corinthians 3:18)

Such 'image Christology', as exegetes and historians of theology call it, was, it may be surmised, the more acceptable to Christian Jews because, relatively early in the common era, and despite the official aniconicism, a Jewish religious art – at least at certain times and in certain places – had begun to express divine action – and therefore presence – in painterly images. This is the message of the synagogue frescoes of Dura-Europos in the Euphrates Valley in modern Iraq, 'the Pompeii of the Syrian desert'.[10] The patristic scholar and historian of archaeology W. H. C. Frend describes the content of the murals as follows:

> [They] were dominated by scenes from the life of Moses, starting with a vivid representation of Pharaoh seated on his throne, with Moses' mother nearby in the act of placing her son in a basket on the banks of the Nile. Moses grown-up was painted twice the size of the Israelite soldiers in the act of leading them to liberty across the Red Sea. Future generations were to behold the Lawgiver and Servant of God. Other paintings reminded worshippers of great moments in Israel's history: the recapture of the ark of the covenant from the Philistines, and the destruction of Dagon's temple, demonstrations of God's will as shown in the sacrifice of Isaac and the story of Job, and the hope proclaimed by Ezekiel for the restoration of the people in this world and the next.[11]

---

10 J. Leveen, *The Hebrew Bible in Art*, p. 22.

11 W. H. C. Frend, *The Archaeology of Early Christianity* (London 1997), p. 236.

That is not in fact an exhaustive list of the tableaux, and the number and variety of scenes treated has naturally invited speculation. What, if anything, holds them all together?

To some extent they can be regarded as a running commentary on texts from the Hebrew Bible read on Sabbaths and festivals. The particular prominence given to the vision of Ezekiel, the single largest fresco, might be explained by the intensified interest in eschatology, and the doctrines of resurrection and immortality, to which the inter-Testamental literature bears witness. Another proposal is that the frescoes are visual realisations of the closing chapters of the book of Ecclesiasticus which concern the praise to be given to 'famous men'. Again, salvation in times of trouble is a shared leitmotif of many of the pictures, and may reflect a Jewish prayer for forgiveness used in synagogue worship.[12]

The historian of the Hebrew Bible in art Jacob Leveen, commented:

> It is quite clear ... that the wall-paintings of Dura are not to be considered as an isolated and possibly unique example due to the liberal attitude adopted by the local heads of the community, but rather as the hitherto sole surviving specimen of a form of art common to many synagogues of the time.[13]

That is a confident statement, and its confidence reposes not just on collateral evidence, widely spaced if not so stunning, from synagogues at Beth-Alpha, Jerash and Na'aran in Palestine, as well as in Greece and North Africa,[14] but also on two texts from the Talmud, which permit respectively painting and mosaic. 'In the days of Rabbi Jochanan [reads the first] men began to paint pictures on the walls and he did not hinder them' – a reference to one Jochanan bar Nappaha who died in AD 279, and so is in fact contemporary with the Dura frescoes.[15]

However, Leveen does not deny that rabbinic permissiveness in these cases is grudging. Right down to the Middle Ages and beyond, rabbinic judgements express distrust for representational art, considered too apt to distract congregations from the business of religious devotion. But the artistic use of Jewish symbols was found far beyond synagogue walls. An example is the menorah, the seven-branched candlestick in the Jerusalem Temple that came to be regarded as the symbol of the indestructibility of Israel and its faith and the sign of immortality. The menorah is found on coins and medallions, in sculpture, on gilded glass and in catacombs.[16] Other widespread symbols include the Ark of the Law, the cabinet containing the scrolls of the Law, the palm-branch, and the silver trumpets used on festal occasions. Needless to say, these are far less iconographically ambitious than the frescoes at Dura. Where the Durene

---

12 J. Leveen, *The Hebrew Bible in Art*, pp. 51–6.

13 Ibid., p. 12.

14 E. L. Sukenik, *Ancient Synagogues in Palestine and Greece* (London 1932). For the synagogue of Hammam Lif, which falls outside the scope of Sukenik's study, see the description in J. Leveen, *The Hebrew Bible in Art*, p. 65.

15 Tractate *Abhodhah Zarah*, 48d.

16 J. Leveen, *The Hebrew Bible in Art*, p. 16

frescoes have some posterity, however, is in the Hebrew Bibles illuminated for private use, of which the earliest surviving example, preserved only fragmentarily at St Petersburg, has been dated to around 930. The most ambitious examples, with whole sequences of miniatures representing biblical scenes, come from the Western European high Middle Ages. A number of these are sumptuous and their stylistic similarity to the miniatures in Christian Bibles at the time is probably to be explained by the emergence in the course of the thirteenth century of schools and workshops where lay artists, some of them Jews, could be trained in what had previously been a monastic craft-tradition. The same holds true for illustrated copies of Hebrew prayer-books, rabbinic treatises, wedding contracts, and, above all, the *Haggadah*, the text for the ritual of the Eve of Passover as celebrated in private homes.

It is not so much symbolic art as anthropological representation which interests the Christian – and therefore Incarnationalist – theological observer. The theme of man in the image of God, inherited from the Hebrew Bible, and the object of new interest thanks to the Adam-speculation of some inter-testamental Judaism, enjoyed a predictable renaissance in the wake of the event of Jesus Christ.[17] The result would be, in the patristic period, not only a Christology of the image but a theological anthropology on this basis also.[18] Thus for example that summator of the Greek Christian theological tradition St John of Damascus warms to this theme in his *Oration on the Transfiguration*:

> Then [in the Incarnation, God the Word] took pity on us, and renewed a second communion with us, much more steadfast and wonderful than the first. For while remaining in the excellence of his godhead, he took up what was inferior, recreating mankind to himself, joining the archetype and the image. And today in this image he shows forth his own beauty for his face shines like the sun …[19]

Unsurprisingly, then, in his discourses in defence of the icons, John affirms how the glory of God in the face of Jesus Christ is glimpsed in the appearance of the holy personage – whether Christ, the Mother of the Lord, or one or more of the saints – depicted in the painterly image.[20]

17   J. Jervell, *Imago Dei. Genesis 1, 26 im Spätjudentum, in der Gnosis und in den paulinischen Briefen* (Göttingen 1960); F.-W. Eltester, *Eikon im neuen Testament* (Berlin 1958).

18   For a thoughtful presentation of Image Christology, see A. Grillmeier, SJ, 'Die Herrlichkeit Gottes auf dem Antlitz Jesu Christ: Zur Bild-Theologie der Väterzeit', in idem, *Mit Ihm und in Ihm. Christologische Forschungen und Perspektiven* (Freiburg 1975), pp. 19–75. See for a survey of the anthropological application, A.-G. Hamman, *L'homme, image de Dieu: Essai d'une anthropologie chrétienne dans l'Eglise des cinq premiers siècles* (Paris 1987).

19   John of Damascus, *Oration on the Transfiguration*, 4. The translation is taken from J. McGuckin, *The Transfiguration of Christ in Scripture and Tradition* (New York 1986), p. 209.

20   K. Parry, *Depicting the Word: Byzantine Iconophile Thought of the Eighth and Ninth Centuries* (Leiden 1996), p. 93.

Christian iconography in the early patristic age

In point of fact, the frescoes at Dura are more impressive in scale of conception than any Christian images (as yet discovered) dating from the earliest centuries, prior to the emperor Constantine's 'Peace of the Church'. Combine that with the seeming hostility to religious art shown by the early Christian Apologists, and there seems to be a case for saying that the first generations of the Church's faithful did not in fact draw any artistic conclusions from Christianity's Incarnational structure, or if they did they were negative ones.[21]

Interpreting the Apologists

In his study *The Invisible God*, Paul Finney argues that such a conclusion does not in fact follow.[22] A precondition for developing a public art is some community control of property, in both land and capital. A religion in a state of incipience – just setting out, lacking legal recognition and subject, albeit sporadically, to persecution – did not meet this precondition. Not until around the year 200 did congregations in what was perhaps the largest local community, the church of Rome, grow to the point where they could begin to assert a distinct public identity. Furthermore, the attacks of the Apologists on religious art turn out generally to have other targets in the moral or metaphysical mistakes made, on their view of things, by pagan religion. Insofar as they train their fire on religious images at large, this is, Finney argues, through a strategy of making common cause with philosophically minded pagan critics of popular (pagan) religion. Such critics often accepted the hypothesis found in the Stoic and Cynic schools whereby primitive mankind was said to have enjoyed a state of aniconic innocence. At any rate, where the Apologists *do* touch on the topic of the Church and art (Minucius Felix is an example), their protestations of happy aniconicism are economical with the truth: frescoed walls in Christian catacombs and iconographic schemes for Christian sarcophagi were already a fait accompli in the Roman church at least.

And in any case, a public religion has to have a public face. Paradoxically, the Apologists stressed this.

---

21 Typical studies which take this view are: H. Koch, *Die altchristliche Bilderfrage nach der literarischen Quellen* (Göttingen 1917); W. Elliger, *Die Stellung der alten Christen zu den Bildern in den ersten vier Jahrhunderten* (Leipzig 1930–34); B. Kötting, 'Von der Bildlosigkeit zum Kunstbild', in W. Heinen (ed.), *Bild-Wort-Symbol in der Theologie* (Würzburg 1969), pp.103–18; T. Klauser, ,Die Äusserungen der Alten Kirche zur Kunst', in idem, *Gesammelte Arbeiten zur Literaturgeschichte, Kirchengeschichte und christliche Archäologie* (Münster 1974), pp. 328–37; idem, 'Erwägungen zur Entstehung der christlichen Kunst', in ibid., pp. 347–92; idem, 'Der Beitrag der orientalischen Religionen, besonders des Christentums, zur spätantiken und frühmittelalterlichen Kunst', ibid., pp. 347–92.

22 P. C. Finney, *The Invisible God: The Earliest Christians on Art* (New York and Oxford 1994).

... There is a steady line of development from Jesus through Paul and the apologists in the direction of a continuous early Christian desire for greater visibility and public recognition ... The apologists are the main carriers of this line. They were champions of public and visible religion in a time when Christianity was largely an unknown quantity to outsiders. They sought to put a public face on the new religion, and in considerable degree they succeeded. Without the groundwork laid by the apologists, the Eusebian-Constantinian program of making Christianity visible in dramatic architectural and iconographic forms is simply unthinkable.[23]

This claim is not as paradoxical as it sounds. For the patrons of early Christian art did not renege on the central credal claim of the Apologists that the true God is of his nature, and in his mystery, invisible. Palaeo-Christian art shows the divine allusively, and in mediations. It does not claim to lay bare the essential form of divinity, but rather to provide signs of how God savingly entered human history in commerce with representative human figures who were the recipients or beneficiaries of divine blessing.[24]

There would naturally be *some* version of a 'material culture' as the Apologist Clement of Alexandria admitted in advising on Christianity-compatible designs for such things as signet rings and seals.[25] For an Incarnational religion, this will surely mean, at the centre of material culture, visual artworks, even if the realisation of this entailment takes some time to work out – on the well-known principle of the development of doctrine (or, in our case, doctrinally related practice). There is reason to think that a presumption of the normatively aniconic nature of Christianity (owing to its Old Testament matrix) has distorted the interpretation of a number of early Christian texts from such writers as Eusebius of Caesarea and Epiphanius of Salamis.[26] In somewhat withering terms, Finney compares the highly influential anti-iconographic study of 'The Ancient Christian Image Question according to the Literary Sources' by the Göttingen scholar Hugo Koch to the *florilegia* produced by the Byzantine Iconoclasts. Koch's work is just:

> another example of quotations lifted out of their original literary-historical contexts and strung together in a narrative that is indifferent to the qualifying force of context. It is true [Finney concedes] that Koch assembled more sources (many more) than any of his predecessors, and he also dressed them up in a more scholarly format consistent with modern historical-critical standards. But even these improvements cannot disguise the underlying barrenness of literary and historical evidence cut free of defining environments and contexts ... In the end *Bilderfrage* [that is, Koch's book] is a modern doxography, a catena of authoritative patristic testimonies carefully selected and arranged to illustrate Harnack's Hellenization theory.[27]

---

23 P. C. Finney, *The Invisible God*, p. 289.

24 Ibid., p. 281.

25 See Clement, *The Teacher (Logos Paidagogos)*, III. 59. 2–III. 60. 1.

26 M. C. Murray, 'Art and the Early Church', *Journal of Theological Studies*, new series 28 (1977), pp. 303–45.

27 P.C. Finney, *The Invisible God*, pp. 8–9.

What *is* correct, however, in the Apologists' insistence on the clear blue water separating Christians from pagans using public art is that pre-Constantinian iconography in the Church eschews the portrait, the face. Finney himself ascribes this to the dampening effect of the convention, introduced by Pliny, whereby the emperor's image was to preside over every courtroom. This inhibited (at first) the emergence of venerating the image of a face. [28] Another student who in all essentials agrees with Finney holds, rather, that it took the doctrinal controversies over the Incarnation, beginning in Constantine's reign, to prompt the Church to draw appropriate aesthetic conclusions from the assertion that the face of Christ is the face of God.[29]

Canon, philosophy, audience

Be that as it may, key to this art was the Bible. This was so not just because the Bible is the accredited witness to the Judaeo-Christian revelation the art claimed to serve. The very idea of a vision of the world based on the exegesis of a canon of sacred books helped form, in the Christianised Roman empire, a 'symbolic consciousness' for which everything in the world could be explicated as a symbol of the other world, the world of God. As Jas' Elsner puts it, in such a context, a naturalistic 'secular' art would be, well, in a word, unnatural.

> In a culture which subjected the artefacts it produced to increasingly complex, exegetical and religious interpretations, art was expected to stand for symbolic and religious meanings, rather than to imitate natural things.

And Elsner goes on:

> Not only was the mimetic illusionism of naturalistic art no longer necessary to late antique culture. But its very attempt to deceive was a barrier for those who sought truth or religious edification in images. Art became 'abstract' or 'schematic' not because of a decline in taste or skill, or for simple reasons of political appropriation, but because viewers, patrons – in fact the collective taste and subjectivity of the culture – wanted it that way.[30]

The transition from illusionistic verisimilitude in art to schematic abstraction, is not just a stylistic shift in the direction of formalism. It directly reflects the changing

---

28   Ibid., p. 86. Concentration on the cult-portrait partly explains the negative attitude towards any version of the Iconophile case for the early emergence of Christian art assumed in Hans Belting's insightful study *Likeness and Presence. A History of the Image before the Era of Art* (Chicago and London 1994): note the author's self-restricting caveat at p. xxi.

29   R. M. Jensen, 'Icon or Idol? A Development in Early Christianity', *Art and Christianity Enquiry Bulletin* 28 (2001), pp. 5, 15.

30   J. Elsner, *Art and the Roman Viewer: The Transformation of Art from the Pagan World to Christianity* (Cambridge 1995), pp. 18–19. Elsner has explained that by 'abstraction' is meant here 'less a stylistic "abstraction" than the abstract relationship whereby an image of a fish means Christ' ibid., p. 9.

philosophy – indeed theology – of viewers. By the age of Justinian, the period when the evidence for Christian veneration of images is most copious, the Roman empire especially in the East was what Elsner terms an 'exegetic' culture, that is, as she explains, one in which:

> Every event, text and image could be read as an exegesis of one fundamental and real event – namely, the Incarnation as represented by the narrative of Christ's life and Passion.[31]

It was through the Bible – through a binding to the closed Canon of Scripture – that the allegorising method well known for the communication of meaning in pagan antiquity became something different. It became Christian typology.

> In tying typology to salvation, Christian art was fastening interpretation to salvation, not any particular exegete's version of salvation … but a textually grounded, critically tested orthodoxy.[32]

The Canon and the commentarial tradition that flowed from it in patristic literature: this is what makes Christian art different content wise from pagan.

Averil Cameron has suggested two additional kinds of factor which drew Christianity to the practice of visual art. First of all, there were consonances of a philosophical kind between revelation and art. With its emphasis on salvation in the body and through the body – Christ's own body and his corporate body the Church – the Christian Gospel gave great weight to the figural. Here, in the context of classical antiquity, that Gospel drew naturally on the Platonic language of representation which itself borrowed the language of visual art. Moreover, Christian discourse was predominantly narrative: it exhibited salvation in the lives of the saints, conceived as a symbolic pattern to follow and, once again, readily expressible – if this were desired – in the form of art. Lives were themselves or as biographical texts 'verbal icons'. Putting these two points together, she writes:

> As the Platonic language of representation used in so many Christian texts was translated into concrete expression, Christians were presented with a pictorial world thickly populated by holy people. It would not be long before they became as familiar and as beloved as living friends.[33]

And then secondly, the Christian leadership, unlike its pagan predecessor, was not concerned with the perpetuation of an elite but with 'reaching an audience at all levels', including 'classes of society hitherto successfully ignored'.

> For Augustine, the average congregation is full of confused masses, the 'straw' of the Lord's 'threshing floor'; these pose a problem just as difficult to deal with as the Jews,

---

31   J. Elsner, *Art and the Roman Viewer*, p. 124.

32   Ibid., p. 280.

33   A. Cameron, *Christianity and the Rhetoric of Empire: The Development of Christian Discourse* (Berkeley, Calif, 1991; 1994), p. 151.

pagans, and heretics whom one met outside the churches. It was only natural that religious art came to be seen as a means of reaching such people.[34]

Cameron emphasises that the icon is at once lowbrow and highbrow, and enters equally into private and public spheres. Holy pictures could be 'small and personal as well as impressive and public';[35] and if in private use there may be a special connexion with women – inhabiters of the private sphere par excellence (this is a topic explored by Judith Herrin[36]), in the realm of public use there is expression at the highest social level.

Clearly, the emergence of a Christian art was part and parcel of that wider process that is the Christianisation of the Roman empire.[37] What was Christianised included art,[38] not least sacred art,[39] and ritual,[40] not least the rituals of power.[41] To cite Cameron again:

A massive intellectual adjustment was necessitated by the final demise of the classical world and the new circumstances of the early medieval one. As the traditional systems crumbled, the nature of truth and the foundations of knowledge were themselves called into question ... Truth being redefined as religious knowledge, images were seen by many as one, though only one, of the ways by which access to this truth was possible. They occupied this privileged position not least because of the long struggle in Christian thought to find a language by which God could be represented ... But they also raised fundamental issues about matter and about what [images] could actually be held to represent, in a period concerned about charges of idolatry and still dominated by basic Christological issues.[42]

---

34   Ibid., p. 186, with an internal citation of Augustine, *On Instructing the Simple*, 7. 11.

35   Ibid., p. 202.

36   J. Herrin, 'Women and the Faith in Icons in Early Christianity', in R. Samuel and G. Stedman Jones (eds), *Culture, Ideology and Politics* (London 1982), pp. 56–83.

37   On which see R. MacMullen, *Christianising the Roman Empire* (New Haven and London 1984); R. Lane Fox, *Pagans and Christians* (London 1986); J. N. Hillgarth, *Christianity and Paganism, 350–750. The Conversion of Western Europe* (Philadelphia 1986); A. Cameron, *Christianity and the Rhetoric of Empire* (Berkeley, Calif., 1991).

38   J. Engemann, 'The Christianization of Late Antique art', in *The XVIII International Byzantine Congress: The Major Papers* (New Rochelle 1986), pp. 83–105; A. Cameron, 'The Rise of Icons and Christian Representation', in D. Wood (ed.) *The Church and the Arts* (Oxford 1992), pp. 1–42.

39   J. Huskinson, M. Beard and J. Reynolds (eds), *Image and Mystery in the Roman World* (Gloucester 1988).

40   S. MacCormack, *Art and Ceremony in Late Antiquity* (Berkeley and London 1981).

41   S. R. F. Price, *Rituals and Power* (Cambridge 1984).

42   Idem, 'The Language of Images: The Rise of Icons and Christian Representation', p. 41. The phrase 'the traditional systems crumbled' might take some justifying, granted the persistence of philosophical Hellenism and the Constantinian concept of the civil polity.

The icon floated on potentially stormy seas. Much turned on it, since sacred images, held by Iconophiles to 'represent objective truth', had come to be seen as among the 'guarantors of knowledge'.[43] Where, despite later classicising revivals in East Rome, classical antiquity was something of a 'lost horizon', the images formed part of the 'intellectual framework' in which Byzantine people sought reorientation.

The crisis of early Christian art

Theology and image in the Iconoclast crisis

Attempts to identify a political or social genesis for Iconoclasm – competition with the (aniconic) Caliphate?, an imperial desire to rein in the centrifugal tendencies of monasticism? – have failed to secure general acceptance. Even were that not so, there would still be a need to ask why tensions between various solidarities took this particular theological form.[44] There is no alternative, then, to controversial theology. In its various phases, the age of Iconoclasm brought forth a fine crop of counter-arguments to Iconophile positions (and practice). Iconophobe dialectics sometimes dusted off texts from the early Apologists. But more sophisticated considerations issued from the Christological controversies of the centuries since the Apologists had written.

Five Iconophobe theses predominated in the argumentation offered at the Iconoclast Councils of Hiereia (754) and Hagia Sophia (815), as well as in the stating of the case against images at Nicaea II, the future 'Seventh Ecumenical Council', itself.[45] Firstly, Iconoclast spokesmen cited the danger – or indeed the reality – of superstition, defined in this case as confusing the image with the Imaged. Secondly, there were historical objections to the cult of images, based either on the existence of the anti-iconic commandments in the Old Testament or those patristic texts – from, especially, the Apologists – which appeared to condemn it. Here the Iconoclast scholars had compiled anthologies of anti-image quotations just as modern scholars would later do in nineteenth- and twentieth-century Germany, though with less refined tools. Thirdly, there was, as in the doctrinal definition of the Iconoclast synod

---

43   Ibid., p. 2.

44   R. Cormack, *Writing in Gold: Byzantine Society and its Icons* (London 1985), pp. 106–18.

45   For the often fragmentary sources, see D. J. Sahas, *Icon and Logos: Sources in Eighth Century Iconoclasm* (Toronto 1986). On the Hiereia synod in particular, see M. V. Anastos, 'The Argument for Iconoclasm as Presented by the Iconoclastic Council of 754', in K. Weitzmann et al. (eds), *Late Classical and Mediaeval Studies in Honor of Albert Matthias Friend, Jr.* (Princeton 1955), pp. 177–88. The same author deals with one major aspect of the Iconoclast case in 'The Ethical Theory of Images Formulated by the Iconoclasts in 754 and 815', *Dumbarton Oaks Papers* 8 (1954), pp. 151–60. For the 815 council, see P. J. Alexander, 'The Iconoclastic Council of St. Sophia (815) and Its Definition (*Horos*)', *Dumbarton Oaks Papers* 7 (1953), pp. 35–66.

of 754, the claim that it was an affront to the Mother of Christ and other saints to portray them in a dead, inert medium when they were in fact alive, alive with the immortality won by Christ in his Resurrection.[46] Alternatively, this could be expressed by asserting that verbal depiction of the virtues in the Bible and saints' lives rendered holy people 'living images' which were ethically inspiring – something art could not achieve.[47] (We should note, however, that some Iconoclasts also disapproved of the cult of the Mother of God and the saints even in aniconic form.)

Fourthly, and centrally, the Iconoclasts made great use of argumentation derived from that dogmatic Christology in which the age dominated by the Councils from Ephesus to Constantinople III had specialised. The emperor theologian Constantine V had proposed that the humanity of Christ, owing to its assumption by the divine Word, was essentially 'uncircumscribed', *aperigrapton*, a word derived from the verb 'to draw' and hence implying that which cannot be rendered artistically in the visual medium. This was an idea that readily suggested itself to those affected by Monophysitism, the Christological position which regarded the humanity assumed as absorbed by the divine nature in its union with the Logos. Already in the wake of Constantinople II, the Council called by Justinian, there was concern that some Churchmen clung on to such symbolic representations of Christ as the Lamb of God precisely because they were unwilling to have the humanity depicted as such, for quasi-Monophysitic reasons – or at any rate such concern is one plausible construction of the motivation behind the relevant canon (82). But even those consciously engaged in avoiding both Monophysitism and Nestorianism – such as the bishops at Constantine's own Iconoclast Council of 754 – could have doubts, and more than doubts, as to the feasibility of images of the Word Incarnate. Surely, the flesh and soul of Christ are those of the divine Logos, and cannot be separated therefrom?[48] Alternatively – or additionally – one might link Constantine's démarche to an earlier 'Origenist' critique of images according to which it is impossible to produce an image of Christ since 'the presence of the divine within him, at all stages of his existence, put him beyond the range of mortal images'.[49] During the early ninth-century revival of Iconoclasm, the Council summoned in 815 by the emperor

---

46   J. D. Mansi, *Sacrorum Conciliorum nova et amplissima collectio* XIII (Florence 1767), 277CE. Cited below as 'Mansi, *Concilia* XIII'.

47   See M. V. Anastos, 'The Ethical Theory of Images Formulated by the Iconoclasts in 754 and 815', art. cit. Anastos cites here the 754 Council's sixteenth anathema from the late eighteenth-century printed version in Mansi, *Concilia* XIII, op. cit., at 345CD: 'If anyone venture to set up profitless figures of all the saints in soul-less, speechless images made of material colours – for this is a vain invention and the discovery of diabolical craft – and does not, on the contrary, reproduce their virtues in himself as actually living images, with the aid of what has been recorded about them in books, in order to be stimulated to zeal like theirs, as our inspired fathers have said, let him be anathema.'

48   Mansi, *Concilia* XIII, op cit., 256A–257D.

49   M. N. Anastos, 'The Ethical Theory of Images Formulated by the Iconoclasts in 754 and 815', p. 154, with reference to Eusebius of Caesarea's *Letter to Constantia* on this very subject.

Leo V – hailed as a 'second Noah' sent to a world sunk in the flood of sin since the empress Irene's restoration of the images in 787 – repeated that Iconophiles by painting an image of Christ either circumscribed the divine nature of Jesus or separated off his human nature: equally illegitimate theological strategies.[50]

> Thus the iconoclasts conclude that 'he who venerates the icon divides Christ into two', since although the person represented is worshipped as Christ 'in two natures', he does not appear as such in his icon. The acknowledgement of the icon of Christ as the image of Christ himself is therefore unacceptable.[51]

Fifthly and finally, Iconoclast theologians proposed that the covenant of salvation already included God-given images of salvation thus rendering the painterly image superfluous. They had in mind either the Cross (which continued to be depicted, though without the figure of Christ) or the Eucharist, or both.[52] This *prise de position* was, evidently, determined by an overwhelming preference for non-figural representation, probably on the grounds that the temptation to idolatry was so much less.[53]

The destruction of images for which the range of arguments described above had been deployed was regarded by Iconophiles as a spiritual disaster. The course of events whereby the campaign against the icons was at once imperially spearheaded yet imperially defeated and reversed has been rehearsed many times. It is summed up simply enough by Bertha Diener who wrote: 'Six emperors had fought against them, and two empresses had led them home in triumph'.[54]

An Arab Christian response to Iconophobia

The theological responses of Greek Christian authors will be summarised by a twentieth- century 'theological aesthetician', Hans Urs von Balthasar, in the following chapter.[55] Much of their drift will emerge likewise from the account of the 'Conciliar theology' of Nicaea II, the Seventh Ecumenical Council, in the present

---

50   Our knowledge of the arguments furnished by the 815 Council comes chiefly from the writings of the Iconophile doctor Nicephorus of Constantinople, and notably the *Elenchos kai Anatropê* ('Criticism and Refutation') found in two Paris manuscripts whose relevant sections are printed as an appendix to P. J. Alexander, 'The Iconoclastic Council of St. Sophia (815) and Its Definition (*Horos*)', at pp. 58–66.

51   A. Giakalis, *Images of the Divine:The Theology of Icons at the Seventh Ecumenical Council* (Leiden 1994), p. 93.

52   For the Eucharist, see S. Gerö, 'The Eucharistic Doctrine of the Byzantine Iconoclasts and its Sources', *Byzantinische Zeitschrift* 68 (1975), pp. 4–22. Eucharist and Cross are discussed together in K. Parry, *Depicting the Word*, op. cit., pp. 178–90.

53   Ibid., p. 178.

54   B. Diener, *Imperial Byzantium* (ET Boston 1938), p. 152.

55   For an account by a modern Eastern Orthodox patrologist, see T. Sideris, 'The Theological Position of the Iconophiles during the Iconoclastic Controversy', *St Vladimir's Seminary Quarterly* 17 (1973), pp. 210–26.

chapter's succeeding section. Here a less well-known voice will be echoed. It reflects a source which should be of particular interest to early twenty-first-century readers concerned with the interplay of Islam and the West. A window opens onto Arab Christian attitudes within the territories of the Muslim Caliphate in the form of the treatise *On the Veneration of the Holy Icons* by Theodore Abū Qurrah, monk of Mar Saba and bishop of Harran.[56]

Though Theodore occasionally wrote in Syriac he is of particular interest in being the first Orthodox Christian scholar we know to have used Arabic as his medium of written communication. This distinguishes him from his theological master, St John Damascene, as does also his complete lack of reference to Byzantium. Theodore came from Edessa, the most influential city of the East Syrian Church, and was a Melchite – that is, an Arab-speaking Chalcedonian Christian, who accepted the two natures, one person, doctrine of Christ's being promulgated at the Fourth Ecumenical Council, Chalcedon, in 451. In his wider theology he pioneered the conceptual formulation of Christian orthodoxy in the Arabic language, in part for the benefit of groups outside the Great Church (those he called 'Jacobites' and 'Nestorians'), but also for Muslim consumption too. He wrote his Iconophile treatise around 805 for an official of the church of Edessa. Theodore was concerned for Edessan Christians who, anxious about Jewish and Muslim sensibilities, were abandoning the practice of venerating the Mandylion – Edessa's celebrated image of the Face of Christ – via the gesture of prostration. But his chief intended audience – or at least his main preoccupation – were the Caliphate's Jews and Muslims themselves. From what Abū Qurrah wrote it seems that, in the first place:

> the icon problem which the 'Melchite rites' faced had to do with the public veneration of the symbols of Christianity in an Islamic environment in which the Caliph's policies since the time of 'Abd al- Malik (685–705) had been to claim the public space for Islam.

What made matters worse was that:

> the icons and the cross actually proclaimed what the Qur'ān denies in regard to Jesus, son of Mary, and his mother.[57]

It was natural to seek to play down the role of the images for the sake of social peace. But how were followers of the two faiths interacting anyhow? Then as now in the Near East, some Muslims were not averse to making occasional use of Christian buildings for their prayers. This may be why images of living beings in late-eighth-century Palestine and Transjordan have suffered defacement.

---

56   S. H. Griffiths (ed.), *Theodore Abū Qurrah: A Treatise on the Veneration of the Holy Icons* (Leuven 1997); see also idem, 'Theodore Abū Qurrah's *On the Veneration of the Holy Icons*', *Sacred Art Journal* 13 (1992), pp. 3–19.

57   G. R. D. King, 'Islam, Iconoclasm and the Declaration of Doctrine', *Bulletin of the School of Oriental and African Studies* 48 (1985), pp. 267–77; see also S. H. Griffiths, 'Images, Islam and Christian Icons', in P. Canivet – J.-P. Rey-Coquais (ed.), *La Syrie, de Byzance à l'Islam, VIIe – VIIIe siècles* (Damascus 1992), pp. 121–38.

For Theodore – faithful pupil in this of Damascene – the images are legitimised by the turn the divine Economy has taken with the Incarnation.

> We accord God the purest attributes, but we also recognise his descent, in his mercy, into something other than what is in harmony with the transcendence of his being – wherein is our salvation, for which we thank him.[58]

In the spirit of Leontius of Neapolis's sermon 'against the Jews'[59], or, earlier still in the subapostolic period, the Epistle of Barnabas, Theodore argues that the Old Testament prohibitions on idolatry were addressed to a back-sliding people prone to revert to idolatrous practices. Such negative commands do not touch the Christian practice of venerating images of Christ and the saints. Worshipping the icons gives due adoration to God, due honour to the saints. So all is appropriate.

Theodore is aware that the New Testament record and the earliest Christian literature carry no explicit witness to an art expressive of biblical revelation, which had to await the emergence of the later Church Fathers. His account of *why* this is so is notable for providing a version of the 'development of doctrine' idea through a governing image that seems to be original to him.

> [W]hat the apostles and prophets said bears a resemblance to the wheat from which people get no benefit so long as it is whole. The teachers [the Fathers] resemble a man whose business is with the wheat; he grinds it, he kneads it, he makes baked bread out of it. He brings out its potentiality, hidden from anyone who sees it whole, who has no practical experience with it. When he has prepared it one may get the benefit of it. For this reason, God dignified their rank, and named them fathers to the believers.[60]

More than any other Iconophile author, Theodore elaborates a 'theology of prostration'. It was, of course, a gesture well known to Muslims, and in the course of his criticism of Iconophobes for a misplaced literalism in their thinking about their Iconodule opponents, Theodore cannot forebear from pointing out that prostration in the mosque appears to honour the ground or the carpet, but we all know that is not actually the case!

> It is the same with the Christians; their touching the icon in the process of making their act of prostration is in accordance with what they want to do – to honour Christ, their God, or his saints.[61]

---

58   Theodore, *A Treatise on the Veneration of the Holy Icons*, ch. V, at p. 59. (Page references are to the Griffiths translation.)

59   Leontius, *Sermo contra Judaeos*, in *Patrologia Graeca* 93 at cols 1597–1610. See N. Gendle, 'Leontius of Naples: A Seventh Century Defender of Holy Images', *Studia Patristica* XVIII. 1(Kalamazoo, Mich., 1985), pp. 135–9.

60   Theodore, *A Treatise on the Veneration of the Holy Icons*, Ch. VIII, at pp. 47–8.

61   Ibid., Ch. XI, at p. 60.

Theodore recalls those occasions in the Hebrew Bible when men did prostration before some representation or likeness of God: Ezekiel before the chariot of fire with the one enthroned who had the appearance of a man; Daniel and Isaiah at the theophanies they experienced; David before the Ark. In venerating the images of the saints, moreover, the 'prostration of honour' is what brings about contact with the saint: something pleasing to God who wills to arouse 'the interest of others in enjoying with him what [the saints] enjoy'.[62] Theodore portrays the Iconophobes as sardonically inviting Iconophiles to worship their critics, who, after all, are made in the image of God and thus presumably veneration-worthy themselves. But by abandoning such virtues as patience, self-composure, munificence, kindness, mercy, justice, those who hate the icons have mutilated the divine image within them and are not suited to be bowed down before.[63]

Critics of the icon-cult, Theodore suggests, are inconsistent: if it were an image of their own parent that was threatened with defacement, they would soon be up in arms.[64] And in any case, what about the veneration of the Torah-scrolls (by Jews) or the Gospel book (by the Christians)? If the status of matter changes when writing is stamped upon it (as Jewish and Christian Iconophobes would agree), why is it not the same when images are emblazoned there?[65]

The comparison between the material of the icon and the parchment and ink of the scroll or the codex is not Theodore's only ad hominem argument for Jews. Integral to his theology of the icon and well suited as an argumentative strategy for Jewish readers, is a comparison between the icons and the names of the tribes of Israel as engraved on the emeralds sewn onto the high priest's cloak in the liturgical accoutrements of Exodus 28.

> Evidently the Lord, the knower of all things before their coming to be, in his condescension wanted the names of the sons of Israel as a memorial before him, as if the sons of Israel, at the sight of their names would be standing in his presence beseeching him, and in his mercy he would be favourably disposed toward them ... So how can the Christians be blamed for making icons of the face of Christ in the course of carrying out his ministry, or of the faces of the saints in the entanglement of their affairs, as memorials to motivate them to express gratitude to the Messiah for having become incarnate for their salvation, and to emulate the saints in what they endured for love of him?[66]

And more widely: names are like icons, they function as representations of things. The signs performed by the prophets are also iconic, so Theodore argues, still thinking of the Hebrew Bible; what else was Ezekiel doing in following out the divine command to trace Jerusalem's outline on a brick and encircle it, then making an image of the

---

62 Ibid., Ch. XIV, at p. 67.
63 Ibid., Ch. XXI, at pp. 88–90.
64 Ibid., Ch. XXIII, at pp. 91–2.
65 Ibid., Ch. XXII, at pp. 90–91.
66 Ibid., Ch. XII, at p. 63.

coming divine judgement on Judah?[67] Here he anticipates the sophisticated modern 'biblical theology' of the unity of two Covenants, Hebrew and Incarnational, offered by the German Lutheran Ulrich Mauser.[68]

Finally, Theodore holds that the icon which best expresses the divine Economy in the Messiah's career, and the grace whereby Christians have been allowed to penetrate the incognito of the Humiliated One who was really God, is not just any image of Christ they erect, but more especially when they 'set up an icon of him shamefully crucified'.[69] If this is a specific reference to the Christ image of Edessa, might it suggest an affinity with the Holy Shroud?

Ecumenical resolution: Nicaea II and the reception of its dogmatic definition

An 'ecumenical resolution' which both Eastern Orthodoxy and Western Catholicism would come to find ultimately satisfying was forthcoming in the Church Council which met at Nicaea (modern Iznik) in 787.

Conciliar theology

The basic contention of the Iconophiles at Nicaea II was that Iconoclasts failed to grasp how the relation between the Uncreated, God and the created differs in the Christian image cult, on the one hand, and in pagan idolatry on the other. This had led them to misconceive the iconophobia of Scripture and the early Fathers, applying it to the post-Incarnation veneration of Christian images in a way that was inapt. Their condemnation of the practice of Christians was unwarranted: here we find an appeal to the 'practice of the Church', 'orthopraxis', as a theological criterion.[70] As Ambrosios Giakalis points out, it is hardly to be expected that Byzantine bishops would mount an archaeological enquiry – into the ruins of palaeo-Christian churches? – in order to prove this point. Instead, their case turned on the evaluation of texts in patristic florilegia, supported in a subsidiary way by appeal, positively, to the thaumaturgical power verified in some icons and, negatively, to the telltale rejection of images by groups that were manifestly heretical or schismatic vis-à-vis the Great Church.[71]

Which images, then, did Nicaea II accept? Those, it said, that in the first place, accorded with *historia*: namely, the 'letter' or 'history' – either translation is possible

---

67   Ibid., Ch. XIII, at pp. 66–7.

68   U. Mauser, *Gottesbild und Menschwerdung* (Tübingen 1971).

69   Theodore, *A Treatise on the Veneration of the Holy Icons*, Ch. XXIV, at p. 93.

70   See G. Dumeige, SJ, *Nicée II* (Paris 1978); A. Nichols, OP, 'The *horos* of Nicaea II: A Theological Evaluation', *Annuarium Historiae Conciliorum* 20 (1988), pp. 171–81, reprinted in idem, *Scribe of the Kingdom: Essays on Theology and Culture* (London 1994), pp. 180–91.

71   A. Giakalis, *Images of the Divine: The Theology of Icons at the Seventh Ecumenical Council*, pp. 29–46.

– of the Gospel proclamation. In the words of a speech recorded in the Council chamber:

> That which we have believed to be true through the faculty of hearing, we consolidate through pictorial imitation for our greater assurance. For being compounded of flesh and blood, we are compelled to confirm that which affects our assurance in regard to our souls through the faculty of sight.[72]

Writing of the icon as 'agent of truth', Giakalis, who considers the 'educational ideal' of the Iconophiles to be an evangelical transformation of the Greco-Roman tradition of *hairesis biou*, the choosing of a (way of) life, remarks that:

> so long as the Christian educational ideal does not aim simply at the satisfaction of the information-gathering capacity of the senses, but primarily at the salvation through faith of him who is being educated, it is understandable that the Church's means of teaching should not provide simple information but at the same time, and this is most important, should sanctify the organs of sense which receive the divine and saving teaching.[73]

In the second place, icons were legitimate, for Nicaea II, inasmuch as they confirmed the reality of the Incarnation. The Iconoclasts frequently dismiss the material medium of art as common, ignoble, worthless, whereas Iconophiles, even when not going so far as John Damascene in exalting the status of matter as the means of our salvation, practise a respectful realism in its regard. As Giakalis writes, with reference to Iconophile speeches at the 787 Council:

> That is why we read repeatedly that the representation of created sacred realities (e.g. the bodies of the saints or of Christ, the events of sacred history) follows the nature of things, constituting an immediate realism.[74]

In the Incarnation, thanks to the hypostatic union, the unique person of the Word energises in his human nature with 'concrete results' which must be taken with 'Iconophile realism'.[75] 'Even in the first phase of iconoclasm, it was obvious to both the patriarch Germanus and John of Damascus that the incarnation stood at the centre of the dispute'.[76] But it was only after the 787 Council, in the writings of Theodore of Studios, that an answer came to the question: are, then, the visible character and the uncreated hypostasis one in the imitative icon of Christ (and if not, how can we avoid saying there is a 'second person' there)? In his theology, St Theodore:

---

72 Mansi, *Concilia* XIII. 249E.
73 A. Giakalis, *Images of the Divine*, pp. 55–6.
74 Ibid., pp. 76–7.
75 Ibid., p. 103, 76.
76 K. Parry, *Depicting the Word*, p. 67.

does not identify the visible character with the uncreated hypostasis of Christ, but with a property of the hypostasis which because of the Incarnation is present also in the icon and permits a unity between archetype and icon, avoiding any possibility of division.[77]

Thirdly, for the Seventh Ecumenical Council, truly appropriate icons are those that prove spiritually 'profitable' for believers – a pragmatic appeal, this, to what 'works' to assist the Christian life as a life of virtue, in growing union with God. Giakalis notes the openness of the Council to the psychological value of the icon or, as he puts it, 'a psychological need to give sensible expression to the transcendent certainties of faith'.[78] However, as he realises, in the patristic witnesses adduced by the Council such subjective psychological assistance is intended to buttress the acquiring of objectively desirable attitudes such as religiously founded consolation for evils suffered (Chrysostom) and compunction for sins committed (Gregory of Nyssa).

Fourthly and finally, the Council did not deny the validity of the Iconoclast 'theology of the Cross'; what it did was to place (some) other images in the same theological realm as those for what it called the 'honourable and life-giving Cross'.[79] In point of fact, so far from opposing the high position granted the Cross of Christ as a 'type' or formal sign of the Redemption, the Iconophile interlude between the First and Second Iconoclasm saw the inauguration in Byzantium of a feast of the Adoration of the Cross (*Stavroproskunêsis*), while on the eve of the final and definitive restoration of the icons, the patriarch Nicephorus of Constantinople in his *Third Antirrheticus* would employ in this regard an a fortiori argument. If the Cross of the Lord, though not showing his worshipful body, is deemed worthy of veneration, how much more so the icon that pictures the Saviour in his full reality![80] (The Council's silence on the iconic status of the Eucharist is, by contrast, eloquent. For the Iconophiles the Iconoclast theology of the Eucharist stated both too much and too little. By treating the Eucharist as a natural, rather than imitative, image of Christ [just as the Son is image of the consubstantial Father], the Iconoclasts appeared to remove this sacrament from the order of signs altogether. But in seeing

---

77 A. Giakalis, *Images of the Divine*, pp. 111–12.

78 Ibid., p. 62.

79 Modern Greek Orthodox theology, by linking this statement to a version of St Gregory Palamas's doctrine of the uncreated divine Energies, would have it that while:

> the uncreated energy which deifies is supplied by grace from the Triadic God solely to the angels and the saints, the energy which purifies, illuminates and sanctifies is supplied to *the icons and holy Cross*, the sacred vessels, holy water, holy oils, etc., and is communicated from these and the Church's sacraments to those who are worthy, not to all in the same way and in the same degree, but in proportion to their spiritual state

Ibid., p. 125. Italics added. While reflecting passages of Damascene's *Orations*, this remains at best a tacit conviction among the fathers of Nicaea II.

80 Nicephorus of Constantinople, *Third Antirrheticus* at *Patrologia Graeca 100*, 428C–433C; cf. K. Parry, *Depicting the Word*, pp. 187–8.

the consecrated species as iconic of the Saviour, they also ascribed to the Holy Gifts a reduced status that was true of the *prosphora* only before their consecration.)

The Council's theological reconstruction of the factors involved in contemplating and honouring images would be important for the future. So far as contemplation is concerned, it affirmed that those who look on images are led to the 'memory of, and desire for, their prototypes'. So far as veneration is concerned, it stated that the honour given to them (which might be by a kiss, a bow, prostration, the use of incense or lights) is given to their prototype (it is 'relative', *schetikê*, veneration or worship). Here the Council made good use of a text from St Basil's treatise on the Holy Spirit where in passing the Cappadocian bishop remarks, 'The honour shown to the image is conveyed to its model'.[81] Thus, owing to this relation, someone bowing before the icon is bowing before the 'hypostasis (person) there graphically depicted': *engraphemonos*, from that verb which Constantine V had made key to his Iconoclast argument.

We could put it like this. The hypostasis of the Logos has its visible self-presentation in the face (*prosôpon*) and form (*eidos, morphê*) of Christ, and that face and form are disclosed in their painterly images. The theological fine-tuning of the definition is generally ascribed, more by presumption than evidence, to the contemporary Constantinopolitan patriarch, Tarasios, who was philosophically more an Aristotelian than a Platonist figure. The high theology of the icon as providing an earthly window into the heaven of the divine being, as that is found among the Russian theologians of the icon in the late nineteenth and twentieth centuries, has its patristic antecedents in, rather, the writings of St John Damascene, for whom the image is filled with the grace of the divine *energeia*.[82] But curiously his works do not figure in the patristic *testimonia* of the *horos* of Nicaea II.[83]

The reception of the horos

The question of the *reception* of the Council's teaching – centrally its *horos* or dogmatic definition – is an interesting one. In the East, Iconoclasm would make a 30-year comeback from 814 to 843, but this in turn would lead Iconophiles to a more sustained exploration of what we can call the logic or the ontology of the Christological icon, in writers like Nicephorus of Constantinople and Theodore of Studios.[84] Ever after, the status of the icon in Byzantium was utterly secure, and

---

81 Basil, *De Spiritu Sancto* 18, 45, at *Patrologia Graeca* 32, 149C.

82 On Damascene's theology of the icon, see T. Nikolaou, 'Die Ikonenverehrung als Beispiel ostkirchlicher Theologie und Frömmigkeit nach Johannes von Damaskos', *Ostkirchliche Studien* 25. 1 (1976), pp. 138–65; A. Louth, *St John Damascene. Tradition and Originality in Byzantine Theology* (Oxford 2002), pp. 193–222.

83 Possibly the text of the *Orations in Defence of the Holy Images* had not reached the main Byzantine centres by 787; or there may have been a hesitation about some aspect of their content: here the best candidate may be John's exalted doctrine of materiality.

84 See for a brief account A. Nichols, OP, *The Art of God Incarnate*, pp. 85–7. For Nicephorus, see P. J. Alexander, *The Patriarch Nicephorus of Constantinople: Ecclesiastical*

the faithful of all ranks heard an annual reminder of this Iconophile triumph on the Sunday of Orthodoxy (the First Sunday of Lent).

> We have moved forward from unbelief to true faith, and have been enlightened by the light of knowledge. Let us then clap our hands like the psalmist, and offer praise and thanksgiving to God. And let us honour and venerate the holy icons of Christ, of his most pure Mother, and of all the saints, depicted on walls, panels and sacred vessels, setting aside the unbelievers' ungodly teaching. For the veneration given to the icon passes over, as Basil says, to its prototype. At the intercession of your spotless Mother, O Christ, and of all the saints, we pray you to grant us your great mercy.[85]

In the West, reception of the dogmatic decree had been effortless at Rome. By contrast, a confused situation arose in the Carolingian empire – the lion's share of Western and west-central Europe at the time. Either (on one view) a group of Aachen court-theologians, or (on another) Charlemagne's English adviser Alcuin, or (on that taken not least by the work's most recent editor) the Visigoth Theodulph of Orleans, produced at Charlemagne's behest a partial rebuttal of the dogmatic definition in the so-called *Libri Carolini*, the *Opus Caroli regis*.[86] The author(s) of these books accepted the making of sacred images but not their cultic veneration. Somewhat reworked, their opinion found its way into the second canon of a Carolingian church council held at Frankfurt in 794. Some theologians, like Claudius of Turin, went even further in an outright rejection of Nicaea II comparable to that of the Byzantine Iconoclasts. But others supported the full teaching of the Eastern Council, notably Jonas of Orleans and the Irish scholar Dungal (Dumgáll).

The background is important. The good political relations of the Carolingian house with the early Isaurian emperors inclined Charlemagne to take a benign view of their assault on the image cult – and to be shocked at Irene's patronage of a Council (Nicaea II) that vituperated their memory. That the Council of 787 called for such gestures as prostration before the images convinced Charles (it is speculated) of its unworkability in the barbarian West. Should he accept its ecumenicity he would be obliged to apply its provisions, urging the introduction of new ritual acts

---

Policy and Image Worship in the Byzantine Empire (Oxford 1958); for Theodore of Studios, J. Meyendorff, 'L'image du Christ, d'après Théodore Studite', in *Synthronon: Art et archéologie de la fin de l'Antiquité et du Moyen Age. Recueil d'études par André Grabar et un groupe de ses disciples* (Paris 1968), pp. 115–19. The survey of relevant themes in the work of these fathers in K. Parry, *Depicting the Word*, is comprehensive.

85   Cited in H. Whybrew, *Orthodox Lent, Holy Week and Easter: Liturgical Texts with Commentary* (London 1995), p. 52.

86   A proposal of Theodulph's authorship was made on philological grounds in P. Meyvaert, 'The Authorship of the *Libri Carolini*', *Revue Bénédictine* 89 (1979), pp. 29–57. After a lifetime of study of the 'Books', this was accepted by Anne Freeman in her new edition, in which Meyvaert collaborated: *Opus Caroli regis contra synodum (Libri carolini)*, = *Monumenta germaniae historica, Leges 4, Concilia 2, Supplementum 1* (Hanover 1998).

on clergy and laity in a politically unenforceable way.[87] This may be correct, but it is supposition, given the lack of textual evidence for such a motive, and Charlemagne's willingness to promulgate his celebrated 'capitularies' for the reform of Church life in other areas.

Another suggestion is that there was, in Theodulph, an original 'fundamental theology' at work of a sort hardly reconcilable with the *horos* of Nicaea II. The *Libri Carolini*, ranging as they do over such topics as the nature of faith, the conception of the sacraments, the foundations of a theology of the Cross, the interrelation of the Old and New Covenants, and the inspiration and meaning of Scripture, have not unfairly been described as a kind of 'Summa' of Carolingian thought.[88] The German Jesuit scholar Rainer Berndt prefers a more contemporary flourish in calling them a 'Frankish *Grundkurs* of theology': the comparison was, evidently, with his confrère the dogmatician and philosopher Karl Rahner who gave just such a title to the synthesis of his theological thought.[89] The distinctive character of their general theological approach does not emerge with any great clarity, however, from Berndt's account: principally, it seems to be the notion that the due interpretation of texts from Scripture and fathers requires reference to an ecclesial norm, which the Caroline Books locate for all practical purposes in the Roman authority of the *Decretum Gelasianum*. That was an argument which could hardly withstand the Papacy's enthusiastic adherence to Nicaea II. It has to be supposed that the Franks expected Pope Adrian to rally to their *via media*, approving the making of images but not their cultic veneration. The ensuing disappointment may be the reason why so little attempt seems to have been made to disseminate the texts of the Council of Frankfurt. While its condemnation of the Spanish Adoptionist Felix of Urgel was ratified by a Roman council of 798, it would leave no mark on the history of attitudes to images until it was rediscovered by the first Protestant historians, the Magdeburg Centuriators of the later sixteenth century.[90] From then on, and especially after its enthusiastic embrace by Calvin, it would never cease to be cited by Protestant Iconophobes. Accordingly, it was placed on the (newly created) *Index librorum prohibitorum* where it remained until 1900.

It has usually been held that those responsible for the Caroline Books – and the bishops at Frankfurt – were misled by a faulty translation of the Acts of Nicaea II, notably in relation to the word *adoratio* which could cover both what the Greeks termed *latreia*, a word reserved for worship of a kind due to God alone, and also their *timetikê proskunêsis*, 'worshipful prostration', understood as a gesture with a wide

---

87   M.-F. Auzépy, 'Francfort et Nicée II', in R. Berndt, SJ, *Das Frankfurter Konzil von 794: Kristallisationspunkt karolingischer Kultur* (Mainz 1997), I., pp. 279–300.

88   See P. Henry, 'Images of the Church in the Second Nicene Council and in the *Libri Carolini*', in K. Pennington and R. Somerville (ed.), *Law, Church, and Society: Essays in Honour of Stephan Kuttner* (Philadelphia 1977), pp. 237–52, and here at p. 238.

89   R. Berndt, 'Das Frankfurter Konzil von 794: Kristallisationspunkt theologischen Denkens in der frühen karolingischer Zeit', in idem (ed.), *Das Frankfurter Konzil von 794*, op. cit., II., pp. 519–45, and here at p. 537.

90   W. Hartmann, 'Das Konzil von Frankfurt 794: Nachwirkung und Nachleben', in ibid., I., pp. 331–56, and notably at pp. 347–8.

ambit of giving religiously motivated honour. But Hans Georg Thümmel argues that not only were the Franks perfectly well aware of the difference, they were aware that the Greeks were aware of it too. Their objection was to a 'levelling', *Nivellierung*, of the terms –something inevitable once it was proposed that whatever kind of worship is due to the one represented in the icon is also due to the icon as his or her image.[91] (Aquinas would draw the conclusion explicitly in allowing *latreia* of the image of Christ.[92])

All issues of translation between Greek and Latin apart, the Frankish theology of what was to be venerated proceeded along different lines from that of the Iconodules at Nicaea II. For court theologians in the West, the sacred objects mentioned in the Old Testament are venerable only as types of Christ, not as material things.[93] Here the Caroline Books stress the role of the Ark as type of the glorified Lord in whom humans enjoy a covenant of peace with God (there may be an artistic illustration of this in Theodulph's own church at Germigny-des-Prés[94]), Aaron's Rod as a type of the priesthood of Christ, and the Manna of the New Covenant's heavenly food – the Eucharist. Admittedly, the physical Cross is venerable as the instrument of the Redemption, the relics of the saints as destined to share the Resurrection.[95] But no comparable statement can be made of icons. Above all, the Franks objected to any hint that the icons were in any sense comparable in rank to Scripture: had not the visionary John been told to write what he saw, not paint it?[96] They have, it must be said, a very beautiful theology of Scripture, filled with praise for its sweetness and capacity to bring spiritual quickening. The *Opus Caroli regis* treads a middle path, which it calls, using a common patristic metaphor, a 'royal highway'.

Theodulph's difficulty, which led him to so different a biblical hermeneutic from that of the fathers of Nicaea II, was an over-accentuated dualism between invisible and visible, heavenly and earthly, an insufficient awareness of the way the mysteric reality of the divine economy overarches and relativises these distinctions. That derives, as Celia Chazelle has pointed out, from a highly personal reading of Augustine, whose early writings in Chapter One of this book, so we have seen, lend

---

91   H. G. Thümmel, 'Die fränkische reaktion auf das 2. Nicaenum in den *Libri Carolini*', in R. Berndt (ed.), *Das Frankfurter Konzil von 794*, op. cit., II., pp. 965–80.

92   Thomas Aquinas, *Summa theologiae*, IIIa., q. 25, a. 3.

93   *Libri Carolini* I, 15, 37.

94   On this, see A. Grabar, 'Les mosaiques de Germigny-des-Prés', *Cahiers archéologiques* 7 (1954), pp. 171–89; M. Vieillard-Troiekouroff, 'Nouvelles études sur les mosaiques de Germigny-des-Prés', ibid., 17 (1967), pp. 103–12.

95   *Libri Carolini*, II., 28, 89; ibid. III., 24, 153–5.

96   Ibid., II., 30, 92–5. So sympathetic a student of the Byzantine Iconophiles as Kenneth Parry considers the writers of the Second Iconoclasm (the period from 814 to 843) lacking in balance in the way they stressed the superiority of the painted image over the written record: thus K. Parry, *Depicting the Word*, pp. 94–5. The ground of Parry's anxiety, though unstated, is clearly how to reconcile this with the status of Scripture as Tradition's primary monument for Christian faith. The exaggeration noted does not afflict, however, the theologians of the First Iconoclasm (730–87), nor Nicaea II itself.

themselves to such a view.[97] With Claudius of Turin – and notably in his *Apologeticum atque rescriptum adversus Theutmirum abbatem* (now lost) – we are in the presence of a far more determined foe. But the irritant within the oyster shell produced the pearl in the relevant writings of the Western Iconodule Dungal, the only master of the schools in the West to be singled out by name in that blueprint for public education in ninth-century Italy, the Capitulary of Lothar.[98] Twentieth-century scholarship pieced together the story of this once forgotten figure. The Irishman, 'outstanding among the "Scots"', who taught first at St Denis (Paris), then, from 825, at Pavia, and left his library to St Columbanus's monastery at Bobbio, also wrote a treatise in defence of the icons, the *Responsa contra perversas Claudii Taurinenis episcopi sententias* of around 827. Along with Jonas of Orleans' *De cultu imaginum libri tres*[99] Dungal's is the most important Latin Iconodule treatise of the *Bilderstreit*.[100] Proceeding by way of authorities, common enough in his day, the 'combination of the scriptural, the theological and the factual elements in the exposition [nonetheless] make Dungal's *Responsa*' – so claims their modern editor Paolo Zanna:

> not only one of the clearest statements of iconodule orthodoxy on the *vexata quaestio* of images written in the early ninth century, but also, more profoundly, a powerful illustration of some of the most distinctive aspects of early Christian spirituality.[101]

In any case, Frankish objections cut no ice at Rome. Pope Adrian II rebuked Charlemagne: Nicaea II was in accord with the entire tradition of the Church at Rome.[102] The Roman churches had many images, some of them put there by popes contemporary with the Ecumenical Councils or at any rate by popes who wanted to confirm the decisions of such Councils (presumably Ephesus with its definition of the doctrine of Mary's divine motherhood is mostly in mind), and these images were still venerated by the faithful in Adrian's own day. Against Iconophobes the popes had consistently defended their veneration. In point of fact the pope had just made a serious financial outlay restoring two relevant buildings: *I santi Cosma e Damiano*, with images of Christ, Peter and Paul and the two local patrons, Cosmas and Damian, and *Santa Pudenziana* with its Christ of the Parousia in the apse.

---

97 C. Chazelle, 'Matter, Spirit and Image in the *Libri* Carolini', *Recherches augustiniennes* 21 (1986), pp. 163–84.

98 See M. Ferrari, 'In Papia conveniant ad Dungalum', *Italia medievale e umanistica* 15 (1972), pp. 1–52.

99 To be found in Migne's *Patrologia Latina* volume 106 at cols 305–88. See further E. Amann in the *Dictionnaire de Théologie Catholique* VIII. 2 (1925), pp. 1504–8.

100 One can note, however, such works as: Eginard's *Quaestio de adoranda cruce;* Agobard of Lyons' *Liber de imaginibus sanctorum;* Walafrid Strabo's excursus on images in his *De exordiis et incrementis quarundam in observationibus ecclesiasticis rerum.*

101 P. Zanna (ed.), *Dungal, Responsa contra Claudium: A Controversy on Holy Images* (Bottai 1991), p. CIII.

102 M. Andaloro, 'Il *Liber pontificalis* e la questione delle immagini da Sergio I a Adriano I', in *Roma e l'età carolingiana* (Rome 1976), pp. 69–77; E. Lanne, OSB, 'Rome and Sacred Images', *One in Christ* XXIII. 1–2 (1987), pp. 1–21.

Conclusion

Iconoclasm was never totally defeated in the Christian tradition.[103] In one sense – as criticism, not as ritual destruction! – Iconoclasm, or at least a *reserved* attitude to images, has a necessary task, a purifying function for the Church's attitude to sacred art. It can be compared with the role of negative theology in keeping the Church's positive affirmations about God sensitive to the mystery of a God who is ever greater.

This can come about in a variety of ways, not all of them compatible with each other. We touch here the issue of the divide between an Iconophobic Reformed Christianity on the one hand, and Iconophile Catholicism, Orthodoxy and (up to a point) Lutheranism on the other. For example, the Cistercian criticism of the lavish iconography of Cluny turns on an interpretation of what is specific to Christian monastic life – hardly a concern of Luther's. The chief preoccupations of the Cistercian spokesman, Bernard of Clairvaux, were monastic poverty on the one hand (over against the much favoured use of gold and precious stones in the setting of images in Romanesque reliquaries and vessels) and, on the other, the need to concentrate on *lectio divina*, the studied pondering of the biblical text (to which the more exotic aspects of Romanesque sculpting were at best an irrelevance).[104] Bernard's emphasis is on the threat to specifically monastic sensibility and imagination. He has no general programme for the Church. Unlike the Romanesque black monk abbeys, Cistercian monastic churches were not centres of pilgrimage for the laity.

Quite different is John Calvin's critique of images. In making them he advances, to the mind of one sympathetic scholar, the theology of divine transcendence.[105] Calvin argues that human beings are metaphysically deranged such that they tend always to invert the order of things, bringing God down to their own level. The cultic expression of this failure to let God be God is disastrous, because worship is existentially integral to the knowledge of God, itself the real *raison d'être* of human life. True metaphysical principles applied to the confession of the Gospel issue in 'reverential acts' that escape the idolatrous contagion. That is why his 1543 treatise *De necessitate reformandae Ecclesiae* treats the issue of the 'corruption' of worship by the veneration of images as top of the Reformation agenda. For Martin Luther,

---

103 See for example, H. Feld, *Der Ikonoklasmus des Westens* (Leiden 1990); D. Freedberg, 'The Structure of Byzantine and European Iconoclasm', in A. Bryer and J. Herrin (ed.), *Iconoclasm* (Birmingham 1977), pp. 165–77.

104 E. Melczer and E. Soldwedel, 'Monastic Goals in the Aesthetics of Saint Bernard', in M. P. Lillich (ed.), *Studies in Cistercian Art and Architecture* I (Kalamazoo, Mich., 1982), pp. 31–44.

105 C. M. N. Eire, *War against the Idols: The Reformation of Worship from Erasmus to Calvin* (Cambridge 1986; 1989), pp. 231–3; see also M. Stirm, *Die Bilderfrage in der Reformation* (Gütersloh 1977*)*, and, concentrating on iconoclastic action as the mode in which many first experienced the Reformation, L. P. Wandel, *Voracious Idols and Violent Hands: Iconoclasm in Reformation Zurich, Strasbourg, and Basel* (Cambridge 1999).

by contrast, the image controversy with Catholics was altogether secondary.[106] That made it vis-à-vis other Protestants distinctly primary! Indeed, as the Calvinist scholarGiuseppe Scavizzi has written, 'the problems of images and of the Eucharist were the two most serious impediments to the unity of the Protestant world'.[107]

The response of the Council of Trent was simply to re-affirm, in a brief paraphrase, the teaching of Nicaea II.

> The images of Christ, of the Virgin Mother of God and of other saints are to be kept and preserved, in places of worship especially; and to them due honour and veneration is to be given, not because it is believed that there is in them anything divine or any power for which they are revered, nor in the sense that something is sought from them or that a blind trust is put in images as once was done by the gentiles who placed their hope in idols; but because the honour which is shown to them is referred to the original subjects which they represent. Thus, through these images which we kiss and before which we kneel and uncover our heads, we are adoring Christ and venerating the saints whose likeness these images bear.[108]

The Council Fathers were well aware that they had done no more than echo Nicaea II. (Thinking back, no doubt, to the cautious views of Augustine and Gregory I, Scavizzi terms the Tridentine decree 'the victory of Greek doctrines over those of the West'.[109]) In the post-Tridentine period, the question of how best to understand the 'relative honour' owed to images by virtue of their quasi-sacramental ontology continued to exercise Catholic spokesmen. As the English recusant Nicholas Sanders put it in his *A Treatise of the Image of Christ, and his saints*, the issue was 'really very difficult, because it touches upon philosophical points that are very subtle, not yet decided by the Church'.[110] To put the matter another way, the rationalism of the underlying metaphysic in Calvin's reading of Scripture called for a more searching response.[111]

---

106 See also Calvin, *Institutes of the Christian Religion*, I. x.

107 G. Scavizzi, *The Controversy on Images from Calvin to Baronius* (New York 1992), p. 2.

108 H. Denzinger- P. Hünermann, *Enchiridion symbolum, definitionum et declarationum de rebus fidei et morum* (Freiburg 1991), 1823 (= pp. 579–80).

109 G. Scavizzi, *The Controversy on Images from Calvin to Baronius*, p. 77.

110 N. Sanders, *A Treatise of the Image of Christ, and his saints: and that it is unlawful to breake them and lawful to honour them* (Louvain 1567; Ilkley 1976), p. 180.

111 Actually, a massive iconophile literature characterises Catholic theological production in the years 1560 to 1570 (and to a lesser extent till 1600): see G. Scavizzi, *The Controversy on Images from Calvin to Baronius*, pp. 5–6. Scavizzi points out how the abreaction against Calvinism produced an emphasis on miraculous images, the exaltation of the function of images, and a more comprehensive presence of the Church in the world of art. But he also points to the pluralism of theological explanation from the Catholic side, ranging from the somewhat minimalising position of Martin Perez de Ayala in his (1548) *De divinis, apostolicis et ecclesiasticis traditionibus*, 'we venerate only the prototype of the image, and honour the image merely as a sign created by Christian predecessors to assist us in such veneration', to

Image and transcendence are not to be set over against each other in the way Calvin does. The Irish Dominican Philip McShane writes:

> The background out of which form emerges is not neutral geometric space, nor is the emerging of form the result of some impersonal chance. Rather, the ultimate background is a boundless life beyond all that is seen. Its word is the template of all form and order through which the brimming profusion of the universe is poured. The artistic depiction of form thus understood is not purely factual. It is a continuation in the medium of art of an influence, a presence, a shining, an intent.[112]

In his Neo-Scholastic aesthetics with a difference – to be studied later in this book – Jacques Maritain will argue that beauty draws the soul beyond the created to the transcendental order, to a meditation on God as the extreme Beauty that is the cause of all the being there is. If the artwork's beauty is the opposite of narcissistic, since it points beyond itself to a beatitude which comes from attention to the other, the religiously inspired artwork may bring us to that supreme boundary where the bounded (the creaturely) is both divided from and linked to the Boundless (the Creator).

And if religion needs art, art likewise needs religion. When the great narratives that religion provides begin to disappear, art is in imminent danger of trivialisation. The contemporary religion-substitute, infinite consumption, would turn art into entertainment. True religion will always remain relevant to serious art because both take seriously the human predicament as, in the last analysis, metaphysical in kind.

> [W]e believe ... [wrote the principal philosopher of the movement called 'New Metaphysical Art'] ... that man is a predicament and not a problem to be solved. We see man as a predicament because through the power of consciousness he has become aware of his paradoxical state, moving from birth to death, torn by contrary impulses, searching for some kind of unity in the disparate and some kind of meaning in the contingent and some kind of timelessness in time. For us art is one of the great means of exploring and amplifying these tensions and, at times, resolving them. We believe that art does this through the creation of sensuous metaphors addressed to the imagination.[113]

The purveyors of these images, it may be suggested, need the canonical images of the Judaeo-Christian tradition as a measuring rod for their work. If the basic forms of an artist's personal imagination interact with the major themes of religious iconography, a desirable purgation can occur.

> The mythic power of certain aspects of his own vision is freed from the shadow of dubious forces. The form of the Judaeo-Christian story is like a stream which purifies and liberates

---

Matthew Ory's maximalising counter-argument in *De cultu imaginum* (1550) that the same worship goes from 'intellect and desire' both to the *res* and to its sign.

112 P. McShane, OP, 'Patrick Pye's Vision: Humanism within Theo-Drama', in The Arts Council, *Patrick Pye, RHA* (Dublin 1997), pp. 5–10, and here at p. 5.

113 Peter Abbs, *Open Letter to Richard Wollheim on behalf of New Metaphysical Art* (Brighton 1997), p. 2.

the strange backwaters in which personal mythologies get held up. Without this influence, without this interplay, much seemingly non-religious art can be in fact the unaware plaything of mythological forces – all the more insidious for being unrecognised. What the contemporary religious artist does is not something strange and deviant in the world of art. It is just his way of doing what is absolutely necessary.

Not that the role of revelation here is exclusively that of negative therapy. There is an eminently positive side to it as well.

[The] result when he succeeds is often the opening up of Dantean spaces for the imagination. No longer is the soul trapped hovering over the breakfast table or struggling in a personal closet. It is led forth onto a public stage where much has already happened, where great forces have long been at work. There is a sharper air, images are restored and a primal power engages us anew.[114]

There are of course limits to what an icon can express.[115] Yet Jas' Elsner could write:

The importance of Christian art on a social level lies in its brilliant visual ability to transmit the meanings and connections of typological thinking in Christian culture to anyone who took the trouble to *look*. In doing so, it transmitted Christianity itself.[116]

In the next three chapters, I consider how a trio of master theologians of the twentieth century – Hans Urs von Balthasar, Sergei Bulgakov, and Joseph Ratzinger (subsequently Pope Benedict XVI) – treated along these lines the theological claims of Christian art.

---

114 P. McShane, OP, 'Patrick Pye's Vision', p. 6.

115 K. Onasch, 'Recht und Grenzen einer Ikonensemiotik', *Theologische Literatur Zeitschrift* 111 (1986), pp. 241–58.

116 J. Elsner, *Art and the Roman Viewer*, p. 286.

PART 2
Twentieth-Century Theologians of the Image

Chapter 3

Hans Urs von Balthasar on Art
as Redemptive Beauty

Introduction

How did twentieth-century theologians approach this issue? For reasons the opening chapter of this book has touched on – he is the founder of contemporary 'theological aesthetics' on the grand scale – we should begin with Hans Urs von Balthasar.[1]

In the opening volume of *Herrlichkeit*, his theological aesthetics, Balthasar, not unnaturally, declares his support for Iconophilia. The Second Council of Nicaea, which dogmatised the legitimacy of making and venerating sacred images, is reckoned, after all, the Seventh Ecumenical Council of the Catholic – as of the Orthodox – Church.[2] But at the same time he evinces a surprisingly negative attitude to the patristic *apologiae* for icons.[3] Using positively English understatement he remarks:

> We cannot say that the theological arguments proposed in favour of icons always sound very convincing.[4]

Balthasar lists five kinds of argument commonly met in Iconophile writings. First, taking a cue from Basil the Great's theology of the relation between the Father and the Son, Iconophiles reasoned there must always be some relation, as well as distinction, between a likeness, *Abbild*, and the original image, *Urbild*.[5] Just so the consubstantial yet hypostatically distinct Son is indeed the 'image' of the Father. Secondly, Iconophiles drew on the corpus of writings left by the sixth-century Syrian

---

1   For an analytic survey of his multi-volume masterwork on this topic, see A. Nichols, OP, *The Word Has Been Abroad: A Guide through Balthasar's Aesthetics* (Edinburgh 1998). A pertinent account of some of his earlier writings can now be found in idem, *Scattering the Seed: A Guide through Balthasar's Early Writings on Philosophy and the Arts* (London 2006).

2   See idem, 'The *horos* of Nicaea II: A Theological Evaluation', *Annuarium Historiae Conciliorum* 20 (1988), pp. 171–81; reprinted as 'The Dogma of the Image at Nicaea II', in idem, *Scribe of the Kingdom: Essays on Theology and Culture* I (London 1994), pp. 180–91.

3   For the wider patristic 'defence of the icons', see V. Fazzo, *I Padri e la difesa delle icone: Complementi interdisciplinari di patrologia, a cura di A. Quacquarelli* (Rome 1987).

4   H. U. von Balthasar, *The Glory of the Lord: A Theological Aesthetics. Volume I: Seeing the Form* (ET Edinburgh 1982), p. 40.

5   Basil, *De Spiritu Sancto* 17. 44 and 18. 45.

monk who wrote under the name 'Dionysius the Areopagite' – Denys – so as to stake out the claim that a humanity which perceives through the senses and not only by the mind needs religious symbols in its ascent to God.[6] Thirdly, the simple point was made that whoever despises an image will naturally be taken to despise, likewise, that reality of which the image *is* an image. Fourthly, the Incarnation of the Word in real humanity suffices by itself to justify the cult of images – or at any rate images of the person of the Saviour. (Balthasar finds this a *petitio principii*. It is no use putting forward as an argument the conclusion that remains to be proved.) Finally, in a particularly unconvincing ploy, some icons at least were held to be *acheiropoietai*, 'not made by human hands', their heavenly provenance being attested by their wonder-working powers.[7] Even taken cumulatively, remarks Balthasar, we do not have here an adequate basis for overturning the anti-iconic commandment in the Ten Words of the Hebrew Bible, a prohibition on imaging the divine which the New Testament never contested and whose continuing force the 'dearth' of images in earliest Christianity attests.[8] Contrastingly, Balthasar finds the case of the Iconoclast lay theologian, the emperor Constantine V, to be impressive. According to Constantine: since the divine aspect of Christ's being is beyond representation, Christological images inevitably depict only a separated humanity. They are, therefore, inescapably Nestorian.[9]

We notice that Balthasar largely assumes the weakness of the five historical Iconophile arguments he enumerates. Only in one case – the fourth – does he bring a counter-argument of his own to bear. By and large, he simply states that Iconoclast arguments deserve better counter-arguments from Iconophiles, who for their part should recognise the strength of the opposing case. Indeed, to the theologian cognizant of Church history, the whole phenomenon of Iconoclasm serves as a timely reminder that 'the Image of himself that God made to appear in the world' – namely, the Image that is his Son, Jesus Christ – should not just be extended 'without any critical distance whatever' into other images. The 'transcendental beauty of revelation' is not the same as 'inner-worldly natural beauty'.[10] Writing in 1961, Balthasar was inclined

---

6   See for instance, Denys Areopagiticus, *De hierarchia ecclesiastica* I. 2. In the sixth century, Neilos Scholastikos and Hypatius of Ephesus may be cited as defenders of the images who apply Denys's general notion of *anagogê* or 'rising up' through material symbols to the immaterial and divine.

7   Cf. H. Belting, *Likeness and Presence*, pp. 47–77.

8   H. U. von Balthasar, *The Glory of the Lord* I, op. cit. For the Old Testament texts, see C. Dohmen, *Das Bildverbot: Seine Entstehung und Entwicklung im Alten Testament* (Königstein/Bonn 1985); recent revisionist scholarship has maintained that images develop in the early Church at the rate of its material culture generally: thus P. C. Finney, *The Earliest Christians on Art* (New York and Oxford 1994). Groundbreaking here was M. C. Murray, 'Art and the Early Church', *Journal of Theological Studies*, N. S. 28 (1977), pp. 303–45.

9   True so far as it goes, this is only a part-reproduction of Constantine's position; for the fragments in which his theology has come down to us, see D. J. Sahas, *Icon and Logos: Sources in Eighth Century Iconoclasm* (Toronto 1986).

10   H. U. von Balthasar, *The Glory of the Lord* I, p. 41.

to say of 'other' images than Jesus Christ that, after all, they belong of themselves not to the sphere of revelation but to that of aesthetics *tout court*.

By 1965, however, he had nuanced this position. His essay on Christian art and proclamation, 'Christliche Kunst und Verkündigung', which was published that year, came out exactly halfway through the writing of the seven-part theological aesthetics,[11] as a contribution to the opening volume of a multi-authored Catholic dogmatics entitled *Mysterium Salutis*, 'The Mystery of Salvation'. In this essay, far from relegating Christian art to a quite different – and evidently inferior – realm to that of revelation, Balthasar seeks to explain how sacred art can be regarded as sharing with the Liturgy, dogma and Christian proclamation the task of mediating revelation and so making revelation present.

For *this* Balthasar, then, Christian art is essentially a 'form' – with the naturally aesthetic connotations of that word – in which divine revelation is presented. His own version of Iconophile theology will consist in the attempt to show how this is so. Balthasar thinks progress in this domain depends on contextualising the issue of images in a wider theology of revelation in creation and redemption. The crucial connecting link between revelation and sacred art lies in that concept of *form* – a concept at once biblical and philosophical, and it enables Balthasar to lay out a theology of analogously ordered beauty in not only nature but also redeeming grace. He proceeds by putting in place not only a theology of man as in the image of God but a philosophy of images generally. An appropriate treatment of these themes, to his mind, is a desirable – not to say indispensable – preliminary to an account of the biblical revelation it is the task of sacred images to serve. These will be, then, the ingredients for a theology of redemptive beauty relevant to the human arts: a theology of beauty; a theology of the image of God in man, and a theology of the saving Incarnation as the centre of the revelation images must serve – not forgetting on the way a philosophy of the image at large.[12]

A theology of beauty

For Balthasar, creation supplies for divine glory an analogy of its own in beauty. When being – as found in the world and in the relation between God and the world – is investigated, it will be found to have certain all-pervading constitutive properties. Notable among these are unity, truth, goodness and beauty, without which a comprehensive appreciation of the particular classes of things that make up creation is hardly thinkable. These 'transcendentals' are interrelated. Here Balthasar seconds the judgement of Aquinas, who himself follows Denys the Areopagite, on whose treatise *On the Divine Names* Thomas had produced a commentary. Beauty is closely linked

---

11 Idem, 'Christliche Kunst und Verkündigung', in *J. Feiner – M. Löhrer* (eds), *Mysterium Salutis: Grundriss heilsgeschichtlicher Dogmatik*, I (Einsiedeln-Zurich-Cologne 1965), pp. 708–26.

12 Elements of the same programme may be found, worked out in different fashion, in A. Nichols, OP, *The Art of God Incarnate.*

to goodness: it has to do with the indwelling perfection and preciousness of some thing. Beauty is also bound up with truth: by its strikingness, it favours the evidence whereby a thing presents itself to the mind. Beauty is related to unity as well: the fine order or 'proportion' of some thing lights up as 'clarity', and this attests its unity which in the last analysis is a participation in the uniqueness of the absolutely One, the Creator. The beauty found in created things is, then, a 'shimmer of the absolute, fascinating preciousness, *Kostbarkeit*, of God' himself.[13] It is because the world shines with beauty that it can be known not to come from nothing or from evil. Such a 'doctrine of the transcendentals' is philosophical truth. Revelation cannot dispute it. Yet, so Balthasar thinks, that doctrine can be 'thrown open to a measureless extent' by the 'self-disclosure of the depths of God in the Trinitarian Word'.[14] Inner-worldly beauty, taken in its highest sense, irrupts into human experience, as witness pagan religion, whether the latter be mythopoeic or philosophical in kind. It does so from out of the mysterious depths of being, its 'God-proximate primal grounds'. This is what grounds art – the art of the peoples – and continues to nourish it. Revelation does not negate – how could it ? – such ontologically rooted art; rather, it fulfils or super-fulfils these often unclear or beclouded intimations from the 'world's depths'. Indeed insofar as it accepts the formal resources of the created and the human world it 'legitimates the speech of images'.

For Balthasar, then, there is no valid reason for limiting the domain of beauty to sensuous appearances – no more, indeed, than the domain of the good or the true. On the contrary, the beautiful requires by its very idea what Balthasar calls:

> A hidden spiritual depth dimension (*fond*) which, by appearing, by revealing itself in the sensuous, lends to its expression a mysterious and quasi-divine value, a value that is all the higher the more the idea which comes to expression is noble, and the more the mode of expression is adequate.[15]

He declares it to be impossible to be attached to form while neglecting or failing to respect what it is that thus comes to expression in it. Hence the 'infinite nostalgia' that shapes all great art. An 'acosmic mysticism' may seek, falsely, to strip away the material integument, but that integument is essential to the artwork not least because, in language taken from the French poet and publicist Charles Péguy, it is in the 'concrete, historical, carnal [*charnel*]' that the spiritual dwells. For a believing Christian aesthetic, every divine manifestation will be approached *a priori* as beautiful, just as it will as true and as good. The entire self-revelation of the Trinity in its economic manifestation in the Church comes under this rubric.

---

13   H. U. von Balthasar, 'Kunst und Verkündigung', p. 711. Balthasar has made use here of what was at the time the best study of Thomas's account of beauty: F. J. Kovach, *Die Ästhetik des Thomas von Aquin* (Berlin 1961).

14   H. U. von Balthasar, 'Kunst und Verkündigung', p. 711.

15   Idem, 'Religion et aesthétique', *Sciences ecclésiastiques* [Montreal] 12 (1960), pp. 299–305, and here at p. 301.

There is in Christianity a divine phenomenon – it is the Son of God, to whom the Father renders witness, and who is the Bearer of their common Spirit. He is the Bridegroom through whom the Bride finds herself enthroned: the Virgin and Mother of God, the Church-Woman who, according to Paul, is the *doxa*, the splendour, glory, effulgence of man. Then by the Spouse, specifically as Spouse, the whole world will be transfigured.[16]

In a theological aesthetics, prayer becomes the aesthetic act par excellence for it is the adoration toward which all admiration of the beautiful tends; theologies will be beautiful inasmuch as they register the incomparable *justesse*, 'rightness', of divine revelation as a revelation of grace freely given to man whom it heals and exalts, and in such an aestetics holiness is the Supreme Beauty on earth. The light, however, which procures us eyes with which to see this comes from God alone.[17]

In his philosophy and theology of beauty, Balthasar draws on both the Scholastic and the Germanist traditions of conceptual thought to forward his reading of divine revelation. Balthasar's linking of the concepts of form and beauty in the service of a Christian aesthetic bears a strong family resemblance to the briefer attempt by Jacques Maritain. Maritain also used axioms and allusions in Aquinas's corpus to furnish the groundwork of a more developed Thomist aesthetic. In *Art et scolastique* he defined form as 'the principle determining the peculiar perfection of everything that is', noting especially its importance for intelligibility and power of irradiation.[18] For Maritain, the creative artist 'discovers … a new way in which the brilliance of form can be made to shine upon nature', for artistic creation 'does not copy God's creation but continues it'.[19] Only when the artist is himself habitually open, however, to the reality of the transcendental order will he be able to produce works of genuine beauty. Meanwhile, in a Christological preview congenial to Balthasar, Maritain notes:

> No form of art, however perfect, can encompass beauty in itself as the Virgin contained her Creator.[20]

With this we can compare Balthasar's other main philosophical source, the classical German philosophy he had studied in the years prior to his entry into the Jesuit Society. Two exactly contemporary authors Johann Wolfgang von Goethe and Johann Christian Friedrich Schiller influenced him. In Goethe's morphology, *Form* denotes the qualitative unity of some living thing. It creates *Gestalt* or configuration in intellectual perception and awakens desire, the impetus of Eros, in the perceiver. For Schiller the aesthetic impulse, combining the 'form drive' of reason and the 'sense drive' of the senses, is essentially a 'play drive' which has as its object 'living form' – for Schiller a concept (in his words):

---

16 Ibid., p. 302.
17 Ibid., pp. 304–5.
18 J. Maritain, *Art and Scholasticism* (ET London 1939), p. 24.
19 Ibid., p. 63.
20 Ibid., p. 46.

serving to designate all the aesthetic qualities of phenomena, and, in a nutshell, what in the widest sense of the word we call beauty.[21]

Such beauty is, wrote Balthasar:

> inherent in things – in degrees from the lower to the higher, from the purely material and functional to the organic and sensible, and so from that of symmetry, proportion and harmony to that shown in vital tension and power, in the alternation of disclosure and concealment, in all the forms of interaction both inside and outside the erotic with its beguiling qualities. It includes all that in nature and in the human sphere serves to deck out bare existence; whatever is agreeable, adornment, clothing: all the apparatus created to serve the purposes of society.[22]

But, he insists, the history of art and culture shows that all this is, as he puts it, 'polarized' through the experience of the *mysterium tremendum et fascinosum*, the mystery of being in its primordial origin as it comes to bear on us – which is why the poet Rilke regarded the beautiful as the onset of the terrible, *das Schreckliche*. The beautiful, like the other transcendentals, opens a way, in fact, for the God of revelation.

> Created being would not be an image and 'outflow' '…' of the sovereign and living God if its transcendentals were static properties, clear and evident to our view, or if, despite their immanence in all contingent being, they did not have something of the freedom and mysterious depths of God's decision to reveal himself.[23]

Beauty, like truth, goodness and unity, has an unfinished character to it. Peter Taylor Forsyth, an English Congregationalist theologian much admired by Balthasar, wrote:

> We have marked in the history and nature of Art the action of certain processes of reconciliation, redemption, spiritualisation and so on. How do we know that these will converge in a reconciliation and glorification of all things? Have we any access already in history to an act which is the final reconciliation and manifestation of the whole creation revealed in advance?[24]

---

21   In the *Aesthetic Education of Man* Schiller calls form 'a concept which includes all the formal qualities of things and all the relations of these to our thinking faculties'. With this he integrated the concept of life, a concept 'designating all material being and all that is immediately present to the senses'. Thus J. C. F. Schiller, *Über die ästhetische Erziehung des Menschen* (1795), Letter 15.

22   H. U. von Balthasar, 'Revelation and the Beautiful', in idem, *Explorations in Theology I: The Word Made Flesh* (ET San Francisco 1989), p. 105.

23   Ibid., p. 111.

24   P. T. Forsyth, *Christ on Parnassus* (London 1911), p. 261.

Yes, he replies: in the person and work of Christ. The Christ who is so mighty in history has the throne in eternity.[25] Balthasar joins Forsyth in emphasising the kenotic means to this *plerosis* or fulness. When the Holy Spirit discloses the power of divine unity, truth, goodness and beauty to Christian contemplation it is above all through the self-emptying of the Incarnation and the Cross and the consequent trial for human faculties which the identification of weakness and torment with One who is divine entails. The art of El Greco Balthasar finds exemplary in this regard: 'the beauty of the human form he portrays is only attainable through the night of faith'.[26]

A theology of the image of God in man

But is it plausible to regard human form as a peculiar concentration of the capacity of the transcendentals to express something of the mystery of God? Balthasar considers it consonant with Scriptural revelation to reply, 'Yes'. Like so many of the Church Fathers, Balthasar is a theologian of the divine image in man. A lengthy excursus on how the key text, Genesis 1:26–7 has been seen by modern exegetes and Christian tradition precedes Balthasar's statement of a 'theodramatic' anthropology in the second volume of *Theodramatik*.[27]

The Genesis text formulates for Balthasar:

> a fundamental truth that is always presupposed in the whole biblical drama involving God and man ...[28]

– the living man as a body–soul totality. He mentions, with respect, the conviction of the author of the Book of Wisdom that the Wisdom of God is the prototype of man. While not developing this in a sophiological direction (contrast another modern theologian he greatly appreciated, Sergei Bulgakov), he maintains nonetheless that the Genesis text has a frankly mysteric intention:

> Just as the original, God, cannot be defined, neither can the copy, the 'image', whose distinctiveness comes from the fact that it represents, in worldly and created terms, this nondefinable divine reality.[29]

---

25 Congenial to Balthasar is Forsyth's rejection of a merely historical–critical approach to the central Figure of the New Testament writings: 'It should be clear that the Christ merely historic and humane is not equal to the perennial control of an interest so great and unusual as Art's treatment of nature's text ... Nothing less than a dogmatic Christ is adequate to the spiritual control of the greatest aspects and interests of mankind in every age', ibid., p. 288.

26 H. U. von Balthasar, 'Revelation and the Beautiful', art. cit., p. 102.

27 H. U. von Balthasar, *Theo-Drama: Theological Dramatic Theory. Volume II. The Dramatis Personae: Man in God* (ET San Francisco 1990), pp. 316–34.

28 Ibid., p. 318.

29 Ibid., p. 320.

And yet the two, the Uncreated and the created, God and man, are 'essentially ordered to each other'. The entire message of Scripture is that man has an imperishable nature yet has turned away from God, so the Fathers of the Church are right to see the 'image' as something given and unlosable, the 'likeness' as something prospective and contingent on how the drama plays out. Balthasar emphasises the importance of *freedom* in image anthropology. But to do justice to the New Testament witness, an 'ascending' theology for which finite freedom moves upwards to God who is infinite freedom must be balanced by a 'descending' theology for which infinite freedom has itself, as he writes:

> produced an Image, the eternal Son, within the Godhead, thus laying the foundation in him for the images of finite creatures.[30]

For the New Testament, as Balthasar reads it, the human vocation is to 'con-form-ity' with the perfect image that is Christ who restores the first, Adamic, image and causes it so to surpass its own possibilities as to attain a totally unexpected likeness to God. In the Incarnation of this Prototype, *Urbild*, the encounter between ascending image and descending Prototype leads not to identity but to nuptial union (between God in Christ and humankind in the bridal, 'Marian' Church).[31] In the biblical volumes of his theological aesthetics Balthasar describes man as 'the figure, *Gestalt*, of God's hands'.[32] As he explains:

> The beautiful does not live in splendour alone; it also needs figure and image, even if what figure does is attest to him who set it up, even if image is beautiful only as the imaging forth of that splendour which is beyond all images ... [I]f in the end all worldly aesthetics needs a theological foundation, we can say in anticipation that only biblical theology provides a final, non-tragic justification for worldly beauty, since it is only here that the image, which finite worldly reality is of necessity, can be taken up and secured in the eternal Image, which is the archetypal image even as it is the image that transcends all images.[33]

Balthasar makes much in this connexion of the eighth Psalm with its declaration that YHWH has 'crowned [man] with glory, *kavod* and honour, *hadar*', expressing the fact that 'man bears a noble beauty within himself that becomes manifest precisely

---

30 Ibid., p. 330.

31 The Son, the Prototype, 'encompasses and reworks all the copies (*Abbilder*) in himself; yet it is not a question of absorbing and extinguishing the finite images but of setting them within the embracing Idea; for it is within this Idea, from all eternity, that they were conceived and created as individuals, ibid.

32 Idem, *The Glory of the Lord: A Theological Aesthetics. Volume VI: Theology: The Old Covenant* (ET Edinburgh 1991), p. 87.

33 Ibid.

in his form', which is a share in God's 'theophanous form', God's radiation of beauty from his being.[34]

Balthasar stresses the unfinished character of man's divine imagehood. The image is 'in suspense', in *Schwebe* – in effect, in flux until it is stabilised in Jesus Christ. Only with him does the 'definitive image' appear and 'gather up into itself the meaning of all the suspended fragments of the image that is man ... Adam's glory as God's image is truly resplendent and becomes legible as form only prospectively ...'.[35] Balthasar's treats the divine image in man as specifically the image of that Son who is at all times the *Trinitarian* Son: thus the image carries reference also to the Father and the Holy Spirit. He suggests, moreover, that the two-gendered nature of the image of God in humanity ('Male and female He created them', (Genesis 1:27b) will be realised fully only in the relation between Christ as the Man and the Marian Church as the Woman.

A theology of the saving Incarnation as centre of the revelation images must serve

For Balthasar, in a revelation based on divine Incarnation – Flesh-taking – and the Resurrection of the Body, there will obviously be no presumption that abstraction from the image enhances theological meaning.[36] In any case, man must accept the measure found in God's self-expression if he is to judge with a suitable eye the images that clothe the revelatory form.[37] That form cannot be seen aright without a degree of sharing in what it represents, the sharing we term 'conversion', and its experiential verification is dependent on its ecclesial transmission in the apostolic tradition. In what is surely the master-idea of his theological aesthetics, Balthasar insists that revelation itself has a 'form-character'. In Jesus Christ, the revelatory events attested in the Old Testament have found the ultimate 'meaning-giving,

---

34   P. Brunner, 'Der Erstgeschaffene als Gottes Ebenbild', reprinted in idem, *Pro Ecclesia: Gesammalte Aufsätze zur dogmatischen Theologie* (1962), p. 91, cited ibid., p. 95. Balthasar speaks of the psalm's:

> great wonderment at the fact that the exalted God has condescended to come so low as to put something of his own divine glory into man's tiny being. It expresses an incomprehensible oscillation between lowliness and exaltation, between God's glory, proper to God alone, and the reflected splendour of the glory that emanates from God and enfolds man, without the human form ever being able to contain this splendour within itself

Ibid., p. 94.

35   Ibid., p. 101, 102.

36   Idem, *The Glory of the Lord* I, pp. 607–9.

37   Balthasar appeals here to the articles on 'Les yeux de la foi' by Pierre Rousselot, SJ, brought out in book form in German translation as *Die Augen des Glaubens* (Einsiedeln 1963). An English version is available: *The Eyes of Faith, and Answer to Two Attacks* (New York, 1990).

all recapitulating centre', which bestows on the total biblical revelation not only ordered unity but intelligibility of form – which is graspable yet without suppression of revelation's mysteric character.[38] In its unity and determinateness, this Christ-centred form is then to qualify or 'trans-form' believing humanity: the Church at first but eschatologically the world.

The form of existence taken by the Word in his Incarnation and Atonement – a servant form, through kenosis (compare Philippians 2:6) – is the adequate expression of the divinely free Lord in his redemptive attitude to sinners. It sums up and clarifies all the past 'act-events' in which the sovereign glory of God engaged itself in covenant relations with his people. Its form, *Gestalt*, can, however, only be read aright when Jesus's entire existence is interpreted against the background or 'horizon' of love (compare Acts 10:38), whereby he can be seen as the unsurpassable revelation not just of what is in *human* nature but of what is in divine (compare I John 4:16), for this is the Trinitarian Love than which no more ultimate mystery can be (compare I Corinthians 2:10–13).[39] Thus St John can declare Jesus's passion and death – which in an obvious sense are the loss from view of both his divinity and his humanity – as actually the supreme epiphany, *Aufscheinen*, of the love–glory of God.[40]

This climactic revelatory disclosure is made to the senses as a whole (the *Prima Johannis* speaks of 'what we have heard, what our eyes have seen, what we have looked on and touched with our hands', 1:1), and if, in this context, the disclosure is described as the *Word* of God, this means it is God's free self-expression, his *Aussage*. When we speak, then, of the primacy of the Word in biblical revelation, what we mean – or should mean – is that a person infinite in being and action makes himself known through a *Gestalt* that is of this world. Such a *Gestalt* typically involves all the senses, for there is not only poetic form and musical form in hearing but also visual form in seeing, and indeed tactile form – not least because, by touching, the blind can perceive the form that the non-blind see.

Balthasar underscores the paradoxical character of this divine revelation in form already signalled by speaking of its climaxing on the Cross. As the prophet Isaiah foresaw in the Songs of the Suffering Servant, this *Gestalt* is to natural eyes *Gestaltlosigkeit*, the deprivation of form, for the Crucified 'had no form or comeliness that we should look at him, and no beauty that we should desire him' (53:2). But what this points to is not less than form, it is super-form. When the Lord himself is 'made sin' (II Corinthians 5:21), accepting for himself the 'likeness of sinful flesh' (Romans 8:3), the loving agency of God in Christ penetrates with its light the chaotic darkness of the world's sin and transforms it. In the words of Paul's Letter to the Colossians, the One who is the 'icon' of the invisible God (1:15) is so in terms not only of the reality of creation (1:16) but of the reality of redemption (1:13–14), both in its present opportunities and in its final, eschatological outcome (1:18). What St Paul calls the 'righteousness' of God, Balthasar paraphrases as 'full

---

38   H. U. von Balthasar, 'Kunst und Verkündigung', p. 708.

39   Idem, *The Glory of the Lord* I, pp. 609–10.

40   Idem, 'Kunst und Verkündigung', p. 709.

adequacy between God and the world', and this adequacy or perfect correspondence is made available, accessible, through the form of Christ, so that whoever responds appropriately to this form will himself be re-formed by it to the point of becoming spotless, immaculate. This is the real ground of the Church's existence as the Bride of Christ as it is of the holiness of the saints. 'Beholding the glory of the Lord, [we] are being changed into his likeness from one degree of glory to another' (II Corinthians 3:18).

A philosophy of the image at large

Balthasar presents a philosophical ontology of the image as a key feature of the foundations of his theological logic. For the Balthasar of *Theologik*, as for Hegel, 'logic' means chiefly ontology: it is concerned with truth, yes, but above all with the truth of being. The context for his discussion of a philosophy of images is his account of the mystery-character of being. It is being's nature to be richer than what, of being, one can see and grasp. In the real order to know an object is to be enriched by a lasting mystery. Now in concrete reality, the primary way in which object and subject are open one to the other interactively is that of images. As he writes:

> The human spirit, gazing on images, contributes a dimension of depth, which they do not of themselves possess. It draws from them a wholeness of form (*eine Ganzheit der Gestalt*) which is more than the simple contours of the appearance alone.[41]

Phenomenalism, the notion of a world of images as sheer surface – a world with no depth of existence or essence – is purely an abstract thought which would never occur to instinctive awareness. The human spirit passes via images to the depth of the object the images re-present. But if empiricism seeks truth in an image without an idea, Platonism wants the truth in an idea without an image. Both alike arrive at an empty mystery. This is Balthasar's version of Kant's celebrated dictum, 'Thoughts without percepts are empty; intuitions without concepts are blind'. The upshot is that, when people fail to approach truth as sensuous image clothing real intelligibility, the world for them is deprived of all graspable figure. Then consciousness seeks salvation within its own resources and tries to create an order by personal effort. In such a 'Copernican epistemological revolution', as Balthasar describes it, all 'objective interiority' disappears into that of the subject, and the images become no more than incomprehensible externalisations of inner space.

If on the other hand, truth really is the unveiling of being – and this is the principal claim of the opening volume of Balthasar's theological logic, subtitled 'The Truth of the World' – then this aporia can be resolved. Balthasar's claim runs: being is able to *appear as it is*. If this is so, then naturally, truth does not have its seat in images – appearances – *as such*, for these can only have meaning if the centre to which they relate is situated beyond them. However, no more is it to be expected that

---

41 Idem, *Theologik I. Wahrheit der Welt* (Einsiedeln 1985), p. 147.

truth lies *beyond* the appearances, for that is the non-disclosed which by definition does not appear. The truth of the matter is that the world of images constitutes the means whereby the non-apparent being of objects interprets itself. Thus, whereas aestheticism falsely thinks that images are the be-all and end-all, anti-aestheticism equally falsely disregards them as of no avail.

Balthasar calls this environing world of images in which we live a 'single field of significances'. The reality expressed there can never be adequately described, for nature's *Ausdruckssprache*, her 'expressive speech', is addressed not to conceptual antennae but to antennae Balthasar terms, paying homage here to Goethe, *gestaltlesende*: 'form-reading'.[42] Our most important epistemological equipment is, accordingly, a capacity for a *comprehending seeing* which can read off, and so assimilate, the significant forms of things.

A Neo-Iconophile theology of the artist

What, then, to Balthasar's mind are the consequences for the relation between revelation and art? Scanning the Old Testament shows us at once how various human arts have been drawn into the expression of revelation: literary arts of all kinds, music, architecture and the plastic arts. The prohibition on visual images for God in the Hebrew Bible reflects one particular historical moment – the need for Israel consciously to reject 'other' gods, and should not be used for a speculative construction of the divine nature.[43] We notice that the Jerusalem Temple, and its archetype – the 'tabernacle' shown to Moses on Sinai, receive prescriptions, at once detailed and lavish, in the applied arts. Why Balthasar so emphasises the art of the Temple becomes plain when he comments that, since the body of Christ is the true and abiding Temple (compare John 2:21), the entire realm of sacred art in Israel should be regarded as on its way to final focussing in Christ, the Head of his Church-members in whose bodies the Holy Spirit also dwells as in a temple (I Corinthians 6:19).

First of all, we can attend to how this 'Neo-Iconophile' theology centred in a biblically informed fashion on Jesus Christ, treats the person and work of the *artist*. Balthasar's habit of including holy images within the wider circle of the arts at large enables him to put forward, by reference in the first place to *literary* art in Scripture, his notion of the 'analogy of inspiration'. In Catholic (as Orthodox) doctrine, the inspiration of the hagiographs – the writers who contributed to the biblical canon

---

42   Balthasar's early love of Goethe – and notably his philosophical fascination with the latter's emphasis on the 'vital form' of concrete, living things – had been confirmed by his study of Romano Guardini at Berlin. For that Catholic philosopher, things cannot be grasped in their originality without *both* intuition which gathers in their 'existential' richness *and* a conceptual apparatus that registers the depth of their 'essence', R. Guardini, *Der Gegensatz: Versuche zu einer Philosophie des Lebendigen-Konkreten* (Mainz 1925).

43   H. E. Bahr, *Poiesis: Theologische Untersuchung der Kunst* (Stuttgart 1961), p. 309, cited H. U. von Balthasar, 'Kunst und Verkündigung', p. 712.

– is unique. For the corpus of literature they produced to be the attestation of divine revelation, they necessarily wrote by virtue of a supernatural charism, albeit using their natural human powers. As Balthasar points out, this by no means prevents our ascribing an analogous inspiration to those creative powers themselves. Though only on the natural level, and hence distinct from the charism of inspiration, such artistic inspiration could be – and was – divinely taken up in an instrumental way to assist in the articulation of revelation and the human response to it. Balthasar speaks of the:

> incomprehensible interior [reciprocal] penetration of the free, all-configuring divine Form-giving, and the free human being who, endowed with all his capacities for aesthetic formation, is already co-operating in the primary act of revelation itself.[44]

Thus, for example, the evangelists, considered as hagiographs, exercise not only practical reason but aesthetic reason in deciding which scenes and sayings of Jesus are to be included in the Gospels. Their meaning is to be found not by critical dissection of the atomised elements of their texts but rather in and through the art form each has made of his Gospel book as a whole. The Gospels are 'proclamation images', *Verkündigungsbilder*, and as the most important books in the Canon thus legitimise in advance all later Christian art – visual art included.

For an artist to work as a Christian, both natural and supernatural inspiration must be present. The divine charism which leads him to re-present in art some aspect of the 'total word' of revelation requires a natural basis in human skill and craft. For this reason, the calling of the Christian artist may be described as existential, and personal, but it is in the service of something objective and supra-personal, namely the ever renewed embodiment, using the means art provides, of the original Incarnation of God in Christ. This may also be expressed by saying that the personal charism given the Christian artist is always at the same time Churchly or ecclesial. Even if the artist is not aiming to produce strictly liturgical art, there is never any question of his entertaining revelation by a 'private tête à tête'. Since ecclesial form belongs to revelation in its objective original appearing – the Word incarnate expressed the union of divinity and humanity in his relation with his Church-Bride, the corporate recipient of revelation – so likewise ecclesial form is a subjective requirement for anyone seeking to give divine revelation subsequent expression.

Between the Christian artist as person and as ecclesial being there is a tension but it must be endured, not attenuated. To glorify the biblical *Offenbarungsgestalt* and be at the disposal of the divine Spirit in Church and Christian community should not be considered a limitation on personal inspiration but the contrary. The Christian metaphysician can see further and deeper with the assistance of faith and doctrine. By the same token the Christian artist should understand more of being with their help and be able to render that 'more' credible in turn.[45] The test will be if the art

---

44   Ibid., p. 714.

45   Theology itself, writes Balthasar, is aesthetic. Great aesthetes fashioned Christian theology – notably Gregory Nazianzen, Augustine, Denys: idem, 'Religion et esthétique', p. 300. Artists, evidently, should learn from theology too.

in question is an art primarily of praise, *Lobpreis*, and secondly of proclamation, *Verkündigung*.

The content of Christian art

That brings us to our final topic, Balthasar's 'Neo-Iconophile' theology of Christian art itself, the work as object and its constituent themes. Balthasar finds the highest task of the Christian artist to be the portrayal of the 'order of Christ' entering and mastering the abyss of sin. Christian art, Balthasar is saying, is above all an art of redemption. The artist must stand by the Cross, like the original witnesses, Mary, John and the holy women, so as to see the glory of Love in the Kenosis – which is possible, desirable and necessary since, in point of fact, 'the Kenosis *is* this glory'.[46]

This redemptive art is for Balthasar essentially an art of proclamation. Art must not serve itself: self-glorification is its besetting sin in a fallen world. When art – even in the extra-ecclesial realm – sees beauty *together with truth* it sees it typically together with tragedy, grace and an intimation of transcendent wholeness. Put biblically, that must mean an orientation not only to protology, the original paradise state, but also to the meta-historical eschatology of the resurrection of the flesh. And these two, the Beginning and End, are connected by the history which reveals the agent in whom the two orders of creation and salvation are held together: Jesus Christ.[47] The nuptial interplay of YHWH and the Daughter of Zion is fulfilled in the New Adam, together with Mary/Church, the New Eve. The Christian revelation points us, accordingly, to the wedding feast of the Lamb at the End of the Ages. Reconciliation in Christ who restores the divine order is already identical with eschatological redemption and the consummation of the creation which at the beginning God pronounced altogether good. The vocation of Christian art is to show forth imagistically how, received by faith, hope and love, the saving eternity of God is now available in passing time, despite man's continuing sinfulness and the consequent need for perpetual repentance (what the ancient aesthetic tradition calls *penthos*).

What sort of artistic manner does this suggest? The weight given here to salvation history, with its distinctive *Offenbarungsgestalt*, more or less rules out abstract art as an appropriate form for sacred artworks. This is not because abstract art is always and entirely without value. What for theology is objectionable about abstract art is not necessarily its non-figural character. Rather is it the way such art considers itself released from the 'single concrete supernatural goal' of humanity revealed by the Bible in the Church's Tradition. What is objectionable is art that has fallen

---

46   Idem, 'Kunst und Verkündigung', p. 718.

47   Such an approach might be regarded as itself an act of patristic *ressourcement*. In the Christian culture of East Rome, 'Every event, text and image could be read as an exegesis of one fundamental and real event – namely, the Incarnation as represented by the narrative of Christ's life and Passion': thus J. Elsner, *Art and the Roman Viewer*, p. 124.

into 'God-forgetting immanence'.[48] Nor did Balthasar think this was a sectarian critique. In its highest expressions, human art has always served the mysteries of being and existence, not been enjoyed for its own sake. Evidently, Balthasar was not enamoured of much modern art: the 'shock of the new' left him cold. He spoke of the birth of 'traditionless man', as Enlightenment chickens came home to roost – for the Enlightenment had been blind to the truth that to belong to humanity is to stand in a tradition. Thus it was not so much that the avant-garde had broken with tradition but that tradition in the West was broken. The notion of the venerable objectivity of the 'great serving crafts' is replaced at the eighteenth century's end by the cult of the creative individual genius. Modern art claims to abandon a mendacious *Schaukunst*, but its objectivity is too often really nihilism, as contemplative play, gratuitous delight and 'streaming pure grace' are ruthlessly removed.[49] In any case, abstraction should be seen as auxiliary, merely, to figural art. Abstraction can no doubt bring to light 'structures' that have their own beauty. Yet such structures are always 'the abstract aspect of something concrete'. They make no sense otherwise. Indeed, the higher some earthly reality stands on the ladder of being, or – what amounts to the same thing – the greater its value, the closer it approximates to what Balthasar calls the condition of a 'spirit-body singularity', and this is eminently concrete. At best, one might compare the role of abstraction in serving the figural arts to the work of the Holy Spirit serving the economy of the Word incarnate with its climax in the resurrection of the flesh.[50]

Balthasar insisted on the *transitive* character of Christian art. Our art passes over into its divine-human object, into what Nicaea II called its 'protoype'.[51] How did he see this working out in practice? Balthasar's *beau idéal* of a Church artist was the Swiss Hans Stocker, born in 1891, dying in 1983.. In 1954 Balthasar noted with enthusiasm Stocker's exhibition in the northern Swiss (but definitely Baroque Catholic) city of Solothurn, capital of the canton of that name.[52] He claimed Stocker as representative of a 'new Catholic art in German Switzerland'. Stocker represented a pleasing contrast to the many artists claiming to serve the Church yet producing 'kitsch', the origins of which Balthasar traced to an unconscious, spiritually unmastered sensuousness, and whose essence he found to be a 'secret capitulation' in cultural mission, an abandonment of creative spiritual effort that took as its pretext the 'givenness' of creation and Incarnation – to which nothing need be added.[53]

---

48 H. U. von Balthasar, 'Kunst und Verkündigung', p. 719.

49 Idem, 'Die Kunst in der Zeit', *Schweizerische Rundschau* [Einsiedeln] 40 (1940), pp. 239–46.

50 Idem, 'Das Weltbild Hans Stockers', in *Hans Stocker: Sakrale Kunst, Band 8*, edited by members of the *Schweizerische Lukasgesellschaft* (Zurich 1957), pp. 129–36, and here at p. 132.

51 Idem, 'Kunst und Verkündigung', p. 720.

52 Idem, 'Hans Stocker', *Solohthurner Anzeiger* 121, 26 May 1954, p. 2.

53 'Periods of flattening, *Verflachung*, into an immanent ideal of beauty call up *Bilderstürme*, iconoclastic attacks, as a natural and necessary reaction': idem, 'Kunst und Verkündigung', p. 719.

Actually, however, what the Christian artist is supposed to do is to 'stand in the movement and continuation of God's becoming man'. He or she must look at things – in world , nature and the body – 'from out of the infinite purity of the gaze of God', and in their depths divine what lies dormant there: a 'word' – *logos* with a lower-case 'L' – issuing from the Logos with an upper-case 'L', the all-creative Word of God. Balthasar describes this 'word' as 'a word of praise of the Creator', a *Gebetswort* or 'prayer-word', which the artist can 'awaken and liberate for form and resonance'.[54] Stocker was well prepared for the tasks of specifically sacred art because even in paintings of landscapes, waterscapes, and domestic interiors, the world for him has religious depth. The world as Stocker portrays it is at once sensuous and mysteric. His art recreates it joyfully in a universe of painterly colour, expressive of real delighting in nature's own 'structural principles' yet inhabited by a childlike simplicity: the simplicity, in a word, of a Christian, in love with both God and creation. Stocker recognises how the cosmos is built out of crystalline, vegetable and organic forms. He does not dictate to nature in Kantian manner the forms he would like it to have – unlike, says Balthasar, Cézanne, for whom the *Sachelementen*, the objective elements of things, were too often substituted by *Bauelementen*, artificial building-blocks for a composition. But Stocker's style is not just lyrical naturalism. Stocker realises that *das Ganze* – 'the whole' of the world and man – includes 'dark threatening powers'. But this does not subvert the world's justification as wonderful.

So for Stocker the transition to painting for the Church was simple. He saw the spiritual universe of salvation history by analogy with cosmic nature. In other words, he was wondrously overwhelmed by its *chiaroscuro*. In this case, the light and the shade are divine redemptive agency vis-à-vis a fallen humanity. His biblical scenes are not depictions of a Paradise lost and refound, as though the 'Kingdom of the Son of Man were only to be understood as an episode in the Kingdom of the almighty Father and Creator'.[55] Stocker would do full justice to the Kingdom of the Son in its redemptive economy; to the communion of saints; to the Church, her sacraments, her functions. Balthasar sees as paradigmatic Stocker's Sankt Gallen fresco of the open Heart of Christ with, arranged around it, scenes of the Old and New Covenants, the Angels, and the 'weeping Key-bearer, Peter'. This extended image testifies to an experience of the *Heilskosmos*, the 'world of salvation', that is central, not peripheral, and the will and capacity to represent it in an original way.

Balthasar evidently considered that Stocker's art satisfied the conditions he laid down in his essay in *Mysterium Salutis*: a right aesthetic reading of the 'form of revelation' can only be achieved in obedience to ecclesial interpretation. Prerequisites include the benefits of appropriate preaching and catechesis as well as the study of the Scriptures in 'the Spirit of the Church'. That art also met his wider criterion that Christian art be an art of 'praise and proclamation'. Its primary aim is doxological – praising God with beauty, in gratitude. There is no conflict between this primary latreutic aim and an apostolic intent, already emerging in the Old Testament and much

---

54   Idem, 'Hans Stocker', p. 2.
55   Idem, 'Das Weltbild Hans Stockers', p. 135.

more amply adumbrated in the Church.[56] 'Let them extol him in the congregation of the people' (Psalm 107:32). Apostolically, art points to the honour of God which doxologically it conveys.

---

56 Compare the paragraphs on sacred art in the Constitution on the Liturgy of the Second Vatican Council, paras 122–30.

Chapter 4

Sergei Bulgakov on the Art of the Icon

Introduction

Bulgakov had, for an Orthodox Christian, an unusual attitude to the Byzantine Iconoclast crisis and the Iconophile theologies it produced. He regarded the outcome of that crisis – the declaration of the legitimacy of making and venerating sacred images in Christianity – as right and proper. But at the same time, he considered the argumentation offered by the historic defenders of the images to be theologically inadequate. This combination of attitudes is rare. By and large, those critics who approve of the victory of Iconophilia also approve of the arguments offered by such Iconodule doctors as Germanus of Constantinople, John of Damascus, Theodore of Studios, Nicephorus of Constantinople and their articulate sympathisers at Rome and elsewhere in the Western patriarchate as well as in the non-Greek East.[1] Scepticism about the theological, philosophical and historical value of Iconophile argumentation normally typifies those who consider the triumph of Iconodulia an unconvincing volte-face by the late patristic Church. Bulgakov supported the conciliar outcome of the Iconoclast crisis and yet it is remarkable that he remained unimpressed by its accompanying theological justification. As a constructive theologian, he took it as his right and duty to work out a more satisfactory theology of the artistic image than the one he found in possession. The manner in which he did so is instructive.

Attitude to Nicaea II and the Iconophile doctors

Bulgakov's study of the Christian image opens abruptly with a rather brusque dismissal of the strictly theological (as distinct from disciplinary or doctrinal) value of the conciliar teaching on the status of the icon at Nicaea II, the Seventh Ecumenical

---

1   For the theologians of the storm centre, the Byzantine East, see C. von Schönborn, OP, *L'icône du Christ: Fondements théologiques* (Fribourg 1976); for the papal theology, E. Lanne, 'Rome and Sacred Images', *One in Christ* XXIII, 1–2 (1987), pp. 1–21; Iconodule theologians elsewhere in the West, include Jonas of Orleans, *De cultu imaginum libri tres* (= *Patrologian Latina*, CVI, cols 303–87) the Irishman Dungal, *Responsa contra Claudium: A Controversy on Holy Images*, ed. P. Zanna; for the non-Greek East, see Theodore Abū Qurrah, *A Treatise on the Veneration of the Holy Icons*, ed. S. H. Griffiths. For the general background, still useful is E. J. Martin, *A History of the Iconoclastic Controversy* (London 1930; 1978).

Council, 787.[2] At the same time, he likewise expresses a poor opinion of the work of the Iconodule doctors who prepared the way for the Council or subsequently defended its affirmations in their writings.[3] Bulgakov found the *horos* of Nicaea II, its key doctrinal statement, insufficiently connected with the main corpus of Trinitarian and Christological doctrine issuing from the earlier ecumenical Councils to count as a dogmatic definition in the fullest sense of that phrase. As he puts it:

> Although the Church has justified the veneration of icons, she has not established the dogmatic foundation of this.[4]

Hence the whole matter is open to theological study. And while claiming to look at the work of the Iconodule theologians of the patristic epoch 'respectfully and seriously', Bulgakov's conclusion will be that, owing to accepting too much by way of initial premise from their Iconoclast opponents, they cannot in fact serve our turn.

The Church had inherited ancient Israel's negative attitude to pagan images and indeed never ceased to share it, as the examples of such Iconophile authors as Nicephorus and Theodore go to show. Yet for Bulgakov the fact of the matter is that the idea of the icon and the basic techniques of its manufacture were received by the Church from paganism. He refused to see this, however, as an example of pagan influence *on* Christianity. It was influence, rather, *in* Christianity: a distinction meant to convey his conviction that a figural art for evoking the divine enjoyed an intrinsic affinity with the Gospel and so – albeit with significant transformations – could readily find a home in the Church. Thus the icon took its de facto place in ecclesial life as an internal feature of the tradition. Only later was it noticed that the Church had in effect lifted an Old Testament interdiction – thus arousing a degree of dogmatic perplexity in which, Bulgakov willingly concedes, instances of superstitious practice by ill-formed Christians played their part.[5] That at the first Iconoclast Council, Hiereia, in 754, as many as 348 bishops could have concluded against the icons shows the scale of the emerging problem for Iconodules. There was a 'legitimate theological perplexity' such that Iconoclasm constitutes to Bulgakov's mind:

> the expression of a necessary moment in the historical dialectics of the dogma of the veneration of icons.[6]

---

2   On this, see A. Nichols, OP, 'The *horos* of Nicaea II: A Theological Evaluation', *Annuarium Historiae Conciliorum* 20 (1988), pp. 171–81; reprinted as 'The Dogma of the Image at Nicaea II', in idem, *Scribe of the Kingdom: Essays on Theology and Culture* I (London 1994), pp. 180–91.

3   For this material, see V. Fazzo, *I Padri e la difesa delle icone: Complementi interdisciplnari di patrologia, a cura di A. Quacquarelli*.

4   S. Bulgakov, *Ikona i ikonopochitanie* (Paris 1931), p. 7.

5   P. Plank, 'Das ambivalente Verhältnis der Alten Kirche zum Bild' in H.-J. Schulz and J. Speigl (eds), *Bild und Symbol – glaubensstiftende Impulse* (Würzburg 1988), pp. 49–93.

6   S. Bulgakov, *Ikona i ikonopochitanie*, p. 17.

Unfortunately, the Iconophile theology did not have the measure of its task. Iconophiles simplified unduly the doctrinal question behind the image-cult. Their attempts to convict Iconoclasts of Christological heresy (Bulgakov notes that icons of figures other than Christ – the saints and angels – received disproportionately small attention in the quarrel) were unsuccessful. The Byzantine Iconoclasts were completely orthodox on such issues. For their part, Iconoclasts hoped to impale their opponents on a fork whose prongs were, on one side, an apophatic argument from the theology of God (who is, they said, essentially beyond representation) and, on the other, a cataphatic argument from the theology of Christ (who is figurable, yes, but only according to his humanity). For Bulgakov the Iconoclast strategy succeeded only too well. He does not accept as an adequate response to the Iconophobe challenge the claim of Theodore in his *First Refutation* – that if Christ is in two natures, then one and the same person, *hypostasis*, is indescribable in his divine being but describable in his human corporeity.[7] How does this do more than license icons of Jesus' humanity, or indeed of the mere external form of his body? Despite the praise Theodore deserves as 'the great defender of the icons and champion of their veneration, who was all his life the servant by high deeds of his faith',[8] the monk-theologian left this crucial question hanging in the air. From his premises one could just as well draw an Iconoclast conclusion, and perhaps better. It remained to be demonstrated that:

> Christ was represented in the unity without either separation or confusion of his two natures, of which one can be figured and the other not.[9]

St John Damascene, writing, unlike Theodore, before Nicaea II, puts forward an argument Bulgakov will exploit in a fashion all of his own. For John, in his *First Defence of the Holy Images*, it is owing to the weakness of the human understanding of the divine and the angelic realms that Scripture presents (literary) images of the divine nature or the spiritual nature of the angelic powers. Thus biblical revelation adapts itself to our feeble condition. So likewise the Church, following suit, licenses (visual) images to the same end and for the same reason as (literary) images are licensed by Scripture itself.[10]

But it was against precisely such concessions or adaptations to human weakness that the Iconophobes raised their protest in the name of true religion. Neither the Seventh Council nor subsequent Byzantine theology – much less that of the mediaeval West where, says Bulgakov inaccurately, the question of the image was neither examined nor even posed – gave a convincing answer to the question the Iconoclasts had raised. His aim will be to show that 'the dogma [of the legitimacy

---

7   Theodore, *First Refutation of the Iconoclasts*, 4 and 7.

8   S. Bulgakov, *Ikona i ikonopochitanie*, p. 34.

9   Ibid.

10   John of Damascus, *First Apology against those who attack the Holy Images*, 11. See more widely, A. Louth, *St John Damascene*, pp. 193–222.

of venerating icons] is essentially a sophiological problem'.[11] If true, this would of course explain why no adequate theological defence of the holy images has emerged hitherto. The Iconodules were barking up the wrong tree. The key is a sophiological metaphysic with the light this throws on divine agency in the world and notably on the hypostatic union of divinity and humanity in Jesus Christ. Bulgakov selects a concept at once biblical and philosophical – namely, wisdom, in order to lay out a theology of beauty in nature and grace. And he proceeds by putting in place not only a theology of man as in the image of God but a philosophy of images generally as desirable preliminaries for an account of Christian revelation which it is the task of sacred images to serve. In sum, Bulgakov offers, in the course of writing a theology of the icon: a theology of beauty, a theology of the image of God in man, a philosophy of images, and an account of Christian revelation as that which sacred images must serve.[12]

A theology of beauty

Bulgakov works with a theology where the concept of beauty has an honoured place. Bulgakov's account of beauty can be found in no one location, for it runs like a thread throughout his Great Trilogy: *Agnets Bozhii*, 'The Lamb of God'; *Nevesta Agntsa*, 'The Bride of the Lamb'; *Uteshitel'*, 'The Comforter'. It is a theology worked out in terms of the being and work of the divine Trinity and notably of the Holy Spirit. He knew of the second century Church Father St Irenaeus' repeated claim that the Father makes beautiful by means of the Spirit what he creates by means of the Son.[13] But he wants to take this back beyond creation into the eternal Trinity. The Holy Spirit is beautiful because in him and by him the depths of God become wonderfully 'clear' as the love of Father and Son, the supreme act welling up from those depths, appears in its refulgence in him.[14] This affirmation is made in the context of a theology of the divine persons, an exploration of how in their relations of communion, the hypostases reveal each other. But just as important to Bulgakov is a theology of the divine nature at the disposal of the hypostases who render it personal. *Sofiia*, the Wisdom of God, exists in the first place as the 'world of God', the totality of the divine properties and ideas in all their wonderful coherence. The Spirit, who by his rejoicing in the Father and the Son reveals the beauty of their mutual love, also gives beauty to the world of God, the 'pan-organism' or overall organisation of the divine ideas, the archetypes or patterns of all created things.[15] Only in the second place,

---

11　S. Bulgakov, *Ikona i ikonopochitanie* , p. 40.

12　Elements of the same programme, independently arrived at, may be found in idem, *The Art of God Incarnate.*

13　Irenaeus, *Adversus haereses* I. 22, 1 and elsewhere.

14　S. Bulgakov, *Agnets Bozhii: O Bogochelovechestve* I (Paris 1933), p. 123.

15　Ibid., p. 140. As is well known, Bulgakov was partially indebted for these ideas to his great predecessor, the lay-philosopher and theologian Vladimir Soloviev: see J. Sutton, *The Religious Philosophy of Vladimir Solovyov: Towards a Reassessment* (Basingstone and

does divine Wisdom come to be as created wisdom, when the divine ideas begin to exist in finite form in what was previously nothing. *Beauty* for Bulgakov puts in its second appearance under this heading. In the Word, the pre-existent Son, there is present with the divine nature the ideas of all created things, since it is by him, as the Johannine Prologue declares, that 'all things were made', (1:3). When the Wisdom of God is made known through creation in the Word it shows itself as glorious. For Bulgakov the glory of God is God's joy at the vision of his own being in all its beauty. Extrapolated as created wisdom in the work of the Word, that glory is reflected in the human beings who typically find creation 'precious, desirable, joyful'.[16] Just as following St Paul, Bulgakov links the divine Wisdom in a special way to the Word, the Son, the second divine person; so following the Byzantine Liturgy, he connects the divine glory in a special way to the third divine person, the Holy Spirit. That at any rate is his inference from the doxology 'for the kingdom and the power and the glory are yours to the ages of ages' where, claims Bulgakov, 'the kingdom' refers to the Father, 'the power' to the Son and the 'the glory' to the Holy Spirit. In the English-language summary of sophiology he wrote for Anglican admirers in 1937, Bulgakov defined Wisdom as the content of the Godhead in its revelation, and glory as the manifestation of that same content.[17] The Holy Spirit is that divine hypostasis who invests the work of God the Son with beauty, making the creation in its structure and order a work of art in which the divine Artist can take delight. The Spirit crowns the creative work of Father and Son with the joy which for Bulgakov is essential to his hypostatic character. He enables the Father to have joy in the creation as the manifestation of his Word, his Son. And he allows the Son in turn to rejoice in the creation as the revelation of the Father. But insofar as the world in its painful process of becoming is not as yet the created wisdom of God in its completed state, the world cannot receive the Holy Spirit in his fulness. Accompanying creation on its laborious path from incompleteness to completeness is the particular way in which the role of the Holy Spirit in creation is 'kenotic', 'self-limiting', 'self-humbling', and indeed 'self-emptying'.

Human beings have a good deal to do with this. In the created world, man plays the same role in regard to creaturely wisdom as the Word in his proto-humanity plays for uncreated Wisdom. It is a world meant from the beginning to find its centre and coherence in humankind. Though the Logos contains the archetypes of all things, he is in a special sense the archetype of man, the 'divine humanity'. Man, then, is to be on earth the 'logos' of the world, the one who both understands its order and confirms that order, just as he is also to be the beautifier of the world, the one who makes it as lovely a cosmos as it can be. That is why the Fall of Adam has cosmic implications for aesthetics. Chaos could and did occur so long as man had not yet ratified his special role as the image of God by freely turning his creative powers to

---

   16   S. Bulgakov, *Agnets Bozhii*, p. 132.

   17   Idem, *The Wisdom of God: A Brief Outline of Sophiology* (London 1937), p. 53.

the service of his sophianic vocation of helping bring the creation to its goal, when creaturely wisdom will perfectly reflect its Uncreated origin and counterpart. True, the Holy Spirit already acts in the cosmos as 'the Artist of the world, the Principle of form, and the Form of forms'.[18]

> Nature exists through the sophianic action of the Holy Spirit and it is normal that the hypostasis of Beauty invests it with beauty – which is already the *preliminary* image of God's advent by the Holy Spirit.[19]

In an ontological perspective, beauty is the 'flowering of the creature', [20] but since the Fall it is, alas, morally ambivalent. In his freedom the rational creature gives beauty a moral co-efficient, which consists in the way created beauty is *applied*. The tragedy of a beauty that expresses the Holy Spirit and yet given the right – which means the wrong – conditions can corrupt man is a supreme symptom of the tragedy of the Fall itself. Beauty is found in Sodom as well as Eden. The Spirit patiently – kenotically – accepts the limited receptivity which is all that is offered him by a creation become to a degree deaf to his 'interior calls'.

A theology of the image of God in man

Bulgakov's sophiological approach to the sacred image depends crucially on a foundational doctrine of Christian anthropology, the imagehood of God in man. Though Bulgakov is a theocentric writer, he takes man to be already a theomorphic creation, and the rest of creation to find its appropriate centre in man who is its microcosm.

In Bulgakov's sophiology, given that the world of God transcends mere creaturely existence, it can only be made known if from the beginning God has prepared man to have communion with it. [21] We are hypostases, unique selves, who faintly reflect God's own tri-hypostatic reality. Moreover, our nature is such that it can enjoy solidarity with the divine nature through the divine humanity of the pre-existent all-creative Word. The Wisdom of God as found in the Word is the 'primordial image of man, *chelovecheskii Pervoobraz*, before the creation of the world'.[22] In the Wisdom of God there is a divine idea of humanity at large as well as of each and every one of us as a participation by a human hypostasis in the divine life. The unity of divinity and, before the Incarnation, proto-humanity, has always been present in the heavenly Man, the Word. When Adam was created he was before the Fall, the image of Christ, albeit an image awaiting its 'integral revelation', and 'fulfilment'.[23] That is

---

18   Idem, *Uteshitel'. O bogochelovechestve II* (Paris 1936), p. 233.

19   Ibid., p. 234. Beauty is 'the exteriorised sophianity of the creature, reflection of the mysterious eternal light of the divine Wisdom', ibid., p. 235.

20   Ibid., p. 238.

21   S. Bulgakov, *Agnets Bozhii*, p. 160.

22   Ibid., p. 137.

23   Ibid., p. 161.

no more than the teaching of that early Church Father, influential on both Bulgakov and Balthasar, St Irenaeus, who said:

> The Word of God, the Creator of all, prefigured in Adam the future economy of his own Incarnation.[24]

Though as images of God we were made primarily in the likeness of the Son, this is of the Son as revealing the Father. For Bulgakov, revealing the Father is always what the Son is doing. So our imagehood of the hypostasis of the second divine person is not without some relation to the hypostasis of the Father, the first. And likewise Bulgakov has stressed that the third divine hypostasis, the Spirit, always accompanies and follows up the revelation of the Father in the Son. So there must be some echo in a human hypostasis of the personal being of the Holy Spirit too. Bulgakov speculates that just as the divine humanity in God himself is revealed in history in the Incarnate Word together with his Mother – that is how we see Emmanuel depicted on icons: the Mother and Child, so an echo of the hypostases of Son and Spirit is found in the fact that the totality of human hypostases is not simply male but male and female. The human hypostasis in womankind reflects the hypostasis of the Spirit in the Spirit's relation to the Son in whose image, primarily and fundamentally, all human hypostases, whether of males or females, are made. In these ways we can make sense of the statement that man is the 'living image if the tri-hypostatic God in his Wisdom'. And not just of the Son alone. Now, as Bulgakov writes:

> By its very nature, the image is in an indissoluble liaison with the Prototype it reflects.[25]

From this Bulgakov draws the strong conclusion that the image of God in us is only in any full sense this relation with its Prototype when we are activating the image, when the image is functioning in human activity. Unless we are continually relating ourselves to God, the image of God within us will become ever more distant from its divine Prototype. That our being is sophianic does not mean we are automatically in a positive relation with God. The manner of our creation gives us 'unlimited possibilities of movement, both upwards and downwards'.[26] We need God's Providence to make available to us fresh influxes of the divine energies. We need the grace of God not only to become what we were meant to be as creatures, sophianically. We need that grace even more in the perspective of deification, so that what the Father has offered the world through the Incarnation of the Son and the descent of the Pentecostal Spirit may become a reality for each and all.

---

24   Irenaeus, *Adversus haereses* III. 22, 3.
25   S. Bulgakov, *Nevesta Agntsa: O Bogochelovechestve* III, op. cit., p. 218.
26   Ibid.

A theology of the saving Incarnation

The Incarnation is the divine means of transfiguring the world into greater beauty precisely by redeeming the divine image in man from the deformity of sin.

For Bulgakov, all saving history leads up to the Incarnation or issues from it. For him, the Son's being is in any case essentially sacrificial. As the One through whom all created things exist, the Son has a special affinity with sacrifice. The Son allows himself to be the place where the divine ideas are expressed, and the instrument by which they will be further expressed in creation. He lets himself be used in the service of the Father as the One through whom God's world is made. He puts himself at the service of the Father and the Father's creative plan. Right from the beginning, the world not only of the divine properties but the divine ideas is 'stamped with the seal of the Lamb'.[27] It carries the mark of the self-sacrificing Word of God. Bulgakov sees this service to the world by the Son in obedience to the divine Father as a first sketch of what will happen to the Word incarnate in the Atonement. The Son is, as the Johannine Apocalypse puts it, 'the Lamb slain since the beginning of the world' (Apocalypse 13:8). Though the Son's obedience is thus ordered from eternity to his incarnate role as the Atoner, the Incarnation has an anthropological as well as a theological precondition. From the side of the creation, Incarnation is impossible unless there is in humanity a fundamental capacity to be united with God, however dormant this be owing to sin. For Bulgakov, the doctrine of divine imagehood satisfies this precondition. So at the Annunciation to Mary, the Father who generated the Son now appropriately sends him on his mission into the world, while the Holy Spirit shares in the Incarnation by descending onto the Virgin so that the Logos may become flesh in her womb.

Assuming human nature in the frequently non-sophianic and even anti-sophianic conditions of fallen man, obedience to the Father is now only 'natural' for the New Adam through distress and anguish, struggle and anxiety. But all the time, as Jesus grows in stature, the two natures hypostatically united in his person influence each other ever more, though not without tension, for his divine will, in its kenotic condition, which is one of self-limitation, does not simply over-master his human will, his will as man.[28] Bulgakov notes how, although the Third Council of Constantinople, which dogmatised the duality of wills in the Word incarnate, has nothing to say about their positive inter-relation (only something negative, that they are never counterposed), its successor Council, Nicaea II, the Council of the icon, testified to the possibility of representing the God-man in the theanthropic unity of his person. The icon of Christ, especially in the form of narrative iconography, does not make sense unless his wills are joined in harmonised action as a single theanthropic use of freedom.

---

27   S. Bulgakov, *Agnets Bozhii*, p. 134.

28   The two wills like, as Bulgakov writes, two cords woven together to form a rope, so interact that the 'single theanthropic person wills by a single act of will, even though this comes from a double source in his divine and human essences', ibid., p. 271.

A philosophy of the image at large

Bulgakov thought it important to put in place a philosophical statement about images at large before proceeding to integrate the materials already considered into a Neo-Iconophile theology.

He offers in this context *a general ontology of the image*. Images depend on a first image, some sort of prototype with which they are identical but from which they are different. They are not repetitions of being. Reality does not in fact repeat itself. Rather are they reality's ideal reproductions. What is reproduced is the *eidetic* image of being: that which enables things to have endless reproductions, as the modern photograph or even photocopying machine demonstrates.

Though an image belongs with the reality it images, it belongs *to* its possessor or what Bulgakov terms its 'creative bearer'.[29] In the world, the subject – as distinct from the object – of ideation is man. In this sense, all the images of being are human. *Pace* Damascene, this is not on account of human weakness and the need for ontological concession, but owing to 'the lordly power of man in the world as its eye, its ideal mirror'.[30] Man is the being who sees the images. He is *zôon eikonikon*, as well as the one who makes images, *zôon poiêtikon*. He receives and reflects images. He also acquires them creatively. He takes an active part in the iconisation of being, he discovers the icons of things in himself and through himself. All that is in the world has a reality that is representable for him. He is the 'pan-icon of the world, *vseikona mira*[31]. Where he is this in a creative sense, we have man the artist. Bulgakov declares himself strongly against a naturalism that is merely *trompe l'oeil* which 'replaces by a subterfuge the fundamental task of the iconisation of being, *ikoniatsii bitiy*'.[32] At the least, we should surely want to say that art aims through the surface of things to show their ideal form as manifested by the natural image in question. The artist tries to point to the authentic being of things by giving them a more fully iconic expression than they enjoy in nature. For Bulgakov, one just has to accept that there is in art a real *noesis* (understanding) of form, that all genuine art grasps in one way or another the 'world of noetic beauty', the beauty of the primal ideal image of things. This is how Bulgakov would take Damascene's comment in his eighteenth oration that 'every image is a revelation and a witness of what is hidden'. Adapting a Kantian axiom, things without prototypes are blind (this is the mistake of naturalism); prototypes without things are empty and abstract (this is the error of all non-realist schematism). Thus Bulgakov reaches the important programmatic statement that:

> The creative act of art, by iconising a thing, consists first of all in perceiving by means of it its prototype; then, in expressing that protoype in appropriate media ... The icon is

---

29 Idem, *Ikona i ikonopochitanie*, p. 65.
30 Ibid.
31 Ibid., p. 66.
32 Ibid., p. 67.

the expression of the true primal image which, by way of the thing represented, has a real being in the world.[33]

This takes Bulgakov into what is recognisably the world of Platonic ideas which he understands, not, however, as with some interpreters of Plato's corpus in quasi-logical terms, but as:

existent noetic images, possessing an energy of being and realising themselves in being as the entelechies of things – their interior final causes.[34]

Put theologically, the philosophical theory of ideal protoypes of the world signifies the *sophianity of the created* which has as its own primal image and foundation the divine Wisdom, the pan-organisation of the ideas. At the basis of figurative art lies:

the objective and anthropocosmic foundation of the world, the sophianic prototypes according to which, created by Wisdom, it exists.[35]

A Neo-Iconophile theology of the icon

Bulgakov's theology of the icon is governed by one principal conviction. We had better follow the line of enquiry sophiology opens up because, on the premises taken for granted in the controversy, dogmatic logic favours the Iconoclast side. It is with the *basic premises* that the problem lies. Bulgakov contends that the fork on which the Iconoclasts would prong the Iconophiles is a false antinomy. It is falsely antinomic to contrast on the one hand a God who is essentially beyond representation and on the other the perfect depictability of the humanity of Christ. There is falsity here not because a true sense cannot be given to both of these principles but because the principles themselves *do not belong to the same logical – and even ontological – order*. In each case, we have half of a genuine antinomy. But these particular halves do not belong together. One belongs with theology, the other with cosmology. To try to join them is, in Bulgakov's comparison, like 'adding metres and grams on the pretext that both are measures'.[36] The thesis that God is essentially unrepresentable is a piece of apophatic theology, owed above all to the Pseudo-Denys and drawing attention to the way God is the Absolute, beyond all relation, and thus essentially alien to all correlation or definition – as the rich Greek vocabulary of alpha-privative adjectives indicates. To this thesis, the proper antinomic counter-thesis is not some claim about Christ's human nature. The counter-thesis should read: God is in himself sheer relationship, the Holy Trinity, divine triune life. This does not bear on a 'history' of God – as if a primordial Godhead, an *Ur-Gottheit*, had 'become' the Trinity, as Jakob Boehme and his German philosophical successors would have it. It is quite

---

33   Ibid., pp. 71–2.
34   Ibid., p. 72.
35   Ibid., p. 74.
36   Ibid., p. 44.

as original as the divine nature itself. In God there is in any case no process. There is only eternal act.

This God – and here we move toward a second antinomy where the humanity of Christ *does* play a part – is not only relationship in himself. He is also relationship with what he has created. In himself, God possesses the fulness of life and is all-blessed, all-sufficient. His perfect plenitude neither needs to be nor can be completed by anything beyond himself. And yet, so the second antinomy tells us, God enters into relation with another, with what is not himself, establishing what Bulgakov calls 'an absolutely relative relation in God which is that of Creator with created'. By virtue of the authenticity – the genuine reality – of the world and the world process, God joins himself to the becoming of the world.

Bulgakov insists that the first, theological antinomy has no relation to its second, cosmological successor. 'No causal relation, *prichinno sootnosheniya*, can be established between them.'[37] From God as Absolute, no path leads to creation. But the way is now open to an account of God's self-revelation in the world, and following it we soon come across a third and final antinomy which this time is sophiological. Between God and the created world an unbridgeable gulf is fixed: 'You cannot see my face for no man shall see me and live' (Exodus 33:20). And yet the created world has its being in God who by his creative relation with it is himself in the world. In his Wisdom, the life of the divine nature, God is turned toward the world. And the world itself is created in Wisdom and can have no other principle of being. The world is creaturely wisdom in becoming, in time. Creatures have their prototypes, what the Greek Fathers call their *proorismoi*, in the uncreated Wisdom – even if the world's life is also immersed in itself, in its own semi-being, and so is both sophianic and non- or even anti-sophianic at the same time.

For Bulgakov an implicit sophiology is the background and condition of possibility for orthodox Christology, the Christology of Chalcedon, to which, in the struggle over the icons, both Iconoclasts and Iconophiles wished to remain faithful.[38] The Christological antinomy whereby Christ is both divine and human in a single person expresses 'with the greatest clarity' the general sophiological antinomy. As Bulgakov explains:

> The Creator and the creature, the eternal and the temporal, uncreated divine Wisdom and created wisdom, are bound up in a single being and a single life, but in such a way that each of the two wisdoms keep its independence and its entire metaphysical distance from the other ('without confusion') at the same time as its liaison with the other ('without separation'), granted their ontological identity.[39]

The appropriate antinomy for a discussion of iconography is, accordingly, this: God cannot be figured for he is inaccessible to creaturely knowledge, *but* he can be for he reveals himself to the creature in the creation – as some celebrated words of Paul in

---

37   Ibid., p. 49.

38   Idem, *Agnets Bozhii*, p. 223.

39   *Ikona i ikonopochitanie*, p. 53.

Romans (1:20) declare. God sets in the creation his image and his other traces – what the Latin Fathers call the *vestigia Dei*. The invisible things of God, *ta aorata tou Theou* in the Romans passage, have been made visible, indeed comprehensible, by God's creative work. The antinomy is one of theological cosmology not of theology in itself. Its specifically Christological form is: God in himself is invisible *but* God in the cosmos is revealed by his Son. 'No one has ever seen God; the only Son, who is in the bosom of the Father, has made him known' (John 1:18).

Bulgakov emphasises that both parts of the antinomy are necessary for gaining a true idea of revelation. 'In revelation, the inaccessibility of the mystery is correlative with the knowledge of it.'[40] Where there is no mysteric depth and the putative object of revelation can be sounded to its depths by a unilateral cognitive act, there is simply knowledge, and not revelation at all. But if the mystery does not disclose itself, then it simply does not exist for man. For Bulgakov, apophatic theology, once brought into some attempted direct relation with iconology, spells death to the icon. This is the truth which the Iconodule Fathers failed to see and from whose evident implications they struggled vainly to escape. If the divine is absolutely beyond all images, it is plain that no image of Christ's humanity has any relation with his being as God, albeit God incarnate.

Given that Bulgakov has now shown how, negatively, he would deal with the Iconoclast divines, can he say how, positively, the icon is possible? He begins from the axiom – questionable or not – that the icon is a work of art. God reveals himself, he proposes, not only to human thinking but also to human vision in art. (Bulgakov's statement that Iconoclasts were hostile to artistic representation *in general* is not one Byzantinists familiar with the eighth- and ninth-century sources would accept.) For him, the notion of art and the notion of image are inseparable.

The Colossians hymn acclaims Christ as the 'image of the invisible God, the first born of all creation' (1:15), or in the anti-Arian translation in Bulgakov's Russian Bible, 'born before all creation'. This, the Primary Image, is the pre-existent Son. The Son images the Father 'visibly' because in the Word, whom Bulgakov calls 'Word of all words and Image of all images', appears the content of the divine life and of all that enters created being, the ideal noetic figures of which the Word holds for the world. This Image expresses the Father's Word but unlike other images it has as its bearer a divine hypostasis, the second trinitarian Person. The third Person too is involved here. Patristic literature sometimes calls the Holy Spirit 'the Image of the Son', and this for Bulgakov is because the Spirit accomplishes the image of the Father in the Son, realising the iconic character of the Son in relation to the prototypical Father.

From the bi-unity of the Image of God by which the Father reveals himself in the Son and the Holy Spirit, it is appropriate to pass to the single figuration or content of that Image in the Holy Trinity. The *content* of that Image in the Holy Trinity is the Wisdom of God. This is 'the living and life-giving Idea of all the ideas in their

---

40   Ibid., p. 60.

perfect unity and reality',[41] as attested by no less an authority than sacred Scripture: 'The Lord possessed me at the beginning of his ways' (Proverbs 8:22). Wisdom is the Prototype of the world created by Wisdom. The world is thus a created icon of divinity. By its ontological theme, the created is identical with its prototype. Thus Bulgakov can conclude:

> This relation between the trihypostatic God and his Idea, the divine Wisdom as Prototype of the world, and the relation between this Prototype and the world, its created image, constitutes in general the foundation of all iconicity, *oskovanie vsyakoi ikonnosti*.[42]

Iconology needs as its starting point the sophiological principle by which God is figurable and the world configured in his image.

Now we know from Bulgakov's account of the Godmanhood of the Word and the related theme of the image of God in man that the divine Wisdom is also the eternal humanity of God. The Word of God is the heavenly Adam, the Prototype of a world centred in man. This conformity between God and man is why the Word could become incarnate as human. Seen from below up: humanity in its theanthropic character is the living image of the divinity – the created image of the uncreated Image hypostatised in the all-creative Word. An obscure feeling for this theomorphism is what made possible the pagan art of the divine-in-human form – the form of a human body considered as disclosure of the human spirit as itself bearing a divine likeness. This is the aboriginal image of the kind Greek Christian piety called *acheiropoietos*, 'not made by human hands'. Alas, original sin means it is now decomposed by the fallen passions, bestialised, no longer able to show forth the image of God. For Bulgakov, then, the Old Testament prohibition on anthropomorphic images of God is explicable by the inauthenticity of the image now that man has lost the purity or integrity of his humanity.

This leads Bulgakov, incidentally, to his subtle explanation of the great exception to the aniconicism of the First and Second Temples, the image of the Cherubim, Positively, inasmuch as the angels have features in common with humanity – they too are intelligent, volitional creatures, and have a mission in our regard, they could be represented in human form. But negatively, that *only* the angels should thus be represented indicates the 'occultation of the theomorphic character of man, which is now obscured by sin'.

> The Incarnation of the Word as Jesus changes all this. The one Christ, without sin, the new Adam, has re-established in his humanity the authentic image of man which is that of God. The Lord has shown himself truly man and in him has appeared the true man, the new Adam. He bears the true image of man, the icon of divinity, living and 'not made by human hands', *nerukotvornii*.[43]

---

41   Ibid., p. 81.
42   Ibid., p. 82.
43   Ibid., p. 90.

That is clearly expressed by the 'secret' prayer in the rite of the blessing of icons of the saints in the *Trebnik*, the Slavonic ritual. The Incarnation restores man's iconic quality – that is its real significance for Iconodulia. In his Godhead, Christ is Image of the Father as Prototype of man (compare I Corinthians 15:47 and 49), while 'the man' in Christ is the direct image of Jesus' divinity, which itself has a human figure. The image, then, belongs to Christ's hypostasis *in its unity*. His image reveals itself in a dyadic way: invisibly according to the spirit, visibly according to the body. But this visible human image is nonetheless identical with his invisible divine image. This the *perichoresis* or compenetration of the natures in the single hypostasis tells us, and the Transfiguration on Mount Thabor demonstrates it.

The content of iconography

Bulgakov has a rich account of the desirable content of iconography, reflecting the highly developed visual culture of Russian Orthodoxy. Not surprisingly, he gives pride of place to the icon of Christ. Not that the Saviour's painterly image is without its limitations. A portrait is always a *pars pro toto*, 'fixing' only one of the 'manifestations of the phenomenology of the spirit'.[44] Hence its merely relative value – and the possibility of supplementing it by others. Still, the entire spirit, being indivisible, appears in each. That is the significance of the act of naming the portrait, which establishes a relation not only with the prototype (the sitter) but with other portraits (of the same person). One difference between an icon of Christ and a merely human portrait is that, as New Adam, the Saviour is a super- or pan-individual. In some sense his face 'contains' all particular individuals. Or, conversely, each human face has something of that of Christ about it. That is why there can be portraits of him painted by unbelievers, and why ancient religious art can be said to have created, all unconsciously, a pre-Christian icon. But to represent the God-man the painter must have not only art but an appropriate vision, and this is only possible on the soil of ecclesiality where the 'creative demands of art are joined with ecclesial experience'.[45]

What other images does he admit? As any acquaintance with the disputes over that issue in the Church of Russia might lead us to expect, Bukgakov begins with the difficult question of iconic representation of the first trinitarian hypostasis, the divine Father. Perhaps surprisingly, he has no objection to the portrayal of the *Creator* under human form – the human aspect of *Elohim* corresponds to the eternal humanity in the Wisdom of God. He has more qualms about the *Father* portrayed as a venerable human figure, along with the Son, in images of the Trinity. To signify the Son's likeness to the Father, the Father's iconography has 'attracted' to itself the human iconology of the incarnate Son. Bulgakov prefers to think that what is shown in such icons is an image of the humanity-in-divinity of the pre-incarnate Lord – only by virtue of which could the Father of the Son be humanly portrayed. What

44   Ibid., p. 101.
45   Ibid., p. 107.

of the Trinity as the theophany of three angels at the Oak of Mamre, made famous in the version by Rublev? Again, this is an anthropomorphic representation, but the emphasis lies not on the personal character of each ('angel') but on their trinitarian correlation. The Holy Spirit has no icon of his own. Indirectly, images of the Mother of God, the *Pneumatophora*, after the Annunciation, are such. But the prohibition of a direct image shows that the revelation of his hypostasis, as distinct from his gifts, belongs to the Age to Come.

Moreover, the holy angels can be iconised in human form owing to their 'co-humanity', though an additional set of, purely symbolic, aspects of their iconography is founded on the prophetic visions in the book of Isaiah, Ezekiel and the Apocalypse. Such symbolism enters into various 'dogmatic' icons – above all, those of the Holy Wisdom of the Novgorod variety. Here a central figure of a fiery angel on an altar, with the Saviour and the noetic heaven above, the Mother of the Lord and John the Baptist on either side, symbolises the eternal Humanity of the Godhead revealing itself in the created world. That 'Wisdom' reveals itself first and foremost in the God-man but also in Mary and John, who embody the summits of spiritual humanity, and finally in the world of the angels themselves. Such dogmatic icons derive for Bulgakov from mystical or prophetic illumination: rare but possible as a source for amplifying the iconographic canon.

Images of the saints are easier to deal with. Since Christ is 'formed' in them (compare Galatians 4:19), they represent his multi-faceted visage. Unlike Israel of old (probably Bulgakov did not know of the synagogue art of Dura-Europos), the Church portrays the saints of the ancient Covenant too. This she does, says Bulgakov, because:

> *their* human figure too began to shine in the light of the resurrection of Christ and thanks to the energy of his Incarnation.[46]

As always, the icon portrays the face of the holy person as glorified, not as on earth, even though certain traits of the individual's likeness may be preserved.

Icons of the Mother of God are especially numerous, varied, beloved and beautiful. Given his high Mariology, this does not astonish Bulgakov. He considers them first in relation to Christ. The Mother and Child is the first image of the Incarnation: earthly humanity united to heavenly and so a sophianic image par excellence. He also views them in relation to the Spirit: when Mary appears without the Child it is as the woman who became perfectly transparent to the Comforter. Bulgakov treats the image of the Theotokos in relation to the Church, most clearly expressed in the Kievan image of Wisdom where Wisdom's 'temple' is represented by a Mary surrounded by prophets and apostles. Finally, he deals with Marian images in their relation to the cosmos: through Mary – so such icons as the *All Creation Rejoices* tell us, the sophianity of the entire created realm finds voice. In all this the Mother of God remains herself, Mary of Nazareth. She is not shown as 'a lovely lady', as in much

---

46   Ibid., p. 147.

Western sacred art, even in its best examples, but beyond her earthly fate as well as in it. Tender beauty is no less as a result. It strikes Bulgakov that her 'miraculous' or 'revealed' icons are more numerous than those of Christ himself who, after all, gives himself to us in the Holy Eucharist as well as the Gospels, his verbal icons, and in his holy Name. The sheer quantity of the Marian icons also speaks of Mary's closeness to the world whose life and suffering she shares. She is 'the Protecting Veil'. Her motherly love leads her to weep for the world from which as a glorified creature she is differentiated but not distanced.

Bulgakov affirms the descriptive or didactic role of the icon, but he associates this more with the fresco which so often takes as its subject wider biblical themes or motifs of Church history or even, in the entrance to church buildings at least, the pagan philosophers and sibyls seen as Christians before Christ. He notes how in the way landscape is shown on the icons, the division between nature and humanity seems to vanish. For Bulgakov, nature has acquired an undue independence or apartheid from humanity owing to the Fall. In such icons as the Transfiguration of the Lord, we see non-human nature in its destiny of participating in the transfiguration of all things. Finally, there is the Cross, which even Iconoclasts did not touch. It can be seen as, quite simply, the image of the Crucified, or in more complex fashion as signifying the sacrificial kenotic love of the Trinity, as well as the suffering love of God for the world. The sign of the Cross, traced by the hand in the air, and joined with the Trinitarian Name, has already a power of sanctification. Bulgakov calls it the seed from which the icon grew, the original indissoluble union of power and image, the heavenly and the earthly, and in this sense the Cross too is a sophianic image – an image of the Church as the union of heaven and earth – hence the Cross's place above every church building. It is 'the type of every iconic quality, the icon of the icon', *ikona ikoni*.[47] This draws attention to the true centre of all Bulgakov's sophiological speculations: the kenosis of the Trinity on the glorious Cross.

Painting an icon is a theurgic act, requiring prayer and askesis. The iconic canon expresses objectively the tradition of the Church. The Church's iconography is a 'treasury of the Church's living memory of the visions and representations' by which her artists have imaged the divine world in form and colour as testimony to her own 'creative, common activity'.[48] The iconic canon should not be seen, then, as an external rule, requiring a servility of mere copying. This was the mistake of the Russian Old Believers from the late seventeenth century onwards. Colour photography, though practically useful, cannot replace authentic iconography. That the canonisation of new saints requires new icons should alone suffice to dispel this misunderstanding. And just as the life of the Church is inexhaustible thanks to the Holy Spirit, so new icons appear: the Rublev Trinity, the Novgorod icons of Wisdom, the various 'cosmic' images of the Mother of God. But ancient icon-types should themselves be painted – and inevitably are – in a fresh manner, by an accumulation of tiny changes. True copying is properly creative.

---

47 Ibid., p. 164.
48 Ibid., p. 108.

Coda: icon and blessing

That icons belong to ecclesial tradition is attested by their *consecration* through a liturgical act. The inscribing of a name is also an essential element of the act of representing the icon performs. It seals the icon with the copula: this representation '*is* Christ; it belongs to him'.[49] Here iconology belongs with 'onomatology', the veneration of the icon with the glorification of the divine Name (*to onoma*). The name is the verbal icon of the hypostasis. Hence to name the image is already in some wise to consecrate it to the prototype, to actualise the representation. But only the Church can do this, by the power of the Spirit. In giving an icon a name she consecrates it and only then does the icon become truly itself. The Church's sacramental act consists precisely in naming. It signifies that the image is assimilated ecclesially to the Primal Image. (In his footnotes, Bulgakov rejects the modern Greek Orthodox notion that consecration of an icon is unnecessary, a false accommodation to Latin practice – even if, as he accepts, the need for such consecration was only felt comparatively late in the consciousness of the Church.)

What are, then, the limits of veneration of such an icon, if any? For Bulgakov, consecration makes an icon communicate in the being of its prototype as a 'special place of the presence [of that prototype] by grace'.[50] Praying before an icon of Christ we pray to him directly, salute him, kiss him. And here the Iconoclasts were right to raise the question of comparison (and contrast) with the Eucharistic Gifts. The Lord appears in the icon for a prayer presence; he appears in the sacramental mystery of the Holy Gifts for communion. There his presence is substantial but without image (Bulgakov feels that the Latin church treats the Elements as if they were an icon of Christ, evidently in the Elevation at Mass but also in Eucharistic devotions). The icon is Christ's image, but not his substantial being. However, though the materials of the icon are not transubstantiated, as are the bread and wine of the Eucharist, Bulgakov allows a transfiguration of the painterly image into the true image of the Prototype. Once consecrated, the image:

> becomes 'not made by hands', it is like the figure of the Saviour which, by his own will, was imprinted on a cloth for king Abgar.[51]

Every consecrated icon is thus miraculous since the divine power is present here even if this is only actively expressed in certain of their number. Nicaea II, not knowing consecration as a rite, has no doctrine of the power of icons – only of their being a commemoration of the primal images, to arouse love for them. Trent, so Bulgakov believes, through ill-advised concession to Protestantism, underlined even more strongly the merely commemorative aspect. But it is as Christ's ideal presence and in this sense his living image that the icon merits veneration. After the Ascension, Christ keeps a bond with the world in two modes – substantially in the Eucharist,

---

49   Ibid., p. 117.
50   Ibid., pp. 124–5.
51   Ibid., p. 130.

ideally in the holy icons. Both of these enjoy eschatological significance. Just as, by transforming this world's substance into Christ's Body and Blood the Eucharist has a cosmic significance that points to this world's final transfiguration, just so, through the iconic assimilation of images to the primal Image, Christ traces his figure in the world that it may shine out there when 'the times are accomplished'.[52] Bulgakov's exposure, in Russia, to the trials of the Bolshevik Revolution and, in France, to those of the Second World War naturally kept him from supposing the Eschaton is in every sense now.[53]

---

52   Ibid., p. 136.

53   For a brief account of Bulgakov's life, and a survey of his wider dogmatics, with an earlier version of some of this material, see A. Nichols, OP, *Wisdom from Above: A Primer in the Theology of Father Sergei Bulgakov* (Leominster 2005).

Chapter 5

Benedict XVI on Holy Images

Introduction

A pope, who is at once a theologian by métier and a man of wide personal culture, is likely to address at some point or other the topic of holy images. For this topic exists at the intersection of two vital lines: the presentation of the economy of creation and redemption through divinely elected signs and the human practice that is visual art or – if the word 'art' has acquired excessively virtuoso associations – then, at any rate, painterly craft.

As Cardinal Ratzinger, Benedict XVI has addressed these issues from two perspectives which broadly correspond to my proposal of two (intersecting) 'lines'. In his Christology, he considers holy images as a continuation of the divine presentation of salvation through the incarnate Word, Jesus Christ, who is the living Icon of God and his human Face – a Face the traits of which can still be captured iconographically, by a meta-empirical seeing, through visionary painting. In his study of the Liturgy he takes holy images to belong with the way the Church, in her worshipping spaces, allows the divine signs issuing from revelation to be themselves signalled and thus transmitted through human art. In the first case, the emphasis lies on the holiness of the image: it is continuous with the divine action. In the second case, the stress lies rather on the image-character of sacred art: it is a sign that is humanly constructed though for a God-given purpose.

We can call these two perspectives, then, Christological and liturgiological respectively. While we may employ the two perspectives alternately in quick succession – as we shall see, Benedict does not keep them hermetically sealed from each other, the distinction between them is plain. Though the material content discussed in one or the other perspective will overlap, the formal entertainment of that content is proper to each. At the same time, as Ratzinger handles these matters, other major themes of philosophical and theological importance also make their appearance.

The Christological perspective

The Christological perspective is well-evidenced in Ratzinger's essay on 'The Face of Christ in the Holy Scriptures' which takes as its starting-point the Johannine saying, 'He who has seen me has seen the Father' (John 14:9). Ratzinger underlines the Old Testament background of Jesus' conversation with St Philip in the immediate aftermath of the Last Supper Discourse in St John's Gospel.

> The primordial human longing to see God had taken the Old Testament form of 'seeking the Face of God'. The disciples are men who seek the face of God. That is why they came across Jesus and followed him. Now Philip brings this seeking before the Lord and receives a surprising answer, in which the novelty of the New Testament – the new thing that is coming through Christ seems – gathered up as if in a crystal: Yes, man can see God. Whoever sees Christ sees him.[1]

But just how are we to look at Christ in such a way that we can see the Father? Ratzinger refers us back to the earlier incident in the Fourth Gospel where pagan Greeks had approached Philip – himself from a strongly Hellenised region of Palestine – asking to see Jesus, to which the reply, from Jesus himself, is a riddling reference to the fruitfulness of his Passion (John 12:24). The Hellenic world – indeed, the pagan world as a whole – will see Jesus (and through Jesus the Father), but only via his Passion. The Passion is glorification, whereby he will come to them in the risen power of the Holy Spirit, and do so in such a manner that there is 'a new seeing, which happens in faith'.[2] Ratzinger emphasises that this never leaves the Passion behind.

> The seeing happens in discipleship. Discipleship is a life in that place where Jesus stands, and this place is the Passion. In it and no place other is his glorification a present reality.[3]

In the pregnant saying of the Johannine Passion narrative, which finds here the fulfilment of a prophetic prediction (Zechariah 12:10), 'They shall look on him whom they have pierced' (John 19:37).

Ratzinger admits that the Old Testament vocabulary of 'the face of the Lord' does not in fact recur in St John. But he holds stoutly, nonetheless, to a deep underlying continuity between that motif of the Hebrew Bible and Johannine thought. If that is disputed, then at least there is one Pauline text which can support his thesis for the New Testament more generally, since in II Corinthians St Paul makes the connexion quite explicit:

> It is the God who said, 'Let light shine out of darkness' who has shone in our hearts to give the light of the knowledge of the glory of God in the face of Christ. (4:6)

Over a quarter of all uses of the word *panim*, 'face', in the Old Testament Scriptures refer to the divine face, rather than human (or angelic) countenances. That amounts to an astonishing total of 100 texts. Ratzinger comments on the thought-provoking fact that this plethora of references to seeking God's face issues from *an aniconic religion*. Were the divine face to be found embodied in a cult-object, this pervasive

---

1   *Unterwegs zu Jesus Christus* (Augsburg 2003), p. 12.
2   Ibid., p. 13.
3   Ibid., p. 14.

vocabulary would be understandable. But no, 'The image is prohibited, yet the seeking of the face remains.'[4] That is certainly curious. The divinity ceases to be objectified yet its face endures. Precisely as the One who must never be imaged, God can, it seems, be seen. The materialisation of the divine in cult is abolished and yet its innermost direction emerges clearly as never before. Relation to the divine personality: that is what the Old Testament holds out to us, and vividly so, in this paradoxical concatenation.[5]

Ratzinger finds it unsurprising that, as biblically derived discourse mutates linguistically in its passage through Greek to Latin, *panim* becomes in the first *prosopon* and then, in the second, *persona*. The *face* brings us to the mystery of the *person*. God is *ein uns zugewandtes Wesen*, an 'Essence turned towards us'. And Ratzinger hints strongly that the notion of sensuous perception which 'face' suggests ought not to be eliminated – just as it was not so eliminated for Israel's experience of the face of the Lord in the rich cultus of the Jerusalem Temple (compare Psalm 24:6 and the 'liturgical calendars' of Exodus 23, Exodus 34, and Deuteronomy 16). That is so even if the prophets and the psalmists alike emphasise the moral and spiritual preconditions of such seeing in right living and purity of heart – and even if a key text for his account, the beautiful fragment that is Psalm 17:15b, the seeing in question is eschatological, lying beyond our historical existence: 'when I awake, I shall be satisfied with beholding thy form'. For other texts again (for example Psalm 4:7b), the 'light' of God's face means life for Israelites here and now. In any or all of these senses, for God to 'hide' his face is penalisation. The deprivation of God is the contrary of flourishing; it is *tiefstes Unheil*, 'deepest woe'.[6]

The Pauline passage from II Corinthians in which Ratzinger found a safe anchor for his claim to New Testament relevance for this Old Testament material, invokes a more particular comparison, between Moses and Christ. In the dramatic encounter of Moses and the Lord that follows the deviant worship of the Golden Calf in Exodus 32, we are told, seemingly contradictorily, that Moses 'spoke with the Lord face to face' (33:11), and yet was warned by God, 'You cannot see my face, for man shall not see me and live' (33:20), a statement whose opening prohibition is solemnly repeated three verses later. The New Testament writers, so Ratzinger explains, find here a significant ambiguity. Putting together various disparate passages from the proto-martyr Stephen's speech to the Sanhedrin in the Book of Acts, the Letter to the Galatians (at 3:13) and the First Epistle of St John (at 2:1), Ratzinger concludes that the Son stands always face to face before the Father. 'He could see the Face of God and on his face is the glory of God visible for us'.[7] If Moses were told only the Lord's 'back' might be seen, for St Gregory of Nyssa in his *Life of Moses* that

---

4   Ibid., p. 16.

5   Ratzinger points out there is an analogy here with Old Testament talk of the 'Name' of God, referring his readers to his *Einführung in das Christentum* (Munich 2000, 2nd edition), pp. 122–4.

6   *Unterwegs zu Jesus Christus*, p. 22.

7   Ibid., p. 24.

is because we can only encounter God when we follow 'behind' in the manner of disciples. Ratzinger makes this more concrete: Gregory should have written 'in the manner of disciples *of Jesus*'.[8]

What is new about the New Covenant in this regard is not new themes, but a new person: Jesus, the face of God for us. At this juncture one might comment: what Ratzinger is carrying out may usefully be called, in words of Kevin Mongrain about Balthasarian thought, an 'Irenaean retrieval'.[9] According to a key expression of St Irenaeus' *Adversus haereses*, the Son is the visibility of the Father. What we have heard so far in 'The Face of Christ in the Holy Scriptures' is a biblically informed defence of this claim. And Ratzinger's summary conclusion on the difference the Old Testament makes to the Old – 'not new themes, but a new person' – seems a verbal reminiscence from Book IV of Irenaeus' great treatise: 'Know that he brought all novelty by bringing himself who had been announced'.[10]

Out of this awareness, writes Ratzinger, there arose the art of the icon, which however, cannot of course claim to be the end of our quest for the face of God, not even when the icons concerned are miraculous icons, the *acheiropoeitai* or images 'not made by hands'.[11] The crucial question to emerge from the Iconoclast dispute for Ratzinger is, do the icons 'carry the dynamic of transcendence'? Can they 'point beyond themselves'? Are they an 'invitation that brings us onto the [right] road in the search for the Lord's face'?[12] If so, they lead us further on the path of discipleship which in this life has no end. The icons are only seen justly when they are seen in terms of this *eschatological* aim. The love of neighbour and the Eucharistic cultus furnish us with anticipations of the Kingdom we hope for. But we need the holy icons to remind us that the 'true healing and the true repletion' will be looking on God's face.[13]

The Christological perspective – readily sanctioned by a work to which Ratzinger has elsewhere made laudatory reference, Christoph von Schönborn's *L'Icône du Christ*, has the possible disadvantage of concentrating an account of the origin and meaning of the cult of icons on the central Figure of Christianity, to the detriment of the full iconographic range of early Christian art – unless, that is, the additional themes (Mariological, hagiological, sacramental, and the like) are treated as aspects of a wider Christological constellation.[14] Where, however, Ratzinger differs from his fellow cardinal lies in the way he underscores the subjective, rather than objective, significance of iconic making and perception. Whereas Schönborn emphasises the

---

8   Ibid., p. 25, with reference to Gregory of Nyssa, *De vita Moysis* at *Patrologia Graeca* 44, 408D.

9   K. Mongrain, *The Systematic Theology of Hans Urs von Balthasar: An Irenaean Retrieval* (New York 2002).

10   Irenaeus, *Adversus Haereses* IV. 34, 1.The ‚Filius visibile Patris‘ text occurs in the same book at 6, 6.

11   *Unterwegs zu Jesus Christus*, p. 26.

12   Ibid.

13   Ibid., p. 29.

14   C. von Schönborn, OP, *L'Icône du Christ.*

dogmatic foundations of the icon in the Greek patristic Christology of dual nature and single hypostasis, Ratzinger stresses the transformed subjectivity which alone can allow us to grasp and profit by the new Image of God in Jesus Christ. In Balthasarian terms, within the unity of the entire perceived *Gestalt*, always both objective and subjective together, it is the 'subjective evidence' (which is far from 'subjective' in any pejorative, self-referential sense of that word) he prefers, in this context, to explore.

Ratzinger returned to the topic – still in what I am calling the 'Christological perspective' – in an essay entitled 'Wounded by the Arrow of the Beautiful: the Cross and the New "Esthetic" of Faith' which, among other things, shows his debt to the theological aesthetics of Hans Urs von Balthasar just mentioned. He begins from the liturgical use of Psalm 45, the Epithalamion psalm for the marriage of an Israelite king, but applied in the Lenten Psalter to the nuptial relation of Christ and the Church. The acclamation 'You are the fairest of men and graciousness is poured upon your lips' (verse 3) is not, so Ratzinger points out, simply an act of praise of the outer loveliness of the Redeemer. For what appears on his 'lips' is 'the inner beauty of his word, the splendour of his message'. What 'appears' in him is, accordingly, 'the splendour of truth, the splendour of God himself, which carries us away, which so to say inflicts on us the wound of love'. This is the 'holy eros' whereby in and with the Church we can respond to the love that calls us.[15] But in Holy Week the same psalm, when used in the Liturgy, is qualified by juxtaposition with an antiphon that radically changes its sense. The antiphon is drawn from the Servant Songs of the Book of Isaiah: 'He had no form or comeliness that we should look at him …' (53:2). The contrast cannot but strike the attentive worshipper.[16]

The fact to which it draws attention certainly struck one attentive reader: Augustine of Hippo, who concluded from the marring of the Passion, itself the most admirable of events, that in the events of the Great Week the entire Hellenic aesthetic is Christologically called in question. Both Old Testament texts, applied to Christ, are breathed out by the same Spirit. Their contrasting sounds, which lack all audible harmony (so prized by the Greeks), are what place before us the true beauty. The suffering Christ tells us that 'the beauty of truth includes wounding, pain, and even the dark mystery of death itself'.[17]

Actually, the Greeks were not without some distant surmise of this. In the *Phaedros* Plato showed his awareness that beauty has the power to draw us out of our contentment with the everyday, and by unsettling us makes us uncomfortable. Ratzinger goes so far as to say, on Plato's behalf, that 'the arrow of longing strikes

---

15 Ibid., p. 31.

16 The alternation of unlovely and lovely in the *Christusbild* of the Fathers was noted in A. Grillmeier [SJ], 'Die Herrlichkeit Gottes auf dem Antlitz Jesu Christi', in idem, *Mit ihm und in ihm: Christologische Forschungen und Perspektiven*, pp. 19–75, but without the use of Psalm 45.

17 *Unterwegs zu Jesus Christus*, pp. 32–3.

man, wounds him, and in this way gives him wings, and draws him upward'.[18] In his treatise *Life in Christ*, the Byzantine theologian Nicholas Cabasilas baptises this thought. People who have a longing that outstrips their nature are those 'the Bridegroom has wounded; he has despatched to their eyes a ray of his beauty'.[19] That is how God awakens them to their highest destiny.

Ratzinger denies that all this is superficial aestheticism, much less irrationality.

> Beauty is knowledge – yes, a higher kind of knowledge, because it brings home to man the full magnitude of truth.[20]

Contrasting knowledge through true report with knowledge through direct experience of things, Cabasilas, unsurprisingly, privileges the latter, which is a being touched by reality, and in the case of the Gospel, by the personal presence of Christ himself. In Ratzinger's words: 'being overwhelmed by the beauty of Christ is a more real and profound kind of knowledge than would be mere rational deduction'.[21] Through the impact of such beauty 'reason is freed from its stupor, *Betäubung*, and made capable of action'.[22] Ratzinger warns that this should not be taken to devalue careful theological reflection. Yet the latter is of secondary importance compared with the encounter of the heart with beauty. This Ratzinger takes to be the central claim of Hans Urs von Balthasar in the opening volume of his theological aesthetics.[23] Ratzinger regrets that so little response has been made to this central claim, not only in dogmatics but also in pastoralia – for the Church public, and the unevangelised too for that matter, need to meet the Lord in his beauty. People think theological reason is a wax nose; one can make of it any shape one likes. Being wounded by the Lord's beauty gives one a measuring rod for judgements in matters of discourse about revelation, and the capacity to weigh arguments in contemporary theology and, by this criterion, find them, if need be, wanting.

In the art of the Byzantine icon, in the creations of Romanesque and Gothic, one finds oneself vis-à-vis what the palpable power of the beautiful truth of God has made present in the inspiration of the artist. The artist has rendered the reality he experienced something in which we too can partake. This will make demands on us. Ratzinger seconds the proposal of the Russian Orthodox lay theologian Paul Evdokimov that the icon calls for a 'fast of seeing', a going beyond ordinary sense perception, the learning through prayer and asceticism of a 'a new, deeper seeing', since what shines through the sensuous matrix is the radiance of divine glory.[24] What can be said so confidently of the icon can be affirmed of all 'the great images of

---

18   Ibid., p. 33.
19   Nicholas Cabasilas, *De Vita in Christo, liber* II, at *Patrologia Graeca* 150, 553A.
20   *Unterwegs zu Jesus Christus*, p. 34.
21   Ibid., p. 35.
22   Ibid., p. 37.
23   H. U. von Balthasar, *The Glory of the Lord* I.
24   *Unterwegs zu Jesus Christus*, pp. 36–7. Compare P. Evdokimov, *L'Art de l'icône: Théologie de la beauté* (Paris 1970), pp. 153–65.

Christian art'. The beauty our faith has generated forms its chief apologia – along with the reality of the saints. These are our greatest treasures.

Some will say, beauty may provide positive experiences in spots of time, but in the long run reality is more likely to be largely wretched. After Auschwitz who can write lyric poetry? For Ratzinger that objection is to 'Apollo', to the Hellenic aesthetic of beautiful harmony, not to the aesthetic embodied in the glory of the Cross, the thorn-crowned beauty of Christ for which the Shroud of Turin may stand as symbol. This is the beauty of the charity that loved us to the end. Here Ratzinger returns to the starting point of the Epithalamion psalm and its fruitful liturgical ambiguity. The icon of the Crucified liberates us from the prison-house of believing the 'lie' which would make the denial of beauty's ultimacy the last word. And the splendid Passion likewise frees us from that other lie offered us by an aesthetic of hedonistic possession, whose artists would content us with the here and now, stifling rather than stimulating the movement of transcendence to go beyond. When in Dostoevsky we hear that beauty will save the world, we can too easily forget that the beauty concerned is specifically the 'redemptive beauty of Christ'.[25]

The liturgiological perspective

When we turn from the primarily Christological to the chiefly liturgiological perspective, we discover that Ratzinger's liturgical iconology remains distinctly Christocentric, just as his Christological iconology bears significant reference to the Liturgy – whether Jewish, for the cultic context of seeking God's face, or Christian, as in the stimulus he found to such reflection in the use by the Roman Office of the theme of the marred splendour of Jesus, the suffering King.

He sets out from where we would normally expect a theology of images to begin – from the issue of Israelite aniconicism, the anti-iconic commandments in the Hebrew Bible. He points out how, in the making of the golden cherubim to flank the Tabernacle's mercy-seat (Exodus 25:22), the Book of Exodus transgresses the very command it elsewhere (Exodus 20:4) asserts. I note that to speak here, as he does, of an 'exception', *Ausnahme*, assumes the prohibition of the Decalogue to strike unconditionally at *all* graven images and not simply those intended to represent the divine. Be that as it may, by using philosophical dialectic, he counters that to render the guardians of the divine mystery visible is precisely to underline the invisibility of the mystery itself.[26]

The question of the original intent of the anti-iconic commandment is raised again when Ratzinger calls the thoroughgoing aniconicism of rabbis contemporary with the high patristic era a 'radical' interpretation of the Torah, in contrast to the more moderate understanding which permitted the rich synagogue art of Dura-Europos, our fullest surviving example of a sacral figurative art in the synagogues of the early centuries of the Common Era.

---

25 *Unterwegs zu Jesus Christus*, p. 40.
26 *Der Geist der Liturgie: Eine Einführung* (Freiburg 2000), p. 99.

The frescoes of the Dura synagogue come with no handy manual of textual interpretation. Ratzinger offers a 'high' theology of these paintings, accommodating them to the Jewish *haggadah* of the period as its visual equivalent. In so doing he produces a Jewish counterpart for the way the Second Council of Nicaea would treat the icons as the visual counterpart to the New Testament Scriptures – themselves, of course, a 'reading' of the Scriptures of the Israel of old. The representations of Old Testament scenes on the walls of the Dura synagogue are not just 'images of past events'. Rather, they participate in the liturgical re-presentation of the original happenings. That is an ontological possibility since those happenings were not merely moments in human development but 'God's action in time'.[27]

The images in the Christian catacombs, so Ratzinger holds, take up this sort of synagogue art into a 'new kind of presence'. That 'presence' is 'new', because it depends on the Incarnation and the inauguration of the sacramental era. And it is really a 'presence' because the biblical events in which, through sacred art, Christians were sharing are now inserted into the reality of the risen Lord as he masters time through his exaltation to the Father's side. It is from there that he dispenses his life-giving sacraments – in catacomb art so often typologically indicated – via their human ministers in the Church.

This *prise de position* enables Ratzinger to establish a distinctive theology of the image, which he does by treating all Christian images as in some way Easter-oriented, ordered to the Session when Christ receives universal Lordship. He can make good his claim that early Christian art, whatever its limitations of technique, always furnishes 'images of hope', *Hoffnungsbilder*, if the entire iconology of the Church consists in fact of *Auferstehungsbilder*, 'images of the Resurrection'.[28]

A more obvious Christological framework for the discussion of sacred art is surely that provided by the Incarnation itself – which would, no doubt, include a reference to the Resurrection mystery, but not necessarily keep its focus there.[29] And in fact, Ratzinger cannot do without some more pervasive appeal to the sheer entry of the Logos into the sensuous realm – prescinding, then, from the Word's eventual destiny in the return, his humanity glorified, to the Father. The early painterly or sculptural images of Christ as teacher, Christ as shepherd, speak of the wisdom of the Logos now entering the human world, and his pastoral guardianship of the human creation which he carries 'home' on his shoulders, the Church of Jews and Gentiles.[30]

One reason for Ratzinger's anxiety to deflect the iconological centre to the Resurrection soon becomes plain. It is those excessive claims for the continuity of the image with the Incarnation made in the context of images believed to be 'not made by human hands'. The appearance of the *acheiropoeitai* – Ratzinger thinks especially of the Cappadocian image called the *Camuliana* and of the *mandylion* of Edessa whose (controversial) identification with the Shroud of Turin he seems

---

27   *Der Geist der Liturgie*, p. 100.
28   Ibid., p. 101.
29   See for instance, once again, A. Nichols, OP, *The Art of God Incarnate*.
30   *Der Geist der Liturgie*, p. 102.

to favour – led the faithful to ascribe to (at any rate, certain) images, a capacity to yield communion with the Saviour, and indeed the gift of his real presence, thus rendering the holy images competitors and rivals of the Eucharistic mysteries themselves. After all, the affinity in causal origination between the *achieropoeitai* and the Babe of Bethlehem was, to say the least, striking. These 'true' icons no more had a human artist as their author than the Word incarnate himself had a human father as his progenitor. Ratzinger thinks that images modelled on the *acheiropoeitai* – whose supernatural provenance, incidentally, he nowhere denies – became the very 'midpoint of the entire canon of images', *die Mitte der Bilderkanon.*[31] He sees here a twofold danger: that icons could usurp the role of sacraments, and that they might be taken as loci of direct vision of God here and now.

The Iconoclast controversy might be called in the circumstances a cruel necessity. Ratzinger recognises the role of non-theological factors in the official adoption by the Isaurian dynasty of Iconoclasm (though where a theological position is concerned every other consideration necessarily takes on a theological colouring). Essentially, however, the crisis enabled the Byzantine church to grasp the nature of the icon as a vehicle for evangelical faith by teasing out the notion of *a new kind of looking*, a looking which penetrates through the sensuous to the Christological centre of the super-sensuous realm beyond. In Ratzingerian terms, the Iconoclast dispute enabled the Church to grasp the *Resurrection-character* of all Christian images. 'The icon wants to draw us onto an inner path, the path "to the East", toward the Christ who will return.'[32]

As my use of the neologism 'Ratzingerian' suggests, this account reproduces neither the language of the dogmatic definition of Nicaea II, nor that of the Iconophile Fathers who worked for the vindication of the icons.[33] It is a contemporary theological re-presentation, a kind of Roman Catholic equivalent to the Eastern Orthodox theology of the icon which flourished in Russian Orthodoxy in the late nineteenth century (for Russia itself) and the early twentieth century (for the Russian diaspora in the West). In particular, echoing the iconological essays founded on a Christological perspective described earlier, Ratzinger does not hide his admiration for Evdokimov's theology of the icon, which is cited liberally in *Der Geist der Liturgie*. Whereas in the Neo-Orthodox appropriation of the patristic sources (not least for Evdokimov), the icon is dependent – ontologically and epistemologically – on the paradigmatic moment of Christ's Transfiguration as reiterated references to the 'Light of Thabor' make plain, for Ratzinger the key mystery in which to see the icon is the Resurrection. And yet the *manner* of his appeal to the Easter event is entirely Evdokimovian in feel. In both cases the crucial consideration is the 'unity of creation, Christology and eschatology',[34] the coincidence of the light of the 'first' day and the light of the 'eighth' day in the illuminated countenances of Christ and his

---

31   Ibid., p. 103.
32   Ibid., p. 105.
33   A. Nichols, OP, 'The *horos* of Nicaea II'.
34   *Der Geist der Liturgie*, p. 107.

saints. Both Evdokimov and Ratzinger are suspicious of an excessively or unilaterally apophatic theology. The radiance of God streaming forth from the glorified form of the Easter Jesus is – in a phrase of Evdokimov's adopted by Ratzinger – the 'apophatic "Yes"', *ein apophatisches Ja*.[35]

The reason why Ratzinger prefers, in the liturgiological perspective, a Resurrection-centred iconology to an Incarnation-centred one, is not only that it fits better his wider emphasis on the eschatological orientation of the Liturgy itself. It is also because, through that very congruence, we are able to discern the peculiar pertinence of a Paschal iconology to the ultimate goal of the Incarnation, which is not to draw the Logos down here to where we are but to take us up with him to his home. It is at 'human ascent' that 'divine descent' aims. Of course, to maintain continuity with the theological doctrine of the image offered in the Christological perspective, we shall have to remind the reader that the Resurrection is precisely the Resurrection of the Crucified. Ratzinger makes the same point the other way round when he says of even the most anguished Late Gothic images of the Passion that, by finding and communicating consolation even in such horror, they 'carry within them the message of the Resurrection'.[36]

That doctrinal suture forms part of an interesting analytic survey of the chief periods of Western Christian art – issuing in some prescriptions for the future. Ratzinger regards the Romanesque as, despite its emphasis on sculpture, Latin Byzantinism. He considers that Early and High Gothic art, owing to its admirable fidelity to the unity of the Testaments, reproduces much in the ethos of Eastern Christian iconography even if, with the relativisation of Christian Platonism in the high mediaeval West, salvation history now strikes people rather as 'Historie' than as 'Sakrament'.[37] We have seen how he deals with the often agonised Passion paintings of Late Gothic, maintaining by a bold inversion of more conventional interpretations, that these are covertly Paschal images, since only by tacit reference to the Resurrection can ghastliness console. It is curious that he does not mention the well-documented fact that the practice of depicting the dead Christ on the Cross is a tenth-century Byzantine innovation subsequently received in the West through early Franciscanism. (The making in Byzantium of images of the *Christus patiens* – showing the Crucified with eyes closed, head sagging to one side – figured among the charges against the church of Constantinople brought there in 1054 by the papal legate Humbert of Silva Candida.) He offers a glowing testimonial to mediaeval glass, the 'iconostasis of the West', where the church walls, in interplay with the sun, become an image sequence in their own right. As a Bavarian Catholic, Ratzinger naturally defends the Baroque at least in its 'best' forms, which he describes as a

---

    35   Ibid., p. 106. On Evdokimov, see P. C. Dinh Phan, *Culture and Eschatology: The Iconographical Vision of Paul Evdokimov* (Berne 1985). I have provided a brief entrée in my essay, 'Paul Evdokimov and Eschatology', in A. Nichols, OP, *Light from the East: Authors and Themes in Eastern Orthodoxy* (London 1995), pp. 194–204.

    36   *Der Geist der Liturgie*, p. 110.

    37   Ibid., p. 109.

visual equivalent to the jubilation of a melismatic alleluia from the Latin chant. His coldest comments are reserved for the Renaissance, in which he joins hands not only with modern Eastern Orthodox critics but with also internal dissenters in the Western tradition. Not for nothing did the nearest English Victorian equivalent to the Nazarene school call itself the 'Pre-Raphaelite Brotherhood'. Ratzinger excoriates the Church art of the Renaissance. It made no proper distinction between the world of meaning of the Gospels and that of ancient myths. It excluded fear of sin and the pain of the Cross. It pronounced an apotheosis of beauty for its own sake.

It is curious, then, that at the first Synod of Bishops at which he presided as Pope, namely the Synod on the Holy Eucharist which met at Rome in October 2005, Ratzinger arranged for an image from the art of Raphael, the *Disputation on the Sacrament*, to be projected on a large screen above the presider's table in the Synod Aula. He likewise commissioned the American-born but Florence-based art historian Father Timothy Verdon to provide an authoritative commentary on the painting in *L'Osservatore Romano* for 12 October. Though the painting *appears* to confirm Ratzinger's strictures on Renaissance art (notably, it presents its Eucharistic subject in parallel with a companion painting on a patently pagan theme, *The School of Athens*), Verdon's commentary rescues it from the theological dumping ground to which, prematurely, it might have been consigned. For Verdon argues that the principal message of *Disputation on the Sacrament* concerns eschatology anticipated by the Liturgy – absolutely in line, then, with Ratzinger's own theology of the image. The centre of this fresco, after all, is the glorified Christ displaying his wounds – a reminder of the general judgement (compare Apocalypse 1:7), with, below him, the dove of the Holy Spirit fluttering above the Eucharistic altar and the Host to whose conversion from bread to the Body of the Lord the Spirit's work is crucial. (Verdon thinks Raphael intended here an eirenic reference to the Greek theology of the Mass, not long previously adumbrated at the abortive reunion Council of Florence). Even the pagan companion piece contributes to the full effect of this image of the Church gathered in the presence of the Trinity in Eucharistic adoration. Raphael, so Verdon argues, wished to emphasise the intellectual fascination the Eucharistic mystery has aroused. The Christian doctors shown in the one painting are no less animated in their search for truth than are the pagan philosophers portrayed in the other, while the latter have laid some vital conceptual foundations for the work of the former. When the two paintings are seen together, as was intended, they show how even the pagans share in the Church as unwitting co-travellers in her pilgrimage to God.

Evidently, here is one Renaissance image which could be taken to embody, rather than traduce, the prescriptions for sacred art which Ratzinger offers. How in his own conclusion does he sum them up? Briskly. First, iconoclasm is not a Christian option: it is tacit denial of the Incarnation of God. Secondly, the principal topic of sacred art (that is, a doctrinally informed art capable of serving as a monument of Tradition) is the salvation history of the two Testaments, seen as ordered to 'the day of the Resurrection and the Second Coming' of Christ. That by no means excludes as a secondary topic the saints, since they are corporately or individually an 'unfolding of the history of Jesus Christ'.[38] Thirdly, the images qua sacred art are essentially connected to the sacramental Liturgy, which is the enduring visibility of the mystery of Christ on earth. That in turn means the centre of iconography is Jesus Christ in the unity of his Passion and Resurrection – since this is the centre of the Liturgy itself. Ratzinger reiterates his claim that all images must be in some way images of Easter – hinting at the Christ who suffered, rose, will come again and now reigns hiddenly in and over time. Fourthly, the holy images are born of contemplation and issue in contemplation. The eyes of faith they require – and inspire – are the eyes of the Church herself, the primary subject of Christian vision. Fifthly and finally, the Church of the West must make her own the common dogmatic formulation owed in practice, at the Seventh Ecumenical Council, to the Church of the East. The theology of the icon proposed at the Council is absolutely normative – even if stylistically a variety of iconographic manners may be compatible with its affirmations.

Conclusion

Pope Benedict is to be lauded for the rapid way in which, on assuming the office of bishop of Rome, he sought to put into effect his high view of the place of holy images in Christian catechesis and mystagogy. The 14 sacred images included in the *Compendium of the Catechism of the Catholic Church*, presented by Benedict XVI on 28 June 2005, were, the Pope insisted, not merely illustrations but an integral part of the new text. Each image receives a detailed commentary in the *Compendium* with generous citations from the Bible and the Fathers of the Church. The new Pope had learned from the fate of the 1992 *Catechism* issued by his predecessor, John Paul II, whose far more modest total of illustrations (here probably the word was apt) suffered the indignity of mutilation, replacement or elimination in some translations. For the *Compendium*, all translations must reproduce the holy images exactly, and in the position indicated.

As patriarch of the West, Benedict XVI has the right and duty to act as overseer of the iconographic patrimony of the Latin church. Writing as Cardinal Ratzinger, he was correct to draw attention to the continuing importance of the Second Council of Nicaea for Catholics of the West as well as of the East. His statement that its theology of the image is normative sits rather oddly, however, with a certain lack of zeal in investigating that theology in its historical context. The dogmatic definition of Nicaea II and the theological doctrine of the Iconophile Fathers are not the same, after all, as the Neo-Orthodox theology produced by Russian devotees of the art of the icon, however gifted, in the modern period.

Actually, the present writer considers that Ratzinger might have gone further, and declared Byzantine practice (and not simply Greek conciliar thinking) to enjoy

---

38   Ibid., p. 113.

a normative significance likewise.[39] The Byzantine church is the only ritual church in Christendom to have worked out with full liturgical and dogmatic coherence an iconographic scheme for the decoration of church interiors, the setting of the Eucharistic action. That alone grants it a special status which could usefully act as a criterion for the re-conceiving of iconographic schemes in a Latin Catholicism too often haphazard or, more recently, minimalistic in this respect. The Byzantine is, furthermore, the only church whose art shows so consistently (albeit not *entirely* consistently) a 'Paschal aesthetic' in the stylistic manner iconographers employ, combining austere Good Friday and lavish Easter Sunday qualities in a unity of asceticism and salvific fulness. Latins, and other Easterners, would do well to note.

Meanwhile, we can take courage and consolation from the magnificent words Benedict used at the ceremonial presentation of that *Compendium* of the Church's faith, when he declared:

> Image and word illuminate one another in turn. Art always 'speaks', at least implicitly, of the divine, of the infinite beauty of God, which finds its reflection in the icon *par excellence*: Christ the Lord, the image of the invisible God. Sacred images, with their beauty, are also heralds of the Gospel and express the splendour of Catholic truth, showing the supreme harmony between the good and the beautiful, between the *via veritatis* [way of truth] and the *via pulchritudinis* [way of beauty]. While they give witness to the age-old and prolific tradition of Christian art, they encourage all, both believers and non- believers, to discover and contemplate the inexhaustible wonder of the mystery of redemption, continually providing a new impulse for the lively process of its inculturation in time.[40]

How, in the contemporary epoch, to produce artworks that point to the divine beauty and serve the Gospel truth, is not necessarily, however, all plain sailing. The two chapters that follow, drawing on twentieth-century experience on both sides of the English Channel, suggest the difficulties – and the possibilities involved.

---

39   A. Nichols, OP, 'On Baptising the Visual Arts: A Friar's Meditation on Art', in idem, *Scribe of the Kingdom*, II., pp. 183–96.

40   Papal address on 28 June 2006, cited in S. Magister, 'A Catechism for the Culture of the Images', www.chiesa.expressonline.it, 4 November 2006.

PART 3
The Difficulties of Practice

Chapter 6

The French Dominicans and the Journal
L'Art sacré

The next two chapters take as their theme the practical effort in France and England to launch a sacrally relevant art in the twentieth century. To practise a sacral aesthetic, whether as producer or consumer, is not easy in an epoch – still continuing – when the visual arts themselves have left behind not only Church but, for the greater part, the public as well.

The project

Just before the Second World War, some Dominicans in the Province of France became concerned about the poor state of religious art in that country, if not only there.[1] They were especially worried about the nature and quality of artworks placed in churches as a context for the sacred Liturgy, and (often) about the style and disposition of those churches themselves. In 1937 they inherited a new-born review with the name *L'Art sacré* in which they began to work out a policy or programme for the future. The coming of the War in 1939 and the German occupation of northern France, where they were working, led to the suspense both of the publication and of their activities. But after the War they were able to resume, and the journal continued its life until a couple of years after the closure of the Second Vatican Council.

Without a doubt its most ground-breaking and influential period was in the early 1950s. At that time it became embroiled in a quarrel over the nature of sacred art which reached the highest levels in terms of Church authority, eliciting in 1952 interventions both by the French episcopate and by Rome. The Dominicans of *L'Art sacré* were not exclusively concerned with theoretical criteria for the art of the Church. Had they been, it is rather doubtful whether they would have stirred up public opinion among the Catholic population in France and in the French episcopate, in the way they did. High on the list of gravamina against them were the controversial commissions they arranged for new churches and decorative schemes, often from artists who were themselves unbelievers. Like all Dominicans, one trusts, they were, however, primarily theologians, even if the two principal figures had also had a professional training in the visual arts and of these one was a practising artist.

---

1   See S. de Lavergne, *Art sacré et modernité: Les grandes années de la Revue 'L'Art sacré'* (Namur, 1992).

Much of their theological combination remains valid, even if, as we shall see, there were also deficiencies.

Historically, Dominicans are canons regular who, for the sake of the Church's mission, turned themselves into preaching friars. So the solemn celebration of the Liturgy, the proper work of canons regular, and the preaching of the Word, the specific task of an 'order of preachers', have always been constants in Dominican life. It was out of concern for the role of the visual arts in liturgical worship, and their value as a medium in which to communicate the truths of Catholic Christianity, that these men (re-)founded and ran *L'Art sacré* and endured the trials it brought them, even if some of these were to a degree self-inflicted. As one of them wrote, what was at stake was 'the face the Church presents to the world'.[2] Their efforts are instructive in that they were trying to negotiate a passage between Tradition and modernity, which is what all of us are trying to do in different ways.

The protagonists

So who were the principal Dominicans involved? They were two in number.[3] The elder was Pierre Couturier, born in 1897, died in 1954, in religion Père Marie-Alain Couturier. After secondary school at Lyons, he decided to train as an artist, and was accepted as a pupil by the Parisian *Ateliers d'art sacré*, on which more anon. In 1925, when in his late twenties, Couturier entered the Dominican Province of France – sometimes known as the Province of Paris since at this time there were three French Dominican Provinces of which the Province of France was the senior. The French Revolution had wiped out the Dominicans, but a brilliant young diocesan priest, the Abbé Lacordaire, who will come into this story again, had re-established them in the early 1840s. Couturier, despite his Dominican vows and priestly ordination, never gave up practice as an artist. Indeed, following such mediaeval Dominican models as Fra Angelico and Blessed James of Ulm, he was encouraged to see his vocation in these terms. Like Angelico, he specialised in the painting of frescoes – scenes and compositions of figures painted directly onto the plaster of church walls. There are, for instance, a number of these, from the years 1928 to 1929, in the Dominican priory church at Oslo, where the present writer spent some time at the turn of the 1970s and 1980s. In 1932, he was commissioned to paint frescoes for the chapel of the Master of the Order at the priory of Santa Sabina in Rome. Like James of Ulm, Couturier also worked in stained glass, another form of Dominican *muta praedicatio*, 'silent preaching'. On this basis, he made it his business to get to know the professional art world in France, and was especially friendly with the Fauvist Henri Matisse. Matisse was usually regarded as the leader of *Les Fauves*, an art movement which treated painting as an 'alchemy of colour' aiming to explore the

---

2   P.-R. Régamey, *Art sacré au vingtième siècle?* (Paris 1952), p. 8.

3   See F. Caussé, 'Les rapports des Dominicains avec *L'Art sacré:* La revue *Art sacré* des Pères Couturier et Régamey', *Mémoire dominicaine* 14 (1999), pp. 169–97, is my chief source of information on these personalities.

possibilities of pure colour and create harmonies parallel to musical composition. It lies behind the later development of abstract art. In the key years 1949 to 1953, Couturier's writing dominated the journal. It is not easy to get copies of *L'Art sacré* most of whose subscribers were clergy, religious or interested laity rather than public libraries. But in 1983 Couturier's articles from that period were collected and published, under the anodyne title *Marie-Alain Couturier: Art sacré*. The following year, the French Dominican publishing house Les Editions du Cerf brought out an anthology of essays he had placed in various publications from 1939 onwards. The anthology was released under a title more eloquent of his later difficulties with the Church public, *La Vérité blessée*, 'The Wounded Truth', and this was sufficiently successful to be reprinted in 1991. Couturier's death in 1954 is one of the two events that mark the end of the great period of *L'Art sacré*.[4]

The other major figure was Raymond Régamey, in religion Pie-Raymond Régamey, born in 1900 and living on until as late as 1996. Régamey was the child of a French Protestant family already distinguished in the arts and the world of letters. He himself studied literature and the history of art at the Sorbonne, and early showed signs of literary productivity, publishing his first articles, chiefly on nineteenth-century French art, before he was 20 years old. Following his University studies, he trained in art conservation and the year after he became a Catholic (1927) was named as assistant conservator of paintings at the Louvre. In 1928, however, he abandoned this promising career and joined the French Dominicans at Amiens, on the territory of the Province of Paris. Régamey was friendly with many of the leading French art critics of the period and also with such practising artists as Georges Rouault, who, like Matisse, began as a Fauvist though his later work is often described as 'mystical Expressionism'. In 1952 Régamey published a book under the title *Art sacré au vingtième siècle?*, 'Sacred Art in the Twentieth Century?'. This book sums up in chastened form (1952 was the date of a sharp Roman rap over the knuckles for the editors) the aims and experience of the Dominicans of *L'Art sacré*, and was regarded by their admirers as the 'Bible' of the movement they represented. Also well worth reading (where accessible!) is Régamey's lengthy essay on the nature of Tradition from the viewpoint of Catholicism and the arts, entitled 'A la recherche de la Tradition', 'In search of Tradition'. Published in *L'Art sacré* for 1948, it is one of the journal's high points.[5] In 1954, straight after the death of Couturier, Régamey began collecting and eventually publishing some writings and notes by the Dominican whose friend he had been since the noviciate.[6] He had more time to do this in that he had just been relieved of the editorship of *L'Art sacré*, owing to the delayed fall out from the Church controversy of two years earlier. Couturier and Régamey, while –naturally enough – not agreeing on absolutely everything, worked

---

4   See also the issue of *L'Art sacré* devoted to him: 1954, 9–10 (the post-war journal numbered issues by fascicules only, sometimes overlapping the end of the calendar year).

5   P.-R. Régamey, OP, 'A la recherche de la Tradition', *L'Art sacré* 1948, 5–6, pp. 81–107.

6   *Dieu et l'art dans une vie, le P. Couturier* (Paris 1965).

from the same first principles in terms of their programme of a modern sacred art. Their removal, whether by death or superior's decision, brought to a close the most creative period of the journal's history, even if the legacy they left was not happy in all respects.

The context

Before getting into the meat of the contribution it will be helpful, I think, to say something about the context. *L'Art sacré* began in 1935. It needs to be understood, therefore, against the backcloth of the 1920s and early 1930s. In the years immediately following the First World War in France various voices were raised against the sugary and sentimental tone of much mass-produced Church art, often referred to by the location of its main Parisian retail outlets as the 'art of Saint-Sulpice'. Oversweet, anaesthetising any sense of the hard ascetic and moral demands of Christianity, offering pseudo-religious compensation: these were the typical terms in which critics poured scorn on this art and its equivalent in the Germanic countries where a useful one-word term of opprobrium was available, kitsch – etymology unknown. The French had a similar term, *bondieuserie*, but the writers of *L'Art sacré* made the German term popular, notably after the monastic press of Ettal in Bavaria published in 1950 a study called *Kitsch und Christenleben*, 'Kitsch and Christian Living', a work enthusiastically reviewed in the French journal.[7] The word got into the other main European languages as well. In English, it was helped along by a translation of Richard Egenter's book, adapted for the situation in England by Nicolete Gray, interpreter of the art of the Dominican tertiary David Jones.[8] The phenomenon of sugary, sentimental sacred art was not confined just to the two sides of the river Rhine. It is an interesting if perplexing question why what came to be called kitsch arose as it did in the later nineteenth century. Writing as a moral theologian with a good knowledge of art history, Egenter traced its origins to the arbitrary subjection of religious themes to artistic fancy, aided by Rococo emotionalism and, subsequently, Romanticism. Techniques of mass production, made possible by the machine, added the factor of multiplication to the simplification and distortion already present in the studio. Insipid, and frivolous (it was compared with Pop Art in this respect), kitsch turned divine things into commodities for the purpose of spiritual pleasuring. Such 'artistic miscarriage', commented Egenter, gave 'the Father of lies' a 'wonderfully flexible and effective means of turning the masses away from salvation'.[9] In his own analysis, Régamey added for good measure: deviations of piety, aggressive commercial organisation and publicity, the desire to avoid the higher cost of employing good craftsmen, official connivance, the laziness of the clergy and the

---

7   It inspired several succeeding issues devoted to 'Les marchands et le temple', or 'Pourquoi le succès de la bondieuserie?', see *L'Art sacré* 1951, 9–10.

8   R. Egenter, *The Desecration of Christ* (London 1967), based on idem, *Kitsch und Christenleben* (Ettal 1958, 2nd edition).

9   Idem, *The Desecration of Christ*, p. 15.

lack of interest in the Church of the recognised 'living masters' of the arts. The last three factors, at least, *L'Art sacré* might expect to help circumvent.

The writers of the early twentieth-century French Catholic revival – Léon Bloy, novelist and pamphleteer; Paul Claudel, dramatist and poet; Loris-Karl Huysmans, novelist – had long since agreed on the lamentable condition of ecclesiastical architecture, painting and liturgical craftsmanship. In due course they won the support of two active – and pro-active – Catholic artists, Maurice Denis and Georges Desvallières. Maurice Denis, though he had trained with the Pont-Aven group gathered around him by the Post-Impressionist Paul Gauguin, was far from being self-consciously modern. An ultramontane royalist who deplored the secularisation of society and looked to the recreation of a 'Catholic social order' in France, he strongly opposed a number of the avant-garde developments: not simply Fauvism but also Cubism whose best-known figure was Pablo Picasso. Cubist artists began by breaking down objects into angular forms, though later on they abandoned the claim to be interpreting nature. Denis was also hostile to Futurism, originally an Italian movement which sought inspiration in the machine, and tried to convey a sense of high-speed motion by whipping forms out of shape. For Denis the upshot of these movements could only be the total separation of art from nature. His own painting – its style described by the *Oxford Dictionary of Twentieth Century Art* as 'tender and mild, with pale colours and relaxed lines'[10] – aimed to reclaim in some way the spirit of the Italian renaissance understood as a Christian rather than neo-pagan development, though a recent study has also claimed him for the enthusiasts of 'Byzantium re-discovered'.[11] But he was not simply anti-modern. He wanted to simplify form so as to stress symbolic content, a concern that links him to the widespread European style of art nouveau, which flourished in Germany, England and Russia as well as France. He emphasised flatness of surface pattern, like some later members of the School of Paris. His stress on the spiritual nature of art cannot have been simply ecclesiastical because it was taken originally from the group of secular artists called *Les Nabis*, 'The Prophets'.[12] When he was demobbed after the War, Denis took up an idea from the other would-be practical reformer of Church art in the 1920s, Georges Desvallières.[13]

Desvallières, whose dates are 1861 to 1950, had been a pupil of the late-nineteenth- century Symbolist painter and illustrator Gustave Moreau. He was probably attracted to Moreau by the latter's fusion of mystical and romantic imagery, as was Rouault. Before the First World War Desvallières was working on ideas for a Catholic art school, something that came to fruition in 1919 more through the efforts of Denis than anyone else, under the title *Ateliers d'Art sacré*, 'The Workshops of Sacred Art'. As Desvallières envisaged them, these 'workshops' were to be places

---

10   'Denis, Maurice', in I. Childers, *A Dictionary of Twentieth Century Art* (Oxford 1988), p. 167.

11   J. E. Bullen, *Byzantium Rediscovered* (London 2003).

12   For more on this figure, see J. P. Bouillon, *Maurice Denis* (Geneva 1983).

13   A. Garreau, *Georges Desvallières* (Paris 1942).

where practising artists could apprentice the young. He had it in mind that they would be lineal descendants of the artists' fraternity founded in Rome by the reviver of the French Dominicans, Henri-Dominique Lacordaire, in 1839.[14] Rome was the Mecca of most nineteenth-century artists, a situation codified later by the French State when it made submission of an entry for the *Prix de Rome* a condition of official recognition for artists. In 1872 the members of Lacordaire's *Confrèrie de Saint-Jean l'Evangéliste* set up a daughter organisation in France itself. That was when the *Sociéte de Saint-Jean* came into existence, as an instrument for organising conferences, exhibitions and publications all designed to renew the visual arts in the service of the Church. The *Ateliers* were to be in this succession.

The Denis-Desvallières *Ateliers* were consciously modelled on the mediaeval guild system, in which in England at the same time the 'Guild Socialists' were interested. One moved from apprentice to collaborator as one went on. The future Père Couturier was precisely one of these young men, who, typically, were sent out in teams to redecorate village churches and convent chapels or to give talks to 'edify' the faithful and clergy by presentations on sacred art. Although the *Ateliers* were not the only associations of artists with religious concerns, they were the most important ones. Denis formulated their manifesto. The artist was to realise in his work a symbiosis between his life as a believer, his life as an artist and his life as an ordinary human being.[15] *Ateliers* artists were invited to explore the main sources of Christian inspiration, which, describing their set-up, Régamey defined as the Bible and the Liturgy, 'sciences religieuses' (meaning, I suppose, a knowledge of doctrine) and lastly the 'works of art of the great Christian epochs': Romanesque, Byzantine, Gothic and so forth.[16]

Apart from the *Ateliers* of Denis and Desvallières, the other main influence on the origins of *L'Art sacré* was the Neo-Thomist philosopher and lay theologian Jacques Maritain. Maritain's *Art et scolastique*, which so stimulated the sculptor, letterer, engraver Eric Gill and the artist (in various media) and poet David Jones at Ditchling,[17] was held in great esteem in circles dedicated to the renewal of Church art in France. This was true not least among the Dominicans who were Maritain's closest clerical contacts. *Art et scolastique* appeared in 1920. It forms part of Maritain's plea for a new Christendom. In this book, he expressly refused to look for a style or a manner of working or a set of techniques specific to Christian art. This refusal deeply influenced the Dominicans of *L'Art sacré*. Like Denis, Maritain did not think that the

---

14   E. Cartier, *Un Religieux dominicain: Le Révérend Père Hyacinthe Besson, sa vie et ses lettres* I. (Paris 1865), pp. 73–6. Besson was a member of the brotherhood who went on to enter the Order of Preachers in the Province of France.

15   For the influence of the *Ateliers'* philosophy on (especially) the early *L'Art sacré*, see P.-R. Régamey, 'Bilan de l'époque 1920–1940', *L'Art sacré* 1948, 3–4, pp. 50–57, and here at p. 53.

16   Ibid.

17   F. MacCarthy, *Eric Gill* (London 1989), p. 161; R. Hague (ed.), *Dai Greatcoat: A self-portrait of David Jones in his letters* (London 1980), p. 31.For more on this subject, see below, Chapter 7.

'Christian' of 'Christian art' had anything to do with painterly means at all.[18] Rather, the Christian character of art had to spring spontaneously from a 'common renewal of art and holiness'.[19] A truly religious art could not, he thought, exist outside a holy society – that is, a society capable of engendering holiness and recognising it when it saw it.

> To turn away from Wisdom and contemplation, and aim lower than at God, that, for a Christian civilisation, is the first cause of all disorder. In particular, it is the cause of this impious divorce between Art and Prudence which one finds in epochs where Christians no longer have the strength to bear the integrity of their riches.[20]

Like Denis and Desvallières, Maritain insisted on the traditional requirement that in sacred art the artist must himself be a believer. Christian art is 'the art of redeemed humanity'.[21] The effective abandonment by the Dominicans of *L'Art sacré* of this fundamental thesis was going to be in the future the most serious criticism lodged against them. What by contrast was new in Maritain's attitude was the notion that the sacred artist, in order to be fully an artist, must be fully of his own time. Without that commitment to the contemporary, Maritain held, his or her artworks would not be an authentic artistic testimony to the faith.[22] This was the other important 'doctrine' the Dominicans took from him.

The background to the beginnings of *L'Art sacré* was also organisational. In 1934 an umbrella organisation – 'OGAR', the 'Office général d'art religieux' – was established for the various associations of Catholic artists and craftsmen. It had the very practical aim of helping artists to get commissions and at the same time informing the clergy about what was called the 'new artistic production'.[23]

The establishment of *L'Art sacré*

With financial assistance from two benefactors, OGAR established the journal *L'Art sacré* in 1935. Its first editor, Joseph Pichard, was a layman married to an artist who worked in mosaic. Under his editorship *L'Art sacré* did not do overmuch to correspond to Maritain's requirement that sacred art be of its time. The great majority

---

18   J. Maritain, *Art et scolastique* (Paris 1927, 2nd edition), pp. 113–16. There is an analogy here with Maritain's view of Christian philosophy, which is '[simply] philosophy itself [but] in its Christian state, in the conditions of exercise and the lights which are the privilege of the Christian soul'. Thus his speech inaugurating the Louvain memorial to Cardinal Mercier as cited in P. Chenaux, *Entre Maurras et Maritain: Une génération intellectuelle, 1920–1930* (Paris 1999), pp. 195–6.

19   J. Maritain, *Art et scolastique*, p. 119.

20   Ibid., p. 41.

21   Ibid., p. 111.

22   For Maritain's relations with contemporary artists, see M. Cagin, 'Jacques Maritain et les artistes', *Cahiers Jacques Maritain* 27 (1993), pp. 5–30.

23   F. Caussé, 'Les rapports des Dominicains avec *L'Art sacré*', p. 173.

of its articles concerned the history of Christian art, while the others were chiefly chronicles of exhibitions visited. Though Pichard had been criticised for being too commercially minded in the way he ran *L'Art sacré*, the journal went into financial crisis in the summer of 1936. To be fair to Pichard, this was partly owing to the wave of strikes that accompanied the transition from the administration of Pierre Laval, which had failed to cope with the continuing inter-war economic crisis, and the coming to power of the Leftist Popular Front government of Léon Blum. *L'Art sacré* was saved only by the intervention of two wealthy aristocratic ladies who bought it and presented it to the fledgling Dominican publishing house Les Editions du Cerf in 1937.

This was the beginning of the connection between *L'Art sacré* and the Order of Preachers. The French Dominicans were surely the first grouping in Europe to establish a Religious community with as its defining apostolate the running of a publishing house. Originally founded at Juvisy in 1938, it soon moved into the centre of Paris where it still exists today in the same building, the Couvent Saint-Dominique at 29, boulevard de Latour-Maubourg. Les Editions du Cerf has been phenomenally successful and remains the largest religious publishing house in France. A few months after they acquired *L'Art sacré*, du Cerf – of course this must have been with the consent of the French Provincial – made Père Couturier and Père Régamey joint editors. Given their artistic backgrounds, they were, after all, the obvious choice. After the interruption of the Second World War, Régamey would become sole editor, since Couturier had developed an apostolate of lecture tours on the areas represented by the review while he was in North America for the duration of hostilities.

Policy or policies of the Dominicans of '*L'Art sacré*'

Hostilities, as things turned out, were not to be confined to the global struggle between the Axis powers and the Allies. The very first post-war issue announced that the journal intended to be 'severe' in its aesthetic judgements. It declared that its criteria would be no different from those operative in the world of profane art: namely, the quality of art as art. It set out to blame and shame, irritating the parish clergy and, even more no doubt, the proprietors of Catholic repositories and art shops by publishing photographs of what it considered the worst examples of bad Church art, though the editors were sufficiently charitable only to give the names of individual artists when they felt they could praise not damn. The post-war *L'Art sacré* expressed its intention to initiate its readership into an understanding of specifically modern art, and to sensibilise it to the work of even those artists they knew many people would find disconcerting. Although the post-war *L'Art sacré* continued to do various things its pre-war incarnation had done – chronicling exhibitions, reviewing books, sponsoring articles on Christian art history and suggesting practical applications of the arts for the Liturgy – the majority of its pages were devoted to contemporary art: a clear reversal of the Pichard policy.

But the new incarnation was also a reversal of the early policy of Couturier and Régamey themselves. Before the War they had shown themselves, after the manner of Denis, rather acerbic critics of much modern art. Their guns were even trained on the work of Rouault, despite the fact that he saw his vocation as to render in art the crusading, anti-bourgeois Catholicism of Bloy. In 1937, for example, Couturier, writing on Picasso and the present-day conditions of Christian art, had roundly declared that some forms of twentieth- century art were simply incapable of meeting the essential conditions of any Christian art worth the name. Naturalist art, abstract art, Cubist art were, Couturier opined, anti-religious in their very fundaments. Not mincing words, he described Picasso's work as 'malignant': it was *tout chargé de maléfices.*[24] In 1938, while recognising Rouault's Christian inspiration, Couturier deemed his work, which of course had a Fauvist background, full of 'extremes and brutality' (certainly Bloy himself disowned it, probably for its violent, ugly colours). To place his artworks in a church setting could only serve, wrote Couturier, in words which must have been extremely painful to Rouault if he read them, to discourage the 'love of priests and the faithful'.[25] The only moderns the pre-war Dominican *L'Art sacré* liked turned out to be some rather obscure Swiss artists in *la Suisse romande* and some slightly better known church architects in the German-speaking cantons.[26]

True, what we can call the 'first Dominican *L'Art sacré*' was far from bovinely content with the existing state of things. In measured but unmistakable terms it lamented the missed opportunities of *Les Chantiers du Cardinal*, the huge programme of church building in the working-class and suburban districts of Paris which occupied most of the 1930s. It welcomed a joint exhibition of Church artists and other artists – including Marc Chagall, a somewhat unplaceable figure who mixed Surrealist dream images with Judaism and Russian folk art – as arranged by Pichard at the end of 1938. But its policies were essentially the following:

- Firstly, while establishing links with the contemporary art world outside the Church, to avoid where possible the avant-garde, and privilege instead connections with those modern artists who were closest in technique and aim to the pictorial traditions of past centuries. This reflected the position of Denis and Desvallières, the two Ds, but not necessarily that of Maritain.
- Secondly, to insist on the principle that a sacred art could only be created by artists who were themselves religious, which in the case of a Christian sacred art must mean believing and practising Christians. This was taken for granted by the two Ds and forcefully restated, with justificatory explanations,

24   A.-M. Couturier, OP, 'Sur Picasso et les conditions actuelles de l'art chrétien', *L'Art sacré* 18 (1937), pp. 99 ff., cited in F. Caussé, 'Les rapports des Dominicains avec *L'Art sacré*', pp. 176–7.

25   A.-M. Couturier, OP, 'Rouault at le public ecclésiastique', ibid., 33 (1938), pp. 245 ff., cited in F. Caussé, 'Les rapports des Dominicains avec *L'Art sacré*', art. cit., p. 177.

26   On the architects, Fritz Metzer and Hermann Baur, see F. Debuyst, *Le renouveau de l'Art sacré de 1920 à 1962* (Paris 1991), pp. 33–5.

by Maritain.

*   Thirdly, to accept that in a society which had undergone considerable secularisation, it was not to be expected that an art sympathetic to the spiritual vision of the Church, congruent with its Liturgy and useful in its preaching, would ever be generally available. There could only be isolated islands where a successful combination of Church Tradition and modernity was achieved. This was also Maritain's conviction and no doubt helps to explain why across the English Channel the artists and craftsmen of the Ditchling Guild and community found his book so satisfying. Such an island is exactly what they were themselves.

In the French context, we can say that, in effect, the Dominicans of the first or pre-war *L'Art sacré* considered the work of the Denis–Desvallières *Ateliers* to be the way ahead. They merely deplored its small success in convincing those in ecclesiastical authority, as well as donors and patrons, that this and not the 'art of Saint-Sulpice' was what they ought to be supporting.[27]

The change that overcame the review when it started up again in 1945 was not total, but it was marked. It forms part of a general transformation of the French Catholic elites in the later 1940s and early 1950s. Often ascribed to the shared struggle against Fascism in which Communists and secular humanists as well as many Catholics were involved, this change took the form of an abandonment of the hope of a restored 'Catholic social [and we can add, cultural] order'. Not only was such a hope unrealistic, based on nostalgia for a lost Christendom that could never, in fact, be restored. Worse still, it was also dangerous, because it minimalised or denied outright the common ground of basic humanity on which Christians and others walked. That common ground might express the values or spirit of the Gospel better than a dogmatic manual or a liturgical text or an icon or a classical treatise from the history of Christian spirituality. This mindset, which was most obviously present in the upper echelons of Catholic Action, where the majority of engaged Catholics were to be found, also held good for a number of the intellectually more sophisticated clergy of which the French Catholicism of this period could boast not a few. The issues it raised were the issues which, after the Second Vatican Council, led to quite divergent views of what the Council's call for *ressourcement* and *aggiornarnento* – making contemporary by going back to the sources – was actually intended to achieve. Today, it underlies for instance the differences between the two main international theological journals, *Concilium* and *Communio*, and even the divergent attitudes of English Roman Catholics towards the London *Tablet* (whose agenda is remarkably coincident with that of the principal *Concilium* theologian, Hans Küng). Fortunately, we are not concerned with those wider issues globally but only as reflected in one small lens, which the Dominicans of the Province of France recut and polished in the years 1945 to 1948.

---

27   P.-R. Régamey, 'Bilan de l'époque 1920–1940', p. 50.

The Second World War and the German occupation had caused great material hardships in France, and the paper shortage led to a marked reduction in the physical quality of the review. But it was the change in its moral quality that aroused attention. After the War Couturier and Régamey began to extend their contacts with profane artists beyond those who were relatively conservative in matters of the medium if not the message so as to reach out to the real avant-garde. These included, for example, such Modernist or Functionalist architects as Le Corbusier – the name adopted professionally by Edouard Jeanneret for whom deliberate rupture with the cityscapes and building designs of the past was a necessity if men were to embrace cultural modernity – defined, as with the Futurists, by technology – in a thorough-going way. In 1920 Le Corbusier had launched the so-called Purist movement, its magazine entitled significantly *L'Esprit nouveau*. In Le Corbusier's view, artist and architect have not only the right but the duty to induce historical amnesia. It was a mentality reflected not only in Futurism but also in Dadaism which explicitly sought to relegate the art of the past to a mental dustbin. (One of the best known Dadaist paintings is the version of the Mona Lisa by Marcel Duchamp which shows the inscrutable lady wearing moustache and beard.) Couturier and Régamey also cultivated the painter and stained glass artist Jean Bazaine, a member of the Post-War School of Paris who had rejected the entire tradition of representational art as exhausted and moribund and expected the future to lie only with non-figural art. Régamey set up a touring exhibition which went round the country demonstrating what sacred art should be like, in painting, sculpture, metalwork, textiles. For the market towns and villages of *La France profonde* Régamey was careful to include less difficult work, including for instance pieces by the two Ds. But when he took his exhibition to Rome, and put it on in enhanced form, with a subsidy from the French State, for the Holy Year of 1950, he dropped most of the non-avant-garde works thus producing a collection dominated by Rouault, Alfred Manessier (an abstract artist of the Paris School), and the Cubist Georges Braque. This was something of a diplomatic gaffe. The exhibition was noticed, as how could it not be, by Cardinal Celso Constantini, Pius XII's president of the Pontifical Commission for Sacred Art. The baleful eye with which the cardinal toured Régamey's exhibition was relevant to the 'querelle de l'art sacré' which exploded two years later.

A caveat

Before describing that quarrel, which centred on the commissions given to largely agnostic architects and artists to create and furnish three churches to be lightships for the future, Notre-Dame-de-toute-grâce at Assy, La chapelle du Rosaire at Vence and Le-Sacré-Coeur at Audincourt, let me enter a caveat. There is no worse fate for a French intellectual than to be considered not *au courant*. Régamey's cultivation of 'the great and the good' in the world of the arts, irrespective of religious affiliation or outlook, was in part an expression of this perhaps forgivable vanity. That he was less radical than some feared is shown by two sorts of evidence.

The first of these is indirect, and it consists in the difficulties he had in relations with the Parisian *Centre de Pastorale Liturgique*. In the forefront, as it was, of the plans for liturgical revision which issued in the new Roman Missal of 1969 and the introduction of the vernacular, the *Centre* emphasised the need to bring the Liturgy closer to the people rather than the people closer to the Liturgy. Though well intentioned, it was, unfortunately, a harbinger of what by the 1970s would be called, in a useful Americanism, the 'dumbing-down' of Western Catholic worship. In time to come, such evidences as the manner of the post-Conciliar reordering of churches, the kind of music encouraged by pastoral liturgists and the style of translation sometimes brought to bear on the new Latin books would speak volumes for the developing spirit of the age. What the stormy petrels of the 1950s envisaged as the Liturgy of the future had little place for high art. Régamey found he could not work with the *Centre* of which at a certain point, embarrassingly, *L'Art sacré* had become an organ. Not only was it deaf to his appeals for more concern with the quality of liturgical celebration. Its *responsables* did not understand the very purpose of such a concern, which was to facilitate the *contemplative* appropriation of the Liturgy.

> To the extent that the sacred arts assure the material conditions for the most worthy realisation of the [liturgical] Mystery, to that degree do they dispose souls to the Mystery, to that degree do they express its different virtualities for souls.[28]

Only by contemplation, argued Régamey, could the realities hidden in the liturgical action be lovingly held in the mind.[29] The church building, he wrote, as setting of the Liturgy, should be heaven on earth.[30] By the late 1960s, with their emphasis on active participation, liturgical creativity and the continuity of the Liturgy with secularity, this point of view would be considered hopelessly reactionary and *vieux jeu*.

The second reason for not exaggerating Régamey's radicalism lies in the tenor of the major articles he published in *L'Art sacré*. There are five major ones. Aside from the most theologically heavyweight, the 1948 essay on Tradition already mentioned, the others are 'Present-day Tendencies in Christian Art' (1946), 'Modern-day Lessons of the Ancient Arts' (1948) and 'The Artistic Education of the Clergy' (1946), as well as a *bilan* or survey of the arts in the years 1920 to 1940, co-authored with Couturier in 1948.[31]

These essays make it plain that Régamey's artistic credo was a modest one. His opposition was certainly not to figural art as such or even, *under certain conditions*, to an art in conscious continuity with the Christian centuries. What he chiefly opposed

---

28   P. -R. Régamey, OP, *Art sacré au vingtième siècle?*, pp. 24–5.

29   F. Caussé, 'Les rapports des Dominicans avec *L'Art sacré*', p. 182. For his view of contemplation, see *Art sacré au vingtième siècle?*, pp. 51–2; of the Liturgy, ibid., pp. 103–18.

30   Ibid., pp. 114–16.

31   P.-R. Régamey, OP, *Tendances actuelles de l'art chrétien*, = *Cahiers de l'Art sacré* 7; idem, *L'éducation artistique du clergé*, = ibid., 9; idem, 'Leçons actuelles des arts anciens', *L'Art sacré* 1948, 1–2, pp. 3–32; 'Bilan de l'époque 1920–1940', art cit.

was the ecclesiastical version of academic art, a term used by art historians to describe the art favoured in the official salons, and notably by the Parisian *Académie des Beaux-Arts*, at the time of the emergence of the Impressionists whose canvases, notoriously, the Academy rejected, thus leading to the first of the *Salons des réfusés*. For Régamey, academicism is what happens when a creative artistic epoch has passed its zenith and enters a sterile period when formulas replace inspiration. He claimed to discern a law whereby such academic art always tends to become eclectic, and seeks to secure its effects by what he called 'amalgamating' the highest number of qualities possible. 'Only the level of pretention', he wrote, 'distinguishes academicism from *bondieuserie*'.[32] Hence the need for what Couturier, writing in *L'Art sacré* for 1950, termed 'fine images that are very pure' so as to purify and discipline an art that had become, like many pre-Conciliar Catholic churches, too cluttered and all over the place.[33]

It was in this *therapeutic* context, Régamey felt, that the Church in France needed to go to the profane 'masters', *les maîtres*. To ignore what was happening in the contemporary arts outside the Church was to proclaim, in his strong words, that the Church was *attachée à la mort*, 'attached to death'.[34] A detached observer might have thought that those words could with greater justice be applied to some of the more nihilistic movements in the contemporary art world then and later: Futurism, for example, in whose original manifesto, by Filippo Tommaso Marinetti, we are told that art should praise war, the strong and the healthy injustices of life, or, in England, the art of Francis Bacon which treats human flesh as meat and as one historian of modern art has commented, portrays human beings 'decomposing in transparent cages'.[35]

Be that as it may, Régamey's condition for permitting a sacred art in explicit continuity with those of the past to persist in the Church was that any form or technique which had no place at all in the present-day secular arts be sedulously avoided. If a particular kind of artistic form is no longer in the creative sensibility of artists, then artists in the Church should never be tempted to make use of it. What all this actually meant in practice with Régamey – and here he *was* radical in the sense the Roman authorities feared – was a rupture with the centuries-old assumption (or conviction) that Church art must necessarily be the work of believing artists. This 'assumption' was certainly a 'conviction' in the Eastern churches whose hagiology contains a special category for artist saints, the holy iconographers.

---

32 Idem, *Art sacré au vingtième siècle?*, p. 130.

33 A.-M. Couturier, OP, 'Pour les yeux', *L'Art sacré* 1950, 5–6, pp. 3–4, and here at p. 4. In *Art sacré au vingtième siècle?*, Régamey would go to some lengths to specify positive criteria for suitably Christian versions of these: doing justice to divine transcendence and divine immanence alike, to both the Cross and the Resurrection aspects of the mystery of Christ, expressive of the Gifts of the Holy Spirit and the Beatitudes (closely linked in the theology of St Thomas Aquinas), instructed by the Liturgy, and 'Marian' in having their centre of gravity outside themselves.

34 Words cited in F. Caussé, 'Les rapports des Dominicains avec *L'Art sacré*', p. 185.

35 N. Weston, *Kaleidoscope of Modern Art* (London 1968), p. 178.

'La querelle de l'art sacré'

As already mentioned, it was the giving of commissions in the liturgical arts to artists who were agnostics or even atheists which alienated a significant proportion of the Church public in France, quite as much as shock – though there was some – about the actual appearance of some of the art produced.[36] Couturier was most responsible for this. By 1945 he had abandoned his largely negative view of the contemporary art world. Twentieth-century art, he declared, so far from being, as many allege, materialistic, is one of the most spiritual chapters in the entire history of art. He connected modern art's deliberate poverty of means with the self-stripping of such Christian mystics as St John of the Cross.[37] What might we be talking about here? Well, we could be talking about Russian Suprematism, as in Kazimir Malevitch for whom putting a black square on a white ground is painting. Or we could be talking about American Abstract Expressionism, emerging in the 1940s, and best known from Jackson Pollock who worked by dancing on the canvas while dribbling paint on it which he then scuffed with his hands to get the end product, hence his nickname 'Jack the Dripper'. In fact, we are probably talking about somewhat more accessible avant-garde artists, but mention of these names could indicate a certain tendency on the Dominicans' part to look at the art world through rose-tinted glasses.

If Couturier thought that the decorative work and liturgical objects produced by a variety of contemporary artists for the three new churches *L'Art sacré* sponsored – the two parish churches at Assy and Audincourt and the chapel for the Dominican sisters at Vence – were going to be received in his own Sanjuanist spirit, he was soon to be disabused. The completion and opening of these projects in 1951 unleashed a storm of criticism of the Dominicans of *L'Art sacré* which in the event they did not survive. The adverse reaction was not just from the so-called 'simple faithful', among whom at any given time the majority of the hierarchy should no doubt be included. A number of Catholic artists with an *Ateliers* training already felt betrayed by the change of tone in the journal, as did those who took their principles in these matters from Maritain. In April 1952, a Commission set up by the French bishops to look into the matter came down nonetheless on the side of *L'Art sacré*, with some reservations. But unbeknownst to them the Holy Office had also been working on the problem. In June 1952 it issued an Instruction on Sacred Art, accompanied by an authoritative article in *L'Osservatore romano* by the cardinal president who had so little enjoyed his tour of Régamey's exhibition two years earlier. The article interpreted the Instruction as a rejection of the French experiments, and its author would have known if anyone did.

The 1952 Instruction is a somewhat threadbare document which chiefly consists of citations from the 1917 Code of Canon Law and passages from the allocutions of the previous Pope, Pius XI. But at least it has the literary virtue of brevity. It opens

---

36   For the crisis, see S. de Lavergne, *Art sacré et modernité*, pp. 150–60.

37   Writing in *L'Art sacré* 1950, 11–12, p. 25, cited in F. Caussé, 'Les rapports des Dominicains avec *L'Art sacré*', p. 186.

abruptly enough by rejecting the proposition that sacred art should be governed by a sense of what it calls 'the needs and conditions of modern times', *novorum temporum necessitates atque condiciones.*[38] Christian art, it goes on in more positive vein, was brought to birth with Christian society, and it has its own ends, its own intrinsic purposes from which it may not deviate and which, by implication, cannot be learnt from elsewhere. However, what may well be feasible is what the Instruction calls, citing a sermon of Pius XI, 'a just and progressive development, *sviluppo*, of the good and venerable traditions [of the art of the Church]'. 'Development', it goes on, is hardly the word for:

> those representations introduced recently by certain people, representations which seem to be a deforming and depraving of sane art and are even at times openly repugnant to Christian dignity, modesty and piety, and deeply wound the religious sense. They must be removed from our sanctuaries.[39]

This was probably a reference to the hanging crucifix at Assy, by the bronze worker Germaine Richier, an atheist: at any rate, it was the only object actually purged in the three buildings concerned (by the bishop of Annécy).

On church architecture the Instruction warned against trying to assimilate sacred architecture to that of profane buildings. Though regretting the addition of tasteless ornamentation to exteriors, it deplored what it called 'a certain negligence in conception and execution' – possibly an allusion (if so a very mild-mannered one) to the stark and often brutal simplicities of the Modernist school. As to art in the interior of churches, the Instruction reminded bishops of their duty in canon law not to allow the installation of images lacking in intrinsic value, or stereotyped images (meaning, presumably mass-produced objects), or the siting of images in a way that, as it put it, lacked 'order or taste'. On that point, the canon law in vigour, specifically canon 1178, sufficiently agreed, as the Dominicans knew perfectly well, with the editorial approach of *L'Art sacré*. But the editors' post-war plan for meeting the demands of this canon by looking to the secular masters to raise the level of art in Church was categorically rejected when the Instruction declared:

> Let there be commissioned works of painting, sculpture and architecture only from those who are remarkable for their competence and who are capable of expressing a sincere faith and piety, the goal of all sacred art.[40]

One might have thought that there would be a few people at least who could meet this twofold criterion given that, in post-war Paris it has been reckoned that the total number of professional artists living in the French capital was around sixty-five thousand.

---

38   For the text, see *Acta Apostolicae Sedis* XXXXIV (1952), pp. 542–6.
39   Ibid., p. 544
40   Ibid., 545

Naturally, Couturier and Régamey responded. It is not entirely easy to say whether the response should be called defiant or despairing. Apparently, they now publicly doubted the very possibility of what they had for some years defended. In effect, they reverted to Maritain's pre-war thesis: a new sacred art has to await a new society that can recognise the holy. In the introduction to his 1952 *Art sacré au vingtième siècle?*, which was published sufficiently late that year to include a translation of the Roman Instruction, Régamey wrote:

> A *true* renaissance of the sacred arts will not be possible for long centuries, because it will take long centuries – some of them doubtless catastrophic centuries – to re- establish an accord that is *sufficiently habitual, strong and stable* between three sorts of existence which have to be pursued simultaneously: that of living faith, that proper to the arts, and that of the faithful whom those arts are to serve.[41]

But even now, he added, they can come together occasionally, and the result is wonderful.

Interviewed by the national daily *Le Figaro*, at the heart of the uproar in France itself, Couturier had put it more vigorously. In a conversation republished in *L'Art sacré*, he told the interviewer:

> I do not believe in the existence or the possibility of a modern sacred art. To expect a truly sacred art (*un art proprement sacré*) from a society of materialist type, and specifically a Christian art from nations that have become once again for practical purposes pagan, seems to me a chimaera.

But, like Régamey later, he went on to put a twist in the tail, by adding:

> In default of a renaissance of a truly sacred art, I do believe, however, in the appearance among us, and especially in France, of works of very high 'religious' inspiration, but rigorously individual and generally fortuitous … That is to say, I believe in miracles.[42]

When Couturier died in February 1954, he did so two days before the draconian measures taken by the Province of France, under Roman pressure, against the Dominican priest-workers, and those like Père Marie-Dominique Chenu who had provided them and their diocesan counterparts with theological legitimation. The opportunity was taken to pronounce also against the directors of *L'Art sacré*. The Master of the Order, Emmanuel Suarez, who had come to France a few weeks previously to demand the removal from Paris of the theologians of the worker-priest movement, had in fact added for good measure that Couturier and Régamey should go as well. Death had defeated him for the one, though not for the other.[43]

---

41   P.-R. Régamey, *Art sacré au vingtième siècle?*, p. 13.

42   See *L'Art sacré* 1952, 9–10, pp. 24–5.

43   F. Leprieur, *Quand Rome condamne: Dominicains et prêtres-ouvriers* (Paris 1989), p. 103. The official letter from the Master only mentions the younger man, Couturier having just been buried.

In fact, as with many such interventions in the Catholic Church, things – with the exception of the Richier crucifix – seem to have gone on very much as before. The new Dominican editors of *L'Art sacré*, Augustin Cocagnac and Marie-Robert Capellades went on much as before. They arranged for yet another controversial church building, the pilgrimage church of Notre-Dame-du-haut at Ronchamps, by Le Corbusier. They continued to champion 'demanding' artists like Rouault. The authenticity of their 'apostolic succession' to Régamey is equally shown, however, in their less than fulsome welcome for the post-Conciliar liturgical reform, at least as received in France. While not opposing the official liturgical revision, their motto became: *La réforme doit éviter l'informe*, 'the reform must avoid the form-*less*'.[44] They warned against over-hasty measures of liturgical adaptation, deploring the 'chaos' into which the offices of the Church had fallen in not a few parishes. Misplaced zeal was leading the clergy foolishly to dispense with forms and objects which, experience showed, had the power to move people towards faith. This was a period when not only kitsch and *bondieuserie* but things of beauty and true liturgical propriety were transferred from church to marketplace, while other things that really were 'articles de bazar' made their journey in the opposite direction.[45] In its last years *L'Art sacré* registered the crisis into which the very notion of rite and ritual gesture was falling. Régamey returned as a guest contributor to analyse the 'ravages'. His verdict could be summed up in the English phrase 'deeply shallow'. The chickens of deficient liturgical, aesthetic, theological, spiritual discernment, some hatched in an earlier generation, were coming home to roost.[46]

Conclusion

I suppose I have already made plain my preference for one crucial policy of the first *L'Art sacré*. If by 'sacred' art we mean, as the Dominicans of *L'Art sacré* did, an art that exists so as to serve and interpret the Church's faith and worship, it seems inappropriate to seek out practitioners among unbelievers. How can they be expected to have an interior understanding of the Bible and the Liturgy which Régamey himself called the principal pertinent sources of a Christian sacred art? If on the other hand by 'sacred' art we mean an art expressive of the human search for God, or transcendence, then matters look different. One could well install outside a church or even in the atrium (if it has one) works which express a question mark to which the holy images in the liturgical space furnish an answer. To the sibyl and the pagan philosophers in the entrance porches of a number of mediaeval cathedrals there correspond within the cathedral the frescoes and sculptures that illustrate the mysteries of Incarnation and Atonement, and their fruits in the lives of the saints.

But, to my mind, the main lacuna in the thinking of the Dominicans of *L'Art sacré* holds good of both periods of the journal's existence and lies elsewhere. It is,

---

44 Editorial of this title in *L'Art sacré* 1965, 7–8, pp. 3–5.

45 Ibid., p. 5.

46 P.-R. Régamey, 'Les racines du mal et les remèdes', ibid., 1965, 9–10, pp. 21–5.

I think, extraordinary that, so far as I can tell, they never seem to have realised the importance for the church interior of an overall iconographic scheme. To devise decoration for a church interior without having any sense of an overall scheme that presents the content of Christian revelation through painterly images in a way suited to the celebration of the liturgical mysteries can only be to condemn church buildings to incoherence. In his study *Modern Sacred Art and the Church of Assy* (New York and London 1961), William S. Rubin describes that flagship of *L'Art sacré* very negatively as the fruit of a temporary alliance between liberal priests, artists and the French Left. He is on firmer ground in saying it lacks liturgical integrity. As the American Episcopalian John Dillenberger pointed out by way of commentary on Rubin's book, the bringing together of individual works by undeniably great artists – Marc Chagall for a ceramic mural and stained glass, Georges Rouault for more stained glass, the Surrealist Jean Lurçat for tapestry, Georges Braque for the metalwork of the tabernacle door, and so on – but *without ever devising a consistent iconographic scheme* conveys quite as incoherent an impression as any of the fussy church interiors the Dominicans deplored in the pages of their journal. Worse still, it generates the feeling that the church is a gallery or museum. Even a 'cursory glance', writes Dillenberger, at the themes in glass, paint and other media in the church of Assy:

> will confirm that there is no iconographic scheme related to the liturgy and the theological scope of the Church's affirmations.[47]

That would be unthinkable in, for example, an English parish church on the eve of the Reformation[48], or a Greek Orthodox church today[49] or, where post-Conciliar iconoclasm has not triumphed, one of the German churches entrusted to the Benedictines of the nineteenth-century Beuron school.[50] We suffer from this lack; if you wish to see how things could be better, without travelling to the Pelopponese or Baden-Wuerttemberg, and happen to be passing through London, I recommend a visit to the Marylebone masterpiece of Sir Ninian Comper[51], St

---

47   J. Dillenberger, 'Artists and Church Commissions: Rubin's *The Church at Assy* Revisited', *Art Criticism* 1. 1 (Spring 1979), pp. 72–82, reprinted in D. Apostolos-Cappadona (ed.), *Art, Creativity and the Sacred: An Anthology in Religion and Art* (New York, 1992, 2nd edition), pp. 193–204, and here at p. 198.

48   W. Pantin, *The English Church in the Fourteenth Century* (Cambridge 1955), pp. 239–41.

49   For an illuminating description of the developed iconographical scheme recreated in Neo-Byzantine churches, see R. Taft, SJ, 'Byzantine Liturgy', in K. Parry et al., *The Blackwell Dictionary of Eastern Christianity* (Oxford 1999), pp. 103–5.

50   H. Krins, *Die Kunst der Beuroner Schule* (Beuron 1998). Perhaps the best example of a comprehensively worked out iconography is the *Gnadenkapelle* at Beuron itself: ibid., pp. 83–9.

51   A. Symondson, *The Life and Work of Sir Ninian Comper (1864-1960): The Last Gothic Revivalist* (London 1988); idem, 'Unity by Inclusion: Sir Ninian Comper and the Planning of a Modern Church', *Twentieth Century Architecture* 3 (1998), pp. 19–42. I am

Cyprian's, Clarence Gate.[52] Meanwhile, the issues Couturier and Régamey raised, the problem of pious artists producing banal art, and the difficult issue of the relation between spiritual quality and artistic quality, will not go away.

---

grateful to Philip McCosker of the University of Cambridge Divinity Faculty for procuring these materials, as well as locating some of the last issues of *L'Art sacré*.

52   Idem, 'Mediaevalism in the Twentieth Century: St Cyprian's, Clarence Gate, London', *Victorian* 14 (2003), pp. 12–15.

Chapter 7

The English Uses of Maritain's Aesthetics: Eric Gill and David Jones

Maritain's *Art et scolastique* was intended to be a revolutionary (perhaps a better word would be 'counter-revolutionary') work. It was early translated into English by John O'Connor, the Irish-born parish priest of St Cuthbert's, Bradford, whose chief claim to fame in English Catholic history is that he reconciled G. K. Chesterton to the Catholic Church and became the model for Chesterton's priest–detective, Father Brown.[1] Its impact in England was restricted to a small circle of Catholic craftsmen and artists. But that impact was immediate and powerful and set up vibrations which continue well beyond the limits of the Catholic communion to the present day. It has not been so often noted, however, that the impulses *Art et scolastique* gave to practising artists in England – and notably to two men who were major figures in the history of English art – were so different as to verge on but not quite tumble over into, contradictoriness.

What is the message – or, rather, for, despite brevity, this is a complex work, what are the messages – of the book? Maritain's opening chapter sets forth a diagnosis of why his study is needed. Modern aestheticians speak of art only in connection with the fine arts which in French are *les beaux-arts* and so literally the 'beautiful' arts. With like restrictiveness, they treat beauty as though it were the exclusive domain of art: the realm of 'the aesthetic'. In so doing, says Maritain, modern thinkers vitiate both notions: art *and* the beautiful. Maritain intends to return to the mediaevals whose moralists (not aestheticians) studied *ars* in general and whose metaphysicians (again, these were not aestheticians) explored beauty – or what the Scholastics called *pulchrum*. He wants to see what happens when these two enterprises – enquiry into the morals of *ars* and investigation of the metaphysics of beauty – are brought together. He proposes to show the usefulness of recourse to the wisdom of the ancients; to demonstrate the interest-value of dialogue between philosophers and artists; to help tidy up what he considered the 'intellectual disarray' inherited from the nineteenth century; and – this would have been of especial interest to the English Dominican laity of the craft guild of St Joseph and St Dominic, for whom, in the first instance, O'Connor's translation was made – to do something to recreate the spiritual conditions prerequisite to 'honest work' (the French *honnête* having, like the Latin *honestum*, a wider range of ethical resonance than the English

---

1   *The Philosophy of Art*, being *Art et scolastique* by Jacques Maritain, translated by the Rev. John O'Connor, STP, with an Introduction by Eric Gill, OSD, (Ditchling 1923).

'honest').[2] One of the founders of the Lay Dominican craft-guild, the stonecarver and letterer Eric Gill, disciple in these matters of Maritain, remarked:

> What I achieve as a sculptor is of no consequence I can only be a beginning – it will take generations, but if only the beginnings of a reasonable, decent, holy tradition of working might be effected – that is the thing.[3]

Put with Anglo-Saxon simplicity, that is indeed Maritainian 'honest' work.

The virtue of art

Congruent with the moral setting of the mediaeval discussion of *ars*, Maritain argues that art is a *virtue* possessed by the *artifex* in his or her practical intelligence. The virtue of art, he insisted, belongs not to the speculative but to the practical order. No doubt there *are* disciplines we might call 'speculative arts' – logic would be an example – insofar as those disciplines involve some sort of work in hand, such as, in logic, the right ordering of concepts, or the construction of a sequential argument. Nevertheless, knowing – the affair of the speculative intellect – differs essentially from art, above all because knowing is intransitive or immanent and art is not. In knowing truth, the mind feasts on being. This is an action which remains within the human subject. It does not cross that boundary on which anyone stands who proposes to *make* something by the exercise of his powers. Here Maritain appeals not to the Scholastics in general but to his favoured doctor, Thomas Aquinas, in particular.[4]

---

2   *L'honnête homme* was the ideal human being of the French seventeenth century: some light is thrown thereon by Thomas's own definition of *honestum* as 'when a thing has some excellence worthy of honour on account of its spiritual beauty', *Summa theologiae* IIa. IIae., q.145, a. 3.

3   Cited in D. Jones, 'Eric Gill as Sculptor', *Blackfriars* XXII. 250 (1941), p. 73. That phrase, recorded by Jones from conversation, aptly served as title for B. Keeble (ed.), *A Holy Tradition of Working: Passages from the Writings of Eric Gill* (Ipswich 1983).

4   This may be a good point to offer some comments on Maritain's connections with Thomism. Originally, Thomas had no influence on the conversion of the Maritains, which, through the fiery prophetic figure of Léon Bloy, was indebted rather to Scripture, the liturgy, and the mystical writings and lives of the saints to which Bloy introduced them as well as to that curious episode in nineteenth-century French Catholic history, the Apparitions of La Salette. But some four years after her Baptism, received in 1904 coincidently with conditional Baptism for Jacques, Raïssa Maritain had been introduced to Thomas's writings by the Dominican priest she found a helpful guide, Père Humbert Clérissac. By 1914 not only was Jacques's own intellectual position was increasingly Thomist in temper. Together they founded and ran the first of the *Cercles d'études thomistes* from their house in Meudon. Thomas was 'seen as a special assistant of the Holy Spirit in dispensing the graces necessary to achieve the aim of study': thus R. McInerny, *The Very Rich Hours of Jacques Maritain: A Spiritual Life* (Notre Dame, Ind., 2003), p. 72. The Maritains' little book *De la vie de l'oraison* (Paris 1925) with its two parts, 'The Intellectual Life and Prayer' and 'The Spiritual Life', is

But even when, with Thomas, we distinguish between speculative and practical activity, we still need, within the latter category, to make a further refinement, as he did. There is a difference between acting (transitively) and making: between, in Maritain's own vocabulary, *agir* and *faire*. If the intellect knows how to know it also knows, in its more practical moments, how to act. But clearly moral action is not the same thing as making, which is, rather, *productive* action. Just as the Greeks had two words for it (the *prakton* – whence our word 'practicality' – and the *poiêton* – whence our word 'poetry'), so likewise did the Latin Scholastics. They distinguished out first the *agibile*, whereby we use our freedom so as to tend by our action towards the human good as such. This is the stuff morality is made of, and if in this context our acts are good that is because they correspond to the proper norm of distinctively human agency and have in view the true goal of human life. That left the Schoolmen with the *factibile* where the good at stake is rather different. The *factibile* – the 'makeable' – is the good of 'conformity to the rules and proper end of the *work to be produced*'.[5] These rules, goals, values are not those of the human being as such. Rather, they are those of the *work*. This puts the artist – all Romantic exaggeration aside – in a world apart. Of course, the manner of artistic working is human and even all too human. But the goal is not. That is why, writes Maritain, in one of those flashes of psychological insight that set this little book a-shimmer, 'any boredom attached to living and willing stops at the door of the *atelier*', the studio workshop. The work of artistic creation may be, owing to impediments, frustrating. But creation can never be boring.

Maritain does no more than echo his mediaeval Aristotelean sources when he defines art as the 'right determination of the works to be made'.[6] The phrase 'right determination' tells us that intelligence regulates art. Some idea must pass into matter. For this to take place smoothly or at least happily the spontaneity of human powers needs modulating by the kind of stable disposition we call a virtue – in this case, the virtue of art developing the practical intellect in an appropriate direction. Indeed, Maritain goes so far as to say that the artist 'in some way *is* his work before he carries it out'.[7] Art, however, seeks the 'good of the work', *bonum operis*, not the 'good of the worker', *bonum operantis*. This is not a recipe for the glorification of the artist as a special kind of man. It is telling that, when the mediaeval Scholastics thought about art, they did not by and large choose the fine arts for their pre-eminent examples but took such simpler instances as the art of boat building or clockmaking. This was going to be music to the ears of those English Catholic artists who sought above all a renaissance of craft and were dismissive of the 'art nonsense' of dealers and collectors, people who paid inflated sums for what could be considered by its owners alternative wallpaper. The Scholastics, it seemed, had recognised a 'nobility

---

their testimony to this desire for an integrated spiritual–intellectual existence. From across the English Channel this stance was admired.

5   J. Maritain, *Art et scolastique*, p. 10.

6   Ibid., p. 12.

7   Ibid., p. 17. Emphasis added.

of the intelligence' in the smithy and the carpenter's workshop and not only in 'Phidias and Praxiteles', those exalted (and possibly over-praised) artists of classical antiquity.[8] Not by chance, thought Maritain himself, had the Word incarnate become an artisan, and thus revealed the divine Artifex, his Father. Was not the transcendent origin of all craft attested when in the *Summa contra Gentiles*, basing himself on the Book of Wisdom, 7:21, Thomas had declared that there is *ars* in God?

As yet, the fine arts have only been mentioned to emphasise how they are not especially in view. But by the end of the Middle Ages, the rationale for the ancient division of the artists into servile and liberal was falling into oblivion. For the mediaevals, the only issue was, does this or that art produce its effect *in matter*? For them, music, like logic, was a liberal art, whereas sculpture and painting, contrary to later perceptions, were not. Subsequently, sculpture and painting would be elevated far beyond the reach of humble crafts, no longer deemed fine enough to appear in their company. In a lengthy footnote, Maritain traces the fate of the word 'artist', at least in France, until the nineteenth century, and comes to the conclusion that the elevation of the fine arts and the depression of the status of craft was essentially a response to the rise of the bourgeoisie.[9] That Maritain regretted the post-mediaeval dichotomy between the fine artist and the craftsman is apparent from one of *Art and Scholasticism*'s most celebrated passages.

> In the potently social structure of mediaeval civilisation, the artist had only the rank of artisan. And every sort of anarchic development was forbidden to his individualism, because a natural social discipline imposed on him certain limiting conditions from without. He did not work for the fashionable and for the commercial class, but for the faithful people from whom he had a mission to shelter the prayer, instruct the intelligence, and rejoice the eyes and the soul. O incomparable epoch when a simple-hearted people was unconsciously formed in beauty, as perfect Religious must pray without even being aware of the fact, when doctors and iconographers taught the poor with love, and the poor savoured their teaching because all were of the same royal race born of water and the Spirit.[10]

The Renaissance would change all that by making the artist conscious of his own greatness and letting loose on him that wild beast, the 'beautiful', which faith once – but no longer – had power to charm.

Maritainian craftsman extraordinary: Eric Gill

This much of Maritain's message was altogether pertinent to Eric Gill. Gill was born in 1882 at Brighton, the son of a minister in the small Nonconformist body called

---

8   Ibid., p. 31.

9   J. Maritain, *Art et scolastique*, pp. 246–9.

10   Cited from the French original at ibid., p. 34. The phrase about unconscious prayer derives from the eulogy of St Anthony of Egypt in the *Conferences* of St John Cassian, IX, 31.

The Countess of Huntingdon's Connexion. After an architectural apprenticeship, his professional formation lay in masonry at the Westminster Technical Institute and calligraphy – under the main English reviver of that art, Edward Johnston – at the Central School of Arts and Crafts. He immediately found his true vocation: as a letter-cutter, perhaps the greatest of modern times. He married, and moved from London's urban sprawl to the Sussex village of Ditchling the better to bring up a family. His sculpting career, begun in 1909, would reflect his training in lettering: he visualised figures in profiles, not as interrelated volumes. He began to take up the art of engraving, which along with water-colours, is historically the principal strength of English art, with links to lettering and sculpture as Gill conceived them. In 1913 he was received into the Catholic Church, having come to believe (in the words of his friend Donald Attwater) that this was 'the church of the oldest Christian tradition – something which teaches the necessary truths about man's first beginning and last end'.[11] At Ditchling his long association with the Order of Preachers began, as did his acceptance of the principles of the philosophy and theology of St Thomas Aquinas. He channelled his enthusiasm for Thomas into two areas: consideration, in the light of Thomas's doctrine of *ars*, of the material culture of twentieth-century civilisation (fundamentally incompatible with man's natural good as Gill believed this to be), and the related issue of man in society – how to lead a whole, and thus at least potentially holy, life in the human city. His move from Sussex to the Welsh mountains at Capel-y-ffin (dictated by the desire to escape the curious, but also, as a recent biography discloses, growing anxieties at Ditchling over his sexual antinomianism[12]) and subsequently to the more lyrical, yet London-accessible, setting of the Chiltern hills: these relocations conceal the essential homogeneity of his life as artist, essayist and lecturer on social questions until his sudden death from lung cancer in 1940.

Gill's early training as a craftsman offers an important clue to the form his exploitation of *Art et scolastique* might take. The English Arts and Crafts movement, with its roots in the work of William Morris and, behind Morris, John Ruskin, was inseparably an aesthetic and a social affair. Gill had met the real founder of Ditchling, the social worker turned publisher and printer Hilary Pepler, as a neighbour during his early married life at Hammersmith: it was emblematic that an iron handpress used at Ditchling had once belonged to Morris at his celebrated 'Kelmscott Press' in that same district of London. Without Morris and Ruskin, the Gill phenomenon – and how Gill read and utilised Maritain's aesthetics – would be hard indeed to understand.

Morris had learned from Ruskin's *The Stones of Venice* – as well as from Thomas Carlyle's study of a monastic community in that tract for the times *Past and Present*. In the words of one interpreter of his thought, Morris realized how:

---

11   D. Attwater, *Eric Gill: Workman* (London 1941), p. 26.
12   F. MacCarthy, *Eric Gill* (London 1989).

the Middle Ages had been more than feudal chivalry and Gothic art: they had been a coherent way of life with a sound understanding of social and communal duties, and their art was the expression of the free and happy life of their craftsmen[13]

Ruskin, Morris's mentor, had attacked the sharp division of manual and intellectual labour that fostered a society of what he termed:

morbid thinkers, and miserable workers ... It would be well [Ruskin opined] if all of us were good handicrafts-men in some kind, and the dishonour of manual labour done away with altogether.[14]

From Morris's standpoint as craftsman–designer, Ruskin had come to the crucial perception that, under modern factory conditions, work could hardly be anything other than mechanical and shoddy. As for Gill, his writing, public speaking, and entire, well- publicised, personal style could be regarded as an extended commentary on Ruskin's words.[15]

In Gill's career a 'Gothic' tradition, at once social and aesthetic, originating ultimately with A. W. Pugin in the Early Victorian English Catholic Revival was, as it were, repatriated, enriched by other contributions, onto its spiritually native – Thomistic –heath. The keynote of this tradition was the inseparability of aesthetics and social ethos. Mediaeval art, so Morris had asserted, owed its greatness to its social basis. In his words:

It was common to the whole people; it was free, progressive, hopeful, full of human sentiment and humour; ... the outcome of corporate and social feeling, the work not of individual but collective genius; the expression of a great body of men conscious of their union.[16]

The difficulty, however, for would-be revivers of mediaeval artistic style lay in its seeming incompatibility with contemporary techniques of construction, and the ethos of modern labour. Morris – whose workshops in fact combined high-quality machine products with handicraft – had by the end of his life lost confidence in the Gothic revival though there remained for the future the potent example of his designs, marked as these were by 'a fundamental integrity, a respect for material, and a quality of workmanship', things more influential than any single style.[17] Gill would, in effect, make of Morris a proto-Thomist, drawing out of these commitments,

---

13   P. Thompson, *The Work of William Morris* (Oxford 1991, 3rd edition), p. 5. For the debt of Gill's ideas to Morris, see P. Faulkner, *William Morris and Eric Gill* (London 1975).

14   E. T. Cook and A. Wedderburn (eds), *The Works of John Ruskin*, X (London 1904), p. 301.

15   See his expression of indebtedness in 'John Ruskin', *Essays: Last Essays and In a Strange Land* (London 1947), pp. 169–72.

16   M. Morris (ed.), *The Collected Works of William Morris* vol. 1 (London 1910), p. 270.

17   P. Thompson, *The Work of William Morris*, p. 99.

with Maritain's aid, the Thomistic account of artistic making and social prudence he believed to be implicit there. When as a convert Catholic indebted to the Arts and Crafts movement, he sought a way of life that would marry work and spirituality, it was perhaps predictable he would find it in the social form that movement preferred: namely, a *guild* or co-operative association of artists and craftsmen.[18] The twin loyalties of 'the Guild of Saints Joseph and Dominic' – to a renaissance of labour and good making, on the one hand, and, on the other, a contemplative apostolate of preaching Catholic truth – were well captured in its name.

Gill's doctrine was set forth in numerous essays, gradually collected into book form, as well as his *Autobiography* and letters. Never (he thought) until the era of industrial capitalism had the desire for riches been frankly regarded as the sole motive of work. The 'Machine Age' had secularised man, abolishing the Christian criterion of holiness both morally and intellectually. It degraded pleasure and recreation by making them purely self-regarding. It likewise degraded labour and skill by rendering the first despicable and the second superfluous, and through payment of the lowest wages possible disabling the worker from practising almsgiving. It removed tenderness and humanity from the objects made and the buildings that housed them. This was inevitable under capitalism, since a joint-stock company, whose investors had no interest in the quality of the work done, would naturally make saleability the single test of the good. [19] In Aristotelian terms, the practices of the Machine Age were neither virtue-requiring nor virtue-engendering.

Gill described industrial-type machines as pathetico-comic, incongruous with their human environment. A steam locomotive is a caricature of a dray-horse, and the faster it goes the funnier it looks, 'like an aged ballet-dancer playing the fairy'.[20] (Actually, Gill could admire the beauty of an airplane engine. His strictures might not have been so severe on early twenty-first-century machinery, where the 'Heath Robinson' touch he mocked in inter-war industrial design largely disappeared.) He cited approvingly T. S. Eliot's statement that:

> The natural life and the supernatural life have a conformity to each other which neither has to the mechanistic life.[21]

The consequence at home – in clothes, furniture, the landscape of town and village – is vulgarity, while murderous wars – ultimately fought for control of the available markets – are its deadly fruit abroad. The outcome of the Machine Age can only be the (sardonically entitled) Leisure State, where in the world of work machines mind machines, and human beings are consigned to fatuity. To Gill, this was false

---

18   Even if Gill came to pour scorn on any claim for that movement to be of itself socially significant: see his 'The Revival of Handicraft', in idem, *Art Nonsense and Other Essays* (London 1929), p. 118.

19   Ibid., p. 32.

20   Ibid., p. 48.

21   T. S. Eliot, *The Idea of a Christian Society* (London 1939), p. 61, cited in E. Gill, *Christianity and the Machine Age*, p. 57.

angelism, or, worse, aestheticism, which he defined as the worship of the pleasure of sensation.

> Here is no desire for the time when men will have better food and better drink, better and lovelier clothes and clothes more suitable to adorn and protect the darling bodies of men, better houses, and, above all, better places for the worship of God and His proper praise; here, alas!, is commonly no more than a desire for release from the pains thrust upon them by a selfish capitalism and, otherwise, no idea more noble or even more human than to have *a good time*.[22]

Gill's respect for tools and materials, and his desire that every man should have the opportunity to work in a way which licensed intelligent respect for the task in hand, count as his most enduring contribution to 'social aesthetics'. The crisis in the fine arts cannot be resolved, he considered, until the common arts of everyday working have been restored to sanity. As the distinguished American priest–calligrapher Edward Catich put it in an attempt to capture Gill's root idea:

> In our time 'fine' artists, sculptors and musicians for the most part have lost their way. Sentimentally, they think the final end of their crafts is a kind of soul-revealing expressionism in which emphasis is more on *how* and *who* than on the good of the work to be done – the *what* and *why*.[23]

We need this background in order to understand the introduction Gill wrote to the English translation of Maritain's book, which is not at all what, coming from the French original, one might expect. Commending Maritain to the English public, Gill wrote:

> This is one of the worst symptoms of our disease: that we have made Art the province of a specially cultured few and have made the common workman responsible only for *doing* and not at all for *making*; for of no factory article can it be said that such and such a man *made* it – the most that can be said is that the article is the result of a number of men *doing* what they were told.[24]

The contrast of 'made' and 'doing' there picks up, evidently, Maritain's contrast of *faire* and *agir*. And so, Gill goes on:

> The artist has become puffed up with the notion of his intellectual superiority, while the workman has lost all appetite for any thing but the amusements he can purchase in his spare time. Art embraces all making and there should be no need to talk about it. But that blissful state wherein all things are well made and none are called 'works of art' is only recoverable by a total abandonment of our present worship of Riches and Empire and by an acceptance of the philosophy of Poverty, Chastity and Obedience instead.[25]

---

22 Idem, *Essays: Last Essays and In a Strange Land* (London 1947), p. 70.
23 E. Catich, *Eric Gill: His Social and Artistic Roots* (Iowa City, 1964), p. V.
24 *The Philosophy of Art*, p. ii
25 *The Philosophy of Art*, pp. ii–iii.

Art et scolastique in its English dress is, Gill declared, a 'medicine' for the English people. It will need to be powerful if it is going to do anything towards curing the disease from which they suffer, whose causes are first: the Renaissance, which defeated 'Humility'; and secondly, the Protestant Reformation, whose outcome was the 'triumph of the trader'. Gill was not over-optimistic. The most the English are likely to do when faced with Maritain's challenge is offer a compromise, of whose habitual practice they are so unjustly proud. No more is to be expected from us given 'our aptitude for self-deception, our dislike, nay, our refusal of logical thought, our respect for respectability'.[26] England has made too close an alliance with Hell to find the bowels of Repentance easily moved. Yet 'a little Truth humbly assimilated' may go a long way.

For Gill, once the right craftsmanly attitude is in place, 'beauty will look after herself', a favoured phrase of his which was also the title of one of his books of essays.[27] He accepted Maritain's account of beauty not least because he found in it the mind of Thomas. But he left to one side Maritain's account of the beauty of the fine arts in particular – arts whose practice was animated by the 'creative intuition' that would increasingly dominate Maritain's own mind when he considered modern painting and modern poetry too.

The nature of beauty

So here we must return to the text of Maritain's treatise. In *Art et scolastique* Maritain's second key theme, after the nature of *ars*, is indeed *pulchrum*, the beautiful. He starts from a short formula of Thomas's which is, he says, a definition that relates not to essence but to effect. *Id quod visum placet.*[28] The beautiful is 'that which it is pleasant to see'. In Maritain's attempt to tease out the meaning of the Latin: the beautiful is that which gives joy in an intuitive knowing, a joy overflowing owing to the object known. Later in *Art et scolastique* Maritain will go beyond this 'definition from effect'. He will quite frankly declare bestowal of delight in knowing a formal constituent of beauty. The Italian writer Umberto Eco, whose career began with a study of Thomas's aesthetics already mentioned[29], thinks Maritain is over-interpreting. As he points out, what Thomas actually says is, *'people call things beautiful* when they give pleasure on sight'. For Eco this is a 'sociological finding' which 'introduces the problem' rather than solves it.[30] Be that as it may, it brings us to the heart of Maritain's account of the beautiful. He writes:

---

26 Ibid., pp. i–ii.

27 E. Gill, *Beauty Looks after Herself* (London 1933).

28 St Thomas Aquinas, *Summa theologiae* Ia., q. 5, a. 4, ad i.

29 U. Eco, *Il problema estetico in Tommaso d'Aquino.* See Chapter 1 above.

30 Idem, *Art and Beauty in the Middle Ages* (ET New Haven and London 1986), p. 128. Eco's criticism is anticipated in G. B. Phelan's essay, 'The Concept of Beauty in St Thomas Aquinas', in C. A. Hart (ed.), *Aspects of the Neo-Scholastic Philosophy* (New York 1932), p. 139. But there can be little doubt that Maritain is right. In *De vera religione* 32 Augustine

If a thing exalts and delights the soul by the very fact of being given to its intuition, it is good to apprehend, it is *beautiful*.[31]

Beauty is necessarily linked to the intellect, and thus to the infinity of being to which mind gives access. Certainly the historical Thomas considered sight and hearing the senses to which beauty relates *precisely because they are maximally cognitive*. They have the most to do with knowing.[32] Since humans are not angels, the only beauty that is connatural to us is that which delights the intelligence through the senses – though Maritain does not rule out that we might possibly enjoy some sheerly intellectual beauty (one often hears that, of course, of mathematical formulae). That, however, is not the beauty of 'notre art'. 'Our [human] art' works over sensuous matter to bring joy to the spirit. It is in a sense a taste of Paradise, the first Paradise, the Paradise of Eden, because 'it restores for a moment the simultaneous peace and delectation of the mind and the senses'.[33]

But why *does* beauty delight the understanding? It must be to do with the way beauty constitutes some kind of 'excellence' or superbness in the way things bear on our intelligence. Here a fuller definition – or description – of *pulchrum* in the *Summa theologiae* at last comes in handy. Three things are required for beauty, says Thomas, reported by Maritain: integrity or perfection; due proportion or consonance; and, finally, clarity.[34] Maritain interprets:

> Integrity, because mind loves being; proportion, for mind loves order and unity; lastly and above all, clarity (*éclat, clarté*) for mind loves light and intelligibility.[35]

That 'above all' will be Maritain's real Ariadne's thread. Radiance, *resplendissement*, *splendor*, is the beautiful's giveaway sign. With the Platonists one can call it the 'splendour of the true', with Augustine the 'splendour of order', or with Thomas (and best of all) the 'splendour of form'. And what might form be, pray? Emphasising its crucial role in Thomas's metaphysics – and we have a major source here for what will be, forty years on, the theological aesthetics of Hans Urs von Balthasar – Maritain writes:

> [*Form* is] the principle that bestows the distinctive perfection of every existing thing – that which constitutes and completes them in their essence and qualities. Finally, if one may

---

had already discussed the question whether things please us because they are beautiful or are (called) beautiful because they please us and opted firmly for the first. This is not an instance where Aquinas is likely to be un-Augustinian. And in any case the issue is clearly analogous to the question of the good – is the good what all desire, or rather is what all desire (called) good? Thomas makes plain his view that the intellectual appetite – the will – desires as it does because what is desired seems *good in itself*.

31   J. Maritain, *Art et scolastique*, p. 36.
32   St Thomas Aquinas, *Summa theologiae* Ia. IIae., q. 27, a. 1, ad iii.
33   J. Maritain, *Art et scolastique*, p. 37.
34   St Thomas Aquinas, *Summa theologiae*, Ia., q. 39, a. 8.
35   J. Maritain, *Art et scolastique*, p. 37.

put it so, form is the ontological secret they harbour within them, their spiritual being and operative mystery.[36]

Supremely, form is the principle of intelligibility of a thing – and thus its *clarity*.[37] It is 'a vestige or ray of the creative [divine] intelligence at the heart of created being'.[38] As J. W. Hanke, an American interpreter of Maritain's aesthetics helpfully explains:

> If with Aquinas the beautiful properly belongs to the intelligible character (*ratio*) of a formal cause …, form must be understood as *this* ontological configuration or structure here and now operative in a singular concrete existent, and beauty as splendour of form is the splendour of such a being as open to cognition.[39]

In works of art what we confront – here Maritain cites an anonymous mediaeval tract 'On the Beautiful and the Good' – is the 'irradiation of form in the proportioned parts of matter'. In art, form is grasped only in and through the sensuous. The light of being penetrates the mind only by the apprehension of the senses. The highest comes to us through the lowliest.

Maritain stresses how easy it is for the work of art so to delight the mind, surprising it by joy. Poor old Immanuel Kant failed to realise that what is given in the sensuous matrix of the artwork is an *intelligibility* – deriving ultimately, like all intelligibilities from the divine Ideas. True, in the case of a work of art, this intelligibility cannot be *detached* from the sensuous object and set up in conceptual business all on its own. In a deliberately strange coining by Maritain, it is le '*sens intelligencié*' – 'sense fructified by intelligence' – that enjoys the intuition of the beautiful. This is why perception of the beautiful leaves us with a conviction of intellectual fulness even when, asked to provide reasons for the same, we find ourselves hard pressed, or indeed, nonplussed. And yet taste, defined by Maritain as an aptitude for perceiving and judging beauty, can nonetheless be developed by 'education and teaching, study and the reasoned explanation of works of art'.[40] The friends of an artist, remarks Maritain, enjoy his works better than does the public at large – adding in a characteristic aside as do the Angels the work of the Creator. Where concepts *are* relevant, then, is that they can dispose us to an act of intuition of the beautiful. What we know when we enjoy such beauty is not easy to state. That does not prevent it from being divinely founded. The 'essentially delectable' beauty Maritain writes of is ontological beauty. In firm textual dependence on Thomas's commentary on Denys the Areopagite's *The Divine Names*: the loveability of beauty

---

36 Ibid., p. 38

37 In *A Preface to Metaphysics: Seven Lectures on Being* (ET New York 1962), Maritain wrote: 'To the extent to which anything is, it is transparent, communicable, it possesses a certain measure of communicability, a diffusiveness, a generosity', p. 80.

38 Idem, *Art et scolastique*, p. 38.

39 J. W. Hanke, *Maritain's Ontology of the Work of Art* (The Hague, 1973), p. 25.

40 Ibid., pp. 255–6.

goes back to its divine Source, who, for Denys, so Maritain reports in unison with Thomas's reading:

> undergoes in some fashion the ecstasy of love, owing to the abundance of his goodness which makes him spread abroad in all things a participation of his splendour.[41]

When we seek the traces of such ontological beauty in works of art, Maritain warns we must take the notions of integrity (or perfection) and proportion (or fittingness or harmony) highly relationally. The way these concepts will be realised in this or that work of art depends entirely on the goal of the work in question. As Maritain explores this point we realise how utterly, even in English translation, he is leaving the world of Ditchling behind. Thus, he tells us, for example, that a Cubist lady with only one quarter of an eye may meet these criteria triumphantly. It all depends. The single really vital quality – splendour of form – has an infinity of ways of striking through matter. Evidently, Maritainian Thomism is not Neo-Classicism. Equally evidently, the commendation, however muted, of Cubism signals to us that the craft-centred English interpretation of *Art et scolastique*, considered as an overall reading of the book, cannot be correct. It is worth stressing the point that, for Maritain, art has endless variety. That is only what we should expect if beauty is indeed a 'transcendental' – one of those concepts that cuts across the borders of kinds and categories. A study emanating from the Catholic University of Milan had the temerity to deny that Thomas saw beauty in transcendental terms. Maritain was nettled. In response he went the whole hog, calling Thomas's *pulchrum* 'the splendour of all the transcendentals united'.[42] Quite simply, beauty *is* being in a particular perspective. It is being 'taken as delighting an intellectual nature by the sole intuition of it'.[43] Thus everything is beautiful – in some respect, in its own way. Which is as much as to say that a suitable ontology of beauty can only be analogical. All the analogues of beauty have one sovereign analogate where beauty subsists in a 'formally eminent' guide. Beauty is a Name of God.

God in himself, of himself, is not only beauty. He is, in a Latin word-form based on a typical piece of Denys's Greek vocabulary, *superpulcher*, 'beautiful to excess'.[44] It is because his divine excess of beauty is the cause of all things, the

---

41   Ibid., p. 42, citing Aquinas, *Expositio super Dionysium De divinis Nominibus* 4, lectio 10. As Maritain recognises, the Hellenic world, even before Christ, had a profound sense of the unity of goodness and beauty (expressed in the word *kalokagathia*). But Maritain (as Thomas) wants to understand this unity in such a way that he does not sunder (the good and) the beautiful from the true. An existent that, *per impossibile*, had intellect but not will, would still grasp the beautiful *at its root* – but not in such a fashion as to delight in it as the restful goal of spiritual appetite. It takes some subtlety on Maritain's part to indicate the possible coherence in various pertinent references in Thomas's corpus: thus *Art et scolastique*, pp. 258–63.

42   Ibid., p. 266.

43   Ibid., p. 48.

44   Ibid., p. 49.

loveliness of each of those things a participated likeness of his own, that there can be innumerable relative beauties without surrender of beauty's objectivity. All of which helps to explain why the beautiful can seem to carry the soul beyond the created realm. Maritain summons to the witness stand two Romantic writers often seen as proto-decadents, Charles Pierre Baudelaire and Edgar Allan Poe. The 'immortal instinct for the beautiful', wrote Baudelaire, in a passage of *L'Art romantique* (1869) indebted to Poe's *The Poetic Principle*, makes us see the sights of earth as correspondences with heaven, and through poetry and music glimpse a world beyond biological death. Without the transcendentals we would be immured in our private needs. The transcendentals allow us to communicate in a common intellectual and spiritual meaning.

These references to Romantic writers suggest how Maritain is moving towards a certain concentration on the *fine* arts. And so it will prove. All the other arts (which may and should produce beautiful things – to this extent Gill was correct) are ordered to useful making. But the fine arts are actually ordered to beauty.[45] Another way to put this would be to say that the useful arts and the fine arts can be distinguished by the extent to which they are – or are not – in the way of being *signs*.[46] As Hanke puts it:

> [T]he form of a purely useful object would make the object it structures be just what it is as a thing determined in its type by the use to which it is totally oriented. The work of fine art, however, must have an intelligibility which exceeds that of a mere thing or thing of use; and this effulgent intelligibility can come upon the work of human creativity only through representation or imitation, the making present of a sense which the material artifact does not have in its own circumscribed being.[47]

This way of expressing a distinction between useful and fine arts was taken up by Maritain's second early and outstanding artist-reader on the far side of the English Channel, David Jones. He called it the distinction of 'utile' and 'gratuitous'.

David Jones: Maritainian artist of the sign

David Jones was born in Brockley, then Kent, now London, in 1895, the son of a Welsh printer's manager (from farming stock in Clwyd) and an English mother

---

45   Though much influenced by Maritain, the aesthetic of the Anglo-Welsh lay Dominican poet and artist David Jones would want to distinguish the 'utile' from the utilitarian on the one hand, the gratuitous, symbolic and sacramental on the other, and expect, in a flourishing culture, to find the beautiful in both utile and gratuitous things: see, for example, D. Jones, 'Art and Sacrament', and 'The Utile', in H. Grisewood (ed.), *Epoch and Artist: Selected Writings by David Jones* (London 1959; 1973), pp. 143–79; 180–85.

46   Touched on in *Art et scolastique* (see, for example, the 1962 American translation, *Art and Scholasticism* at pp. 54–5), but more fully adumbrated in Maritain's essay 'Sign and Symbol', in *Redeeming the Time* (London 1944), pp. 191–224.

47   J. W. Hanke, *Maritain's Ontology of the Work of Art*, op. cit., p. 45.

(from a family of Thames-side shipbuilders). At the early age of 14, his parents enrolled him at the Camberwell Art School. His teacher, A. S. Hartrick, has been described as follows:

> Hartrick, an accomplished artist, knew Van Gogh and Gauguin, whose portraits he painted and drew, and was on friendly terms with Degas and other French artists of the turn of the century. In his autobiography *A Painter's Pilgrimage* (1939), Hartrick gives a favourable account of the stir caused by the first Post-Impressionist Exhibition (1910, when fifteen-year-old David Jones was beginning the study of art), but thought little of the second (1912), which was [in Hartrick's words] 'full of Cubism, Futurism and other "isms", most of them merely stunts and dead or moribund today'.

Situating Jones against this backcloth, the Canadian literary scholar William Blissett continues:

> David Jones never 'went abstract' and may be described as a gentile Fauve: he clearly belongs to the 1901, not the 1912, movement, though neither show included the modern painter he came to venerate above all others, Pierre Bonnard.[48]

Clearly, this was a very different artistic education to Gill's training in masonry and calligraphy – and it led, as we shall see, to a very different way of reading Maritain's treatise.

In 1915, however, Jones interrupted his training by enlisting in the Royal Welsh Fusiliers, serving as a private soldier on the Western front for most of the remaining years of the First World War. This experience – which left him mentally invigorated rather than scarred – generated his war epic, *In Parenthesis.*[49] It was on the battlefield that he discovered Catholicism, not least through the chance observation of a Mass celebrated in a barn close to the front line.

On demobilisation, a government grant enabled him to resume his artistic formation, this time at the Westminster School of Art. It was probably then that he discovered Bonnard, doubtless through his painting-master the Impressionist Walter Sickert whom he considered the greatest English painter since Turner, while carefully disregarding his influence. In 1921, Jones was instructed in the Catholic faith by Father John O'Connor who was to receive Chesterton the following year. He was much struck by the thought that the 'central Post-Impressionist insight' – a painting is not *of* something but *is* that something under the form of paint, bears comparison with the Catholic doctrine of the Eucharist, where the Real Presence *is* under the form of bread and wine.[50] Encouraged by O'Connor, who was working on his Englishing of Maritain's book, Jones now put his further education – in the first

---

48   W. Blissett, 'Threefold Introduction', *The Chesterton Review* XXIII. 1–2 (1997), p. 3. The book referred to is A. S. Hartrick, *A Painter's Pilgrimage through Fifty Years* (Cambridge 1939).

49   D. Jones, *In Parenthesis* (London 1937).

50   W. Blissett, 'Threefold Introduction', art. cit., p. 6. And see Jones's own account in a letter to the BBC producer Harman Grisewood in R. Hague (ed.), *Dai Greatcoat*, p. 232.

place, as a wood engraver – into the hands of Gill. To be with Gill, Jones moved to Ditchling where he took part in that community of craftsmen both as Dominican Tertiary and, qua apprentice, as 'postulant' in the Guild of Saint Joseph and Saint Dominic.[51] He imbibed Gill's views on industrial society, and took up other ideas in the Ditchling 'air'. Ewan Clayton describes how, when the O'Connor translation rolled off the Ditchling printing press, 'to most Guildsmen, Gill and Jones included, this book became a second Bible'.[52] When he read Maritain, however, Jones drew from *Art et scolastique* not only (with Gill) Maritain's view of the artistic object as something made 'according to right reason' but also, in the case of the fine arts, the artwork's semiotic importance – its status as a sign of realities beyond itself. More widely, he embraced an entire theology, ultimately Thomist in inspiration, of the gratuitousness of creation and, by analogy, the gratuity of the work of artistic man.[53]

Though this produced a very different aesthetic from Gill's, whose emphasis lay on the essentially practical nature of making, Jones nevertheless followed Gill to Capel-y-ffin, which became his home until 1925. When the Gills moved to Buckinghamshire, Jones lived with them there too, at least periodically, until 1933. The intervals he spent in the boarding houses of seaside towns and unromantic parts of Greater London would establish the pattern of his life from the later 1930s onwards. He was to become distinguished both as visual artist and epic and mid-length poet. As an artist, his early period is dominated by his engravings in wood and copper;[54] his middle period by his watercolours, which are often 'magic casements': an interior scene opening through a window onto an exterior (a genre associated with Bonnard and also Matisse);[55] and his late period by his painted inscriptions where Latin, Welsh, Old English and Middle English words, rendered in something between print and calligraphy, seem to take on the character of the meanings they express.[56] The publication in 1952 of his poetic masterwork, *The Anathemata*, a book-length, free-verse poem on the culture of Britain in its pagan and Christian roots, against the background of world history and cosmic evolution, brought David Jones great acclaim, but hardly corresponding wealth.[57] It has been called Jones's:

---

51 See E. Clayton, 'David Jones and the Guild of St Joseph and St Dominic', in D. Shiel (ed.), *David Jones in Ditchling, 1921–1924* (Ditchling 2003), pp. 17–32.

52 Ibid., p.27.

53 R. Hague (ed.), *Dai Greatcoat*, p. 31.

54 D Cleverdon, *The Engravings of David Jones* (London 1981).

55 N. Gray, *The Paintings of David Jones* (London 1989).

56 Idem, *The Painted Inscriptions of David Jones* (London 1981).

57 D. Jones, *The Anathemata: Fragments of an Attempted Writing* (London, Faber and Faber, 1952). The fullest study of Jones's poetry is T. Dilworth, *The Shape of Meaning in the Poetry of David Jones* (Toronto 1988).

most comprehensive work because it contains themes, concepts and illustrations which are present, albeit in a less condensed and convoluted manner, in much of his visual output.[58]

Jones died a recluse, but a much befriended one, in the care of sisters of the Little Company of Mary, at Harrow, Middlesex, on 28 October, 1974. To Jones, Gill was his 'intimate and beloved friend', whose central 'thesis' he was happy to make his own, namely 'That the good of work should come first and be … [men's] natural concern, as also their natural delight'.[59] The critic Adrian Cunningham comments:

> Much twentieth century writing concerns justice *about* work, the conditions under which we work, rather than the nature of the work itself. Both Gill and Jones were concerned with the reciprocity of the *finis operis* and the *finis operantis*; for, in making the world, we make ourselves.[60]

But Jones does not just reproduce Gill. Where his message differed was in its emphasis on human activity as supremely a matter of the making of signs. Whether we are talking about murals or meals there is a right way of making things, and the distinctively human mode of so doing features an element of gratuitousness, which allows *things* to be *signs*. When the material basis and environment of social life becomes merely functional, it is, to that degree, dehumanised – and rendered impervious to the claims, or even the intelligibility, of a sacramental religion, for which signs are crucial.[61] Jones described the subject matter of *The Anathemata* as:

> things that are the signs of something other, together with those signs that not only have the nature of a sign, but are themselves, under some mode, what they signify.[62]

And in his essay 'Art and Democracy', Jones argued that:

> schemes and plans and trends within a civilization may achieve brilliant superficial results, but in the end there will be collapse just in so far as these schemes violate, or are forced to disregard, the kind of creature man is at his deepest foundations – at his determining foundations – the foundations in his nature as the animal-who-is-the-artist.

It will profit a human community nothing to 'gain the whole world of political and social and economic rights and equalities' if it loses 'the habit of art'.[63] Humans are

---

58   A. Price-Owen, 'Text, Texture and Intertextuality in the Art of David Jones', in idem, *The Private David Jones: A Celebration of 'The Anathémata* (Swansea 2002), p. 5.

59   Thus D. Jones, 'Eric Gill: An Appreciation', in H. Grisewood (ed.), *Epoch and Artist: Selected Writings by David Jones* (London 1959), p. 296.

60   A. Cunningham, 'Primary Things: Land, Work and Sign', p. 82.

61   That is the point of his essay 'Art and Sacrament: An Enquiry Concerning the Arts of Man and the Christian Commitment to Sacrament in Relation to Contemporary Technocracy', most easily consulted in H. Grisewood (ed.), *Epoch and Artist*, pp. 143–79.

62   D. Jones, *The Anathemata* (London 1952), p. 19.

63   Idem, 'Art and Democracy', in H. Grisewood (ed.), *Epoch and Artist*, p. 90.

born into a 'form-making species' given to the gratuitous making of culture. Their equality within their own kind, and the inequality of the animals in their regard, resides here.

Jones sought a renewal of culture on the basis of a religious humanism congruent with, but by no means wholly derived from, Catholic faith. To his mind, Western society needed to recover its sense – inherited from the Germanic, Greco-Roman and Judaeo-Christian past – of the significance of artefacts, of what is made. The modern West is a world where:

> the symbolic life (the life of the true cultures, of 'institutional' religion, and of *all artists* in the last resort – however much we may disavow the association) is progressively eliminated – the technician is master.[64]

Contemporary technocracy thus subverts what is distinctively human about society, as well as disabling the Church – which, in dependence on 'circumstances and conjunctions', can only inspire or patronise a 'particular creativity', not bestow the conditions that make its emergence certain. That is not to say that all 'recovery' is impossible. Those recoveries that 'preserve a genuine continuity with "the bests" of their several traditions' are no mere pastiche.[65]

Jones's paintings reflect his vision of a social civilisation expressive of man's nature as the 'creative beast'. Though his work as a watercolourist was indebted to the gentle English tradition to which the art schools had introduced him, he was also moved by a more strong-minded school of 'counter-modernist' artists in inter-war France. These were painters committed, as he was himself, to the 'layering of metaphorical, historical, mythic and ultimately metaphysical meanings'.[66] For Jones, a renewal of society worthy of humanity is impossible without the re-awakening of cultural memory, the reversal of the 'death of the sign'. In substantial artists, in his words:

> Almost all the motifs employed depend upon some apperception of that continuous sign-making which is an entailed inheritance, coming to us from our remote forebears.[67]

Certainly his own artworks do not intend to be merely useful. They correspond exactly to Hanke's description of a Maritainian work of fine art:

> The form of the work of fine art is to be considered at once the form of the work and an intentional meaning-structure which transcends the work. It abides in and animates the work; it is the form of this concrete artifact, apprehended as a thing and as the terminus

---

64   Idem, 'Religion and the Muses', in ibid., p. 103.

65   Ibid., pp. 102–3.

66   M. James, 'Portrait of a Maker', in idem (ed.), *David Jones, 1895–1974: A Map of the Artist's Mind* (London, 1995), p. 20.

67   D. Jones, 'Use and Sign', in idem, *The Dying Gaul, and Other Writings* (London 1978), p. 181.

of cognitive, joying acts; but it also, as a form resplendent with intelligibility caught in things, causes the work to spill out of its bounds as a fabricated object.[68]

It is plain that the judgment of Maritain's most recent American biographer, Professor Ralph McInerny, should stand. *Art et scolastique* was:

> far from being a reconstruction of a possible medieval aesthetics. Maritain was seeking in Thomas principles that could be applied to contemporary art and thus link the effort of the artist to his effort as a Thomist ... [And he adds:] This little book ... was destined to have a tremendous impact throughout the century on working artists ...[69]

Maritain made strenuous efforts to bring a Thomist Catholicism to artists and poets in France.[70] It may be, however, that his actual influence was far more decisive in a country he hardly visited, which was England.

---

68   J. W. Hanke, *Maritain's Ontology of the Work of Art*, p.50.
69   R. McInerny, *The Very Rich Hours of Jacques Maritain*, pp. 94, 92.
70   M. Guérin, 'Jacques Maritain et les artistes', in M. Bressolette – R. Mougel (ed.), *Jacques Maritain face à la Modernité* (Toulouse 1995), pp. 33–64.

Chapter 8

Conclusion: Christ and the Muses

So why are the arts important – not only to human life at large but also for Christianity in particular? Cambridge University Divinity Faculty has an ongoing research project called 'Theology through the Arts', so one can turn to the manifesto of its Director, Jeremy Begbie, for a programmatic statement of why the arts count.

The first point he makes is that, whatever interpretation we want to put on this, artistic practices are more or less coterminous with the human species as such. Wherever you find man, you find art. As one contemporary anthropologist has written:

> It is commonly held that economic activity is a necessity, but that art is a luxury. Yet we can assert empirically the universality of art in man's social history ... Even in the hardest natural environments, art has been produced ... It is easy, then, to refute the idea that at the primitive stages of man's existence the theme of subsistence dominated his life to the exclusion of the arts.[1]

This seems acceptable, and even indisputable. Certainly David Jones thought so.

I am not so happy about Begbie's second argument, which seems a good deal more questionable. And this is the claim that, in Begbie's words, 'scarcely a day passes when a person is not confronted with or surrounded by objects which are generally agreed to be "works of art"'.[2] This may be true in Siena but it seems unlikely to be the case in Scunthorpe, unless it has changed very radically since I was last there. What proportion of people, in any given society, care deeply about the arts is surely a moot point. Mass education does not necessarily bring in its train great responsiveness to high art. As one writer has put it, 'Given a free vote, the bulk of humankind will choose football, the soap opera or bingo over Aeschylus [the Greek tragedian]. To pretend otherwise ... is cant.'[3] These words were not written in the interests of glorifying philistinism. They were written by someone aiming to persuade the relatively few people who (he thinks) make a real effort to come to terms with music, art and literature of acknowledged excellence, to take seriously their responsibility for keeping alive what the arts represent. This is not to say that the arts should be the preserve of an elite, only that in many situations they are

---

1   R. Firth, 'The Social Framework of Primitive Art', in D. Fraser (ed.), *The Many Faces of Primitive Art* (Englewoood Cliffs, New Jersey, 1966), p. 12. Cited in J. Begbie, *Voicing Creation's Praise: Towards a Theology of the Arts* (Edinburgh 1991), p. xvi.

2   Ibid.

3   G. Steiner, *Real Presences: Is there Anything in What we Say?* (London 1989), p. 67

likely to be. In principle, the overwhelming majority of people *could* share these experiences, but are not encouraged to do so. It may even be true to say that most of us could have been poets, artists or composers, but when we were children we allowed the artistic impulse in us to wither away.

Possibly, though, Jeremy Begbie has in mind not high art, what Eric Gill who claimed he wanted none of it, called 'art nonsense'. Possibly he has in mind, as Gill said one should, things, however lowly, such as chairs or knives, which are consciously crafted in a way that delights the mind. But even these in Scunthorpe are unlikely to be littering the streets.

So this argument to the importance of the arts from their supposed omnipresence in daily life seems rather more hopeful than accurate. So far as the generality of society in the modern city is concerned, the most we can say is that elected authorities often recognise the importance of public art. To which we can add there is a trend whereby more and more individuals with an economic surplus tend to look for things that are craftsman-made rather than mass-produced. And this amounts to a good deal less than omnipresence.

A third way of saying why the arts are important, Begbie goes on, is to ascribe to the arts a unique ability to reflect the character of their age. Thus for instance one might say that the disillusion and sense of social hollowness and cultural alienation which followed the First World War in England is reflected with peculiar profundity in T. S. Eliot's poem-cycle *The Waste Land*. This is no doubt true, though it is also the case that literary art can reflect what its author regards as the missing features of his age rather than those that scream out at one. Like Eliot, David Jones was a literary modernist in matters of technique, but he set out to be deliberately anti-modern in writing the *Anathemata*, his evocation of Britain as seen from the Dark Ages on. So perhaps it would be truer to say that art reflects either the character of an age or what people regard as signally lacking to, or needed by, the character of an age. To the extent that this is so – to understand where we are, where we are 'at', what the needs and hopes of human beings in some particular epoch may be – art is, yes, certainly important.

I mention now an argument for the importance of the arts that is not found in Begbie. The arts are an ongoing extension of the original creation and as such they bring new intrinsic value into the world. Natural kinds of things, in all their individual examples, are of value, each in their own way. We recognise this for human beings by speaking of the 'dignity' of human life. Protagonists of animal rights make the case for animal species. Environmentalists make it for other organic life forms, like trees and plants, and, I suppose, even inorganic forms like water as found in rivers and seas. Through artistic creativity, the total value of the world around us is increased, as artists bring into being works that are either imitations of nature ('mimetic' art, which, for example, Aristotle took to be the proper form art should take), or renderings of how nature should be but generally is not (that is what we find in visionary art like Gauguin's painting of people and places in the South Sea islands – Tahiti seen as a new Paradise, which it may be in the age of the new heavens and the new earth but certainly is not now). Both mimetic and visionary art are recreations, supplementary creations. As one aesthetician has put it:

> I take the aesthetic act, the conceiving and bringing into being of that which, very precisely, could not have been conceived or brought into being, to be an *imitatio*, a replication on its own scale, of the inaccessible first *fiat* (the Big Bang of the new cosmologies ...)[4]

It has been suggested that one major reason why there are relatively few women artists (virtually no women dramatists, for instance) is that for women the vocation to continue creation is primarily expressed in motherhood in such a way that artistic creativity pales into relative insignificance by comparison. Be that as it may, artists even or maybe especially in a secular age, sometimes compare themselves to God. When he had finished his paintings for the Dominican chapel of the Rosary at Vence Matisse said, 'I did it for myself'. 'But', objected the prioress, 'you told me you were doing it for God'. Matisse: 'Yes, but I am God'. (An object lesson, perhaps, in why it may be a mistake for the Church to employ unbelieving iconographers.) More acceptably, Picasso declared somewhere, 'God is in reality nothing but another artist (*otro artista*)'.[5] There is something like such artistic creativity in the artistic public, ourselves, too. To take in a text, a painting, a piece of music, and let it live in us in the way the artist intended is to generate it anew, to bring about its resurrection.

But the most important argument for the importance of the arts has still to be considered. The fourth general argument for the importance of art Begbie comes up with (this will be, then, the fifth in my rundown here) is the weightiest one. Unfortunately, it is also the most difficult one to state. And this is the argument, expressed by a number of philosophers in different ways, that in the making and experiencing of art there is some kind of encounter with transcendence, with (that is) what 'goes beyond' the realities we find in our everyday transactions in and with the world.

In his book *Real Presences*, the literary polymath George Steiner speaks of works of art as actualising:

> a root-impulse of the human spirit to explore possibilities of meaning and of truth that lie outside empirical seizure or proof ...[6]

Nietzsche called music 'a metaphysical work', an *opus metaphysicum*. Presumably if music is that, then serious literature and art should be called the same thing. All these arts, writes Steiner, imply a postulate of transcendence. 'Transcendence' is a very slippery word, though. It just means 'going beyond', as a citizen of Cambridge might go beyond Swavesey on the way to St Neot's or for that matter go beyond the third floor in the lift at Addenbrooke's Hospital. What sort of 'going beyond' might be involved here? In the direction of *what* are the arts said to point?

---

4   Ibid., p. 201.
5   Cited ibid., p. 209.
6   Ibid., p. 225.

In the first place, the claim is being made that through the arts we *go beyond* our sense of what this or that thing or event means to something like an awareness that there may be a meaning to experience as a whole. In one way or another, the arts confront us with the affirmation that there is a wondrous or terrible meaning to existence, a meaning that is not arbitrarily thought up or subjectively foisted on the face of things but *really there*. A meaning, too, for existence as a whole. In a huge, hardly chartable, variety of ways, the arts all say to us, This is how the world is and it is wonderful, and they may add, *terribly* so.

We could argue that this is already to make a metaphysical claim of an implicitly theological sort. A world with intrinsic meanings which is also a world that has an overall meaning (even if that meaning is simply to be terribly wonderful) is not a world of chance but a world which has a rationale. It seems to be a world that is in accordance with the Logos (to use a word common to St John's Gospel and the early Greek philosophers), a world that presupposes a Meaning that was in the beginning. So art is a pointer to transcendence in the sense of making us go beyond not only the partial aspects of the world to a characterisation of existence as a whole. It is a pointer to transcendence in the sense even of urging us to go beyond our inchoate awareness of what reality as a whole may be like to the deeper reality on which this world's reality is based, or (if you prefer) the wider reality within which our world is set. Steiner compares the arts to:

> an Annunciation, [as] of 'a terrible beauty' or gravity breaking into the small house of our cautionary being. [And he continues:] If we have heard rightly the wing-beat and provocation of that visit, the house is no longer habitable in quite the same way as it was before.[7]

One sign of this power of art to put us in touch with reality at a deeper level, or in its wider compass, lies in the *moral* potency of art. Steiner (again) speaks of the ways art can affect our sensibility and understanding as 'waking' them, 'enriching' them, 'complicating' them, 'darkening' them, and 'unsettling' them. That range of words suggests, obviously, the different effects that the arts might have on us. Our moral attitudes and actions might just possibly change for the better under the impact of seeing Turner's *Slavers Throwing Overboard the Dead and Dying*, or hearing Elgar's *Dream of Gerontius* or reading Tolkien's *The Lord of the Rings*. Worryingly, they may also change for the worse. Sometimes art may persuade us to action that is not properly virtuous, making us less not more than we were. That is why, over-hasty moralising aside, we cannot accept the blank cheque to art expressed in the slogan, 'Art for art's sake'. As the Scholastics would say, the transcendentals of goodness and beauty must ultimately be convertible, be two sides of the same coin.

So art is, arguably, a disclosure of the overall character of the world, and a pointer to its precondition in a supreme rationale, and it can therefore have its effect, for good we hope, on moral character. But something even more is at stake, Steiner's comparison of aesthetic experience with the Annunciation at Nazareth is evidently

---

7   Ibid., p. 143.

meant to raise in our minds the question: can the arts put us in touch with God? Here I interject an autobiographical aside. When I was young and foolish, I took part in a mission to convert the Swedes to Catholicism. Run by the Legion of Mary, it took the form of going from house to house in a small town in south-west Sweden, offering the occupants cheap copies of the well-known medal of Mary immaculate struck so as to commemorate the apparitions of the Virgin in the Rue du Bac in Paris in the 1830s. Conversation of a suitable kind was then supposed to strike up. One highly cultured gentleman on whom we called struck up something else. Taking his violin off the wall, he said to us, 'You want to know what Catholicism means to me? It means *this*', and he played us Gounod's *Ave Maria*. At least that was better than hitting us over the head with it! But *could* art be in fact a means of communion with the divine? If so, that would take us beyond cosmic musings about the meaning of life and bring us to the threshold of divine presence – and this is the strongest sense which the word 'transcendence' enjoys.

Even art which is not at all overtly religious in its subject matter, is a shining through of divine presence, of the source of being, the meaning of meaning, in such a way as to re-connect time with eternity. That is what, on one view, we are admitting when we call the truth or the meaning expressed in some work of art 'beautiful'. Bertrand Russell said that God has given man too few indices of his existence for belief in God to be plausible. On this view, Russell was metaphysically tone-deaf. He forgot to consider the arts.

And so to sum up this Conclusion so far. Art has been a feature of human society since pre-historic times, even if to speak of its omnipresence in the everyday world after the Industrial Revolution is going too far. Art discloses what we think our society is like, or what it is *not* like but ought to be like. As the main expression (other than childbirth) of human creativity it can be said to take further the original creation by bringing into being new realities of intrinsic worth. Above all, it is or can be a pointer to transcendence in three main ways. The first sense in which the arts can relate us to transcendence was, we saw, by making us go beyond interpretations of this or that thing or event toward an *overall* reading of the world. The second was to see the world as having as its own precondition a fundamental meaningfulness beyond itself. The third (after we had noted the possible moral effects of art in making us go beyond the limits of our present character) was that art might be regarded as a kind of epiphany of divine presence, divine light.

Given the title of my Conclusion – 'Christ and the Muses' – I now have to relate this to the Word incarnate, at any rate schematically. Our first two arguments for the importance of the arts – their ubiquity over time and relative but by no means complete geographical omnipresence (in Begbie's word) through space really only tell us that relating Christ to the Muses as to any other major feature of human life – economics, or the world religions – is a task we need to carry out. Essentially, then, we need to concentrate on the three last arguments or 'suasions'. The arts reveal the human world, either as it actually is or as it ideally is. They express the creativity of man when the artist adds to the things of intrinsic worth in the world, or the art-appreciating public makes the artist's vision of what he has made live again.

The arts point to transcendence, not just the way the world as a whole is wonderful and presupposes a meaning greater than itself, but also by enacting divine presence sustaining the special density of meaning that art, literature, music can contain.

I think we could reasonably relate to these three arguments three aspects of the work and being of Jesus Christ, the God-man, as classical Christian thought presents him. First of all, Christ reveals the true nature of humanity. As the true Adam, he shows us the reality of what the human species should be like and on the Cross discloses the range and power of the evil which inhibits our being as the first Adam was meant to be, in God's image and likeness. This is the first way in which Christ may be compared with a work of art – by disclosing what the human world is unfortunately like and, even more importantly, what it ought to be like.

Secondly, though, the work of Christ goes beyond nature by bringing into being a further dimension of reality in what we customarily refer to as 'salvation': new resources of grace and life, or what the Lutheran theologian Paul Tillich called the 'new being' (and St Paul no less graphically a 'new creation'). This is the second way in which Jesus Christ can illuminatingly be compared with a work of art, which is also (as we saw) an enhancement of natural creation, taking the original creation further.

Thirdly, Christ discloses the meaning of the world as a whole, which is found in the Father's wonderful plan to bring about the nuptials of heaven and earth, the uncreated and the created, in the sacrificial joy of the Kingdom. He points to the source of the world in a pre-existing divine truth, to express which he came forth, so he tells Pilate in St John's passion narrative. Moreover, he actually enacts that truth – the truth which is the Holy Trinity – in his own person. Of course, only the second divine Person, the Son, became incarnate in Jesus Christ, but just as in eternity the Son is co-defined by the Father and the Holy Spirit, so Jesus is always the trinitarian Son, essentially related to the Father and the Spirit in his work on earth. Into the everlasting movement or dance of the Trinity (beautifully captured in St Andrei Rublev's icon of the three angels) the whole redeemed creation is destined to enter. The risen and ascended God–man is the true predestined goal of all creation. Here the capacity of the artwork to be the vehicle of divine presence in the material form of words or sounds or shapes and colours is super-fulfilled.

Christ is, then, the perfect art work in the sense of that reality in whom is realised those goals that all artistic making has as its explicit or implicit ends. Because he is infinite meaning, life and being perfectly synthesised with finite form, the cave-painters at Lascaux, or Hesiod penning his hymns, or Beethoven working on his last quartets, were all gesturing towards him though they realised it not.

If this is true, it is hardly surprising that the Church (and I use this expression to mean the Catholic Church, but it would equally be true of Orthodoxy and much though not all Protestantism) has used the arts for two basic purposes. First, the Church has used the arts to throw light on the supreme art work that is Jesus Christ – hence all that the visual arts, poetry, music can offer by way of showing how Christ has been portrayed in Christian tradition. Thus we get the Byzantine icon, Hopkins' Christological sonnets, Bach's *St Matthew Passion*. And secondly, the Church has used the arts by 'baptising' them – that is, by letting them be transfigured by the light of Jesus Christ, setting them a new mission in the world. And this mission is to do what they did under their old and still continuing mandate, but now with the additional aim of witnessing to the revelation of God and his saving work in Jesus Christ: the novels of Georges Bernanos, the clown paintings of Rouault, the organ music of Messiaen. The arts, once in this sense baptised, become pneumatic. The arts become pnematophoric, bearers of the Holy Spirit, when they carry out their original mandate in order to testify to Christ since all such testifying is carried out by the Holy Spirit's grace and power. No one can say Jesus is Lord, remarks St Paul, except by the Holy Spirit (I Corinthians 12:3).

Is this still happening today? Certainly, though not as powerfully as in the age of the anonymous painters of the icons or of Dante or Rembrandt or even Haydn. Why not? Various reasons might be suggested, of which the most important is the failure of dogmatic Christianity – the only historically valid sort, the only sort worth having -- to commend itself as a unifying framework for all the legitimate activities and aspirations of contemporary culture.[8] Theological evaluations of the world are for the moment out of fashion, and regarded, as when not venomous, then at any rate implausible. There is no one strategy that can deal with that but only a multi-pronged attack or advance – intellectual, imaginative, moral and so forth.[9] There is, however, one reason why the arts so rarely accept a mission that *is* within the power of the Church to alter. In the past, the densest or richest location of baptised art has been the Liturgy. The sacred use of the arts in the liturgical setting has provided inspiration for artists engaged in producing artworks for contexts outside the Liturgy, for consumption beyond the limits of the visible Church. In the modern West, the Muses have largely fled the liturgical amphitheatre, which instead is given over to banal language, poor quality popular music, and, in new and re-designed churches, a nugatory or sometimes totally absent visual art.[10] This deprives the wider Christian mission of the arts of essential nourishment. Where would the poetry of Paul Claudel be without the Latin Liturgy? Or John Tavener's music without the Orthodox Liturgy? Where would be the entire tradition of representational art in the West without the liturgical art which until the seventeenth century at least remained at its heart?

We need today to summon back the Muses to the sacred foyer of the Church, to be at home again at that hearth.

---

8 For an account of how this might function, see A. Nichols, OP, *Christendom Awake: On Re-energizing the Church in Culture* (Edinburgh and Grand Rapids, Mich., 1999).

9 Idem, 'Integral Evangelization', in *Josephinum* 13.1 (2006), pp. 66–80.

10 Idem, *Looking at the Liturgy: A Critical View of its Contemporary Form* (San Francisco 1996).

Index of Names